James Nott

Some of the antiquities

James Nott

Some of the antiquities

ISBN/EAN: 9783337249861

Printed in Europe, USA, Canada, Australia, Japan

Cover: Foto ©Andreas Hilbeck / pixelio.de

More available books at **www.hansebooks.com**

Some of the Antiquities

OF

"Moche Malverne"

(GREAT MALVERN),

INCLUDING

A History of its Ancient CHURCH and MONASTERY,
Engravings of SEALS of the Convent,
and the Publication of GRANTS and DOCUMENTS,
and much other matter never before printed.

BY JAMES NOTT,

AUTHOR OF

"NOTES ON THE ANCIENT STAINED GLASS IN THE PRIORY CHURCH OF GREAT MALVERN.

"There be some who slight and despise this sort of learning and represent it to be a dry, barren, monkish study: but I dare assure any wise and sober man that historical antiquities do deserve and well reward the pains of an English Student."

Bishop Kennett.

"Thou small but favor'd spot of holy ground!
Where'er we gaze, around, above, below,
What rainbow tints, what magic charms are found!"

Byron.

MALVERN:
JOHN THOMPSON, CHURCH STREET:
WOODS & CO., THE ROYAL LIBRARY.

1885.

DEDICATION

(BY PERMISSION.)

To

SIR EDMUND A. H. LECHMERE, BART., M.P.,

THE RHYDD, NEAR MALVERN.

SIR EDMUND,

I have craved permission to dedicate this work on the Antiquities of "Moche Malverne" to you,

First: Because I remember that your forefathers,

"A time-honoured race,"

have dwelt for centuries within the shadow of the Malvern Hills, and have always been associated with the place;

Secondly: Because I know no one who has a better appreciation of the natural beauties of Malvern, or more reverence for its interesting antiquities;

Thirdly: Because, being a native of the place, I thought you might not be displeased to have your name associated with a work on Malvern Antiquities.

I am, Sir Edmund,

Your humble and much obliged Servant,

THE AUTHOR.

CONTENTS.

PREFACE.

For thirty-five years I have lived under the shadow of the Priory Church of Great Malvern, and have taken the greatest possible interest in the building. Its walls, buttresses, and tower, hoar with age, have had a constant fascination for me. To pace slowly round the churchyard, at different seasons of the year, at early morning, or late at night, has been my delight. The church's old stones have become, to me, familiar friends. I have entered the sacred place, and with no one near, have marked its every feature. In hours snatched from a busy life, I have taken my field glass and peered into the mazes of its many coloured, ancient windows: have permitted my eyes to wander over its tracery, up its lofty shafts, and about its roof. I have tried many times to interpret the designs and intentions of the ancient architects. Whilst so doing I have pondered in deep meditation on what has been revealed to me there, and often paused in wonder.

I have long been interested in Malvern's history; and dusty folios, old documents, or books of any kind that were likely to have anything to reveal, I have diligently studied. Till very recently no thought of publishing such work as this ever seriously occurred to me; on the contrary it has often been my lot to urge such duty upon others. Gentlemen of learning, archæological taste, and literary skill, had often been appealed to by me to undertake the task. And I had offered to more than one capable gentleman all the information of which I had become possessed. Years had gone away and nothing had been done, and, as hands more competent would not undertake the work, with such poor skill as I possessed, mine were devoted thereto.

This is the simple and unvarnished history of this book, which is now submitted to the public.

I am indebted to so many sources for information, that I think it useless to attempt to particularize them; but I must mention that to the Rev. Dr. Card's "Antiquities of Malvern Priory Church," to Dr. Thomas's "Antiquitates Prioratus Majoris Malverne," to Chambers's "History of Malvern," and to Mr. Noake's Worcestershire books, I am under obligations. The Rev. McKenzie's Walcot tract on "Church Goods" in the reign of Edward VI, has also been made free use of by me. To the Worcester Architectural Society the public are indebted for the publication of this interesting and valuable document. But above and beyond every one else to Walter de Gray Birch, Esq., of the British Museum, I am indebted. Through him I am able to lay before the reader copious extracts from the "Scudamore Papers." To him I owe the interesting collections of Malvern's Priory seals, now for the first time made public, with their skilful descriptions. From him also I have received the several charters, grants, &c., now published with their exact interpretations; and much besides of valuable matter and assistance. With a kindness and readiness unexampled in my experience, he has given me the benefit of his skill, knowledge and learning, and has placed at my disposal some of the rich treasures of the noble institution to which he belongs. I should like also to express my obligation to Mr. Luther Davis, the son of a respected townsman of Malvern, who has had the kindness to turn aside from his legal studies to make very considerable researches on my behalf in the British Museum.

Other of Malvern's antiquities remain to be explored, and, should the present work be at all acceptable, I purpose, at an early date, giving a revised edition of my "Notes on the Ancient Stained Glass in the Priory Church," as well as to tell something about our unrivalled collection of old tiles.

THE AUTHOR.

CHAPTER I.

MONASTERY AND CHURCH
OF
GREAT MALVERN.

"Nor rough, nor barren are the winding ways
Of hoar antiquity, but strewn with flowers."

I ASK the reader to go back in imagination to the days of William the Conqueror. A great straggling forest of some eight thousand acres then entirely surrounded Malvern. This forest extended to the Severn on the one hand, far down into Gloucestershire on the other, into Herefordshire on the west, and to beyond the site of Bransford Bridge northward. The most we could then say of Malvern was, that it had a name, and it was principally famous for its great camp achievements in the reign of the Saxon king Athelstan, and the Druidical occupation of its (Worcestershire) beacon's crown.

How the place came to be called Malvern, learned men have differences of opinion. Nash, the county historian, thinks the word is derived from "moel" signifying bald, and "wern" alders, importing a bald hill, with alders at the bottom; or else from "moel," which, in British, signifies a mountain. The antiquarian Allies favours the idea that the syllable "vern" is derived from the British word "sarn" or "varn," which respectively means a pavement or seat of judgment. In Doomsday Book, Malvern is spelled "Malferna," and mention is made of "Malveselle," and "Malveshill," county of Hereford. Jones in his "Brecknockshire," makes "moel-y-varn," which he tells us is "pure Welsh," signify the high court, or seat of judgment, "proving Malvern," says Mr.

Allies, "to have been an important station of the Druids." Professor Phillips suggests by way of enquiry, "Moel Hafren," the "Hill of the Severn." Another suggestion is that it is a corruption of "St. Mary-le-Fern," a supposition favoured by the fact that "among the encaustic tiles in the church the monogram of St. Mary the Patron Saint exists with fern leaves intertwined."

The next important fact to be mentioned in connection with the earlier history of Malvern is the existence, in its neighbourhood, of the great camp at Colwall, on the Herefordshire Beacon. The word Colwall is said to be derived from "Collis Vallum," meaning a fortified hill, and appears to have been so named by the Romans, of whose occupation of this neighbourhood considerable evidence exists. Others maintain that the name is more likely to be connected with the Keltic word "coll," hazel, shut-up fruit; hence, a hollow (compare French "col," a mountain pass); and "waal," a British town. This camp is thought to have been formed by Caractacus, and there is every reason for believing that it has been the scene of sanguinary engagements, and, without doubt, it was that of a battle which, in the days of Athelstan, finally extended the Saxon rule from the line of the Severn to that of the Wye. This is intimated in the following quotation from Bruit, translated by Sir Frederick Madden:—"At this time," says the legend, "Margadad, fairest of all men (knight fairest of all), King of South Wales, and Cadwin, or Cadigan, King of North Wales, helde all the goode lande unto the Severne from the upper end that floweth into the sea. In Malverne, near Severne, Magadad, the King, dwelt with very mickle folke, and Athelstan to him advanced—the king of this nation—and held them exceeding hard, and greeted them with harm, and drove them with his weapons over the Wye, and took from them the land that lieth there betwixt; the Severne and the Wye they possessed not afterwards."

At or near the same camp, it may be conjectured another engagement had previously taken place. An ancient crown or bracelet of gold is reported to have been found within a musket shot of the beacon, in the year 1650. This crown was found by a poor rustic when digging in his garden It was sold by the poor

HALL OF MALVERN PRIORY, 1850, NOW TAKEN DOWN.

Glossary of Architecture, Vol. ii, plate 173.

MALVERN MONK AND MARTYR.

From the painted windows of the Priory Church.

man to Mr. Hill, a jeweller, of Gloucester, for £37. Mr. Hill sold it for £250 to a London goldsmith, this goldsmith, in his turn, selling the stones alone, which were deeply inlaid, for £1,500. This coronet, it is conjectured, belonged to a crowned Prince of Wales, of whom we have record in the following quotation:—"Roderick, Prince of Wales," says Caradoc, in Welsh history, "divided his kingdom between his three sons, and because they each wore a coronet of gold indented upwards, and inlaid with precious stones on their helmets, they were called the three crowned Princes." It is inferred that the said crown was either lost in battle, or that it was concealed where found on the approach of an enemy.

The next important events which we have to deal with in the annals of Malvern are the arrival of St. Werstan, and the establishment of a cell or chapel on the hill side near St. Ann's Well with which an interesting history is connected. St. Werstan lived in the early part of the reign of Edward the Confessor, and was a monk of the monastery of Deerhurst. He came to Malvern under the following circumstances:—The monastery he lived in was destroyed by Danish miscreants, who, on errands of plunder, frequently then advanced up the river Severn. St. Werstan, hardly escaping with his life, fled to Malvern. Leland is the authority for this piece of information, a passage in his Itinerary running thus—"Bede maketh mention that in his time there was a notable abbey at Deerhurst; it was destroyed by the Danes; Werstanus fled thence, as it is said, to Malvern."* The reader should notice that this passage records the fact that Bede mentions Deerhurst, Leland himself going on to speak of the destruction of the monastery and the flight of St. Werstan; otherwise the quotation may mislead.

What privations St. Werstan suffered ere he reached Malvern, how long he roamed in the marshes of the forest, and what first

* Leland continues (vol. 5, 2 Deerhurst),—"The olde Priory stode Est from Severn a Bow shotte, and North of the town (*i.e.* of Deerhurst). There remayne yet dyverse Names of Streates, as Fischar Streate, and other. But the Buildings of them be gone. Ther be yet 2 Fayres kept one at eche day in inventione and Exaltatione Crucis."

gave him the idea of locating himself in the fair spot that surrounds it, we are left to conjecture. However, here he came, and in the absence of more definite and reliable information, his legend as pourtrayed in the painted windows of the church must be our guide. From whence we learn, first, that a vision of heavenly messengers pointed out to the Saint the site for his chapel, and that they laid the foundation stones for each corner of the building; secondly, that when the chapel was built these same angels came to its consecration; and for that occasion at least they took upon themselves the apparel of earthly priests, and carried the processional cross, cross staff, and holy water, with which it was usual for priests of that day to perform the rite of consecration; thirdly, that Edward the Confessor conferred upon the monk the legal title to the chapel in question; and fourthly, that last of all the Saint suffered martyrdom at the hands of Danish, or other miscreants, by having his head cut off while looking out of his own chapel window on Malvern Hill side, and that these same miscreants, or others like them, committed the barbarity of scourging the brothers in exile of the sainted martyr.

Presuming that thus much was known of Malvern, and remembering that the brow of its bald hill was then, as now, a conspicuous object throughout Worcestershire—presuming, too, that, in an age of legends and traditions, tales of the druidical occupation of its beacon, of its ancient border warfare and great camp achievements, were plentiful—let us proceed to speak of the circumstances connected with the foundation of its famous monastery.

Probably the martyrdom of Saint Werstan had more to do with the establishment of the Malvern Priory than at first might appear. This is intimated by the church of the Priory being dedicated to the Archangel Michael, showing that the founders wished to have the thought cherished, that the monastery's existence was owing to the vision which appeared to Saint Werstan. I think it not at all unlikely that the shrine of the martyr had something to do with the unusually liberal benefactions, which at the foundation of the monastery so speedily flowed in. Many a noble fane has been reared from benefactions cast upon the tombs of less sainted and devoted martyrs than St. Werstan, and, though such a thing may be incapable of positive proof, it is one way of accounting for the sudden up-rearing of buildings of such dimensions.

There were two important personages in Worcestershire at this time, to whom the place was somewhat indebted. The first was the good Saint Wulstan, the last Saxon bishop of Worcester, a man of singularly upright life and deep-toned piety, the friend and adviser of the last Saxon, and—though by no means a time-server—of the first Norman King. Saint Wulstan's position gave him opportunities of knowing the minds of those in authority. He was a man of keen discernment, and had the happy ability of understanding the spirit and the tendencies of the age in which he lived. St. Wulstan foresaw somewhat of Malvern's future, and had to do with it.

The second personage was Urso D'Abitot, the hereditary sheriff of the county, and the King's representative in Worcestershire. This nobleman, though charged with crimes against religion generally, and though he died with a bishop's curse resting upon him,* toward the sacred enclosure of Malvern had a kindly intention, becoming a benefactor, and, in concert with St. Wulstan, interesting William the Conqueror in its behalf. Bearing the position of these personages in mind, let us note the ordinary account of the foundation of the monastery. It runs thus:—"Before the conquest," says Nash, in his history of Worcestershire, "it (Malvern) was a wilderness, thick set with trees, in the midst of which some monks, who aspired to greater perfection, retired from the Priory of Worcester and became hermits. The enthusiasm spread so fast that their number soon increased to three hundred, when,

* Urso D'Abitot, not content with receiving as a gift about 4,000 acres of land in the county, contrived to possess himself, by force, of much more, and, in particular, some belonging to the Convent of St. Mary's, at Worcester, on which he built his castle. To the monks and clergy he gave great offence and drew down upon him from their great patron, Eldred, Archbishop of York, the following imprecation:—"Have God's curse, and mine, and that of all holy men, unless thou removest thy castle; and know assuredly that thy posterity shall not inherit the patrimony of St. Mary." "This imprecation," says William of Malmesbury, "seemed to take effect, for Urso died soon after, and his only son, Roger, who succeeded him, did not long survive him."

forming themselves into a society, they agreed to live according to the Order of St. Benedict, and elected Aldwyn, one of their company, to be Superior; thus was this monastery founded about the year 1083, with the consent and approbation of St. Wulstan, Bishop of Worcester, and was dedicated to the Virgin Mary." Tanner writes, "Great Malvern was a place of great antiquity, for here, in the wild forest, was an hermitage, or some kind of religious house for seculars, before the Conquest, endowed by Edward the Confessor." The more full detail of the event runs thus—"Two men, Guido—supposed to be a Dane, and perchance in some way implicated in St. Werstan's murder—and Aldwyn, residents of this neighbourhood, a little before the time of the Conquest determined, for some reason, and perhaps because of their sin in the Saint's martyrdom, to become palmers, and visit the Lord's Sepulchre at Jerusalem, or meet with a glorious death at the hands of the Saracens; before doing so however, Aldwin seeks permission from his spiritual pastor, St. Wulstan. St. Wulstan heard his plea, but dissuaded him from the enterprise, speaking to him, as is reported, in words to this effect: 'Aldwin doe not thou go to Palestine, for thou shalt see that God will doe great things for Malvern.'" Aldwin listened attentively to what the Bishop said, returned to Malvern, set himself humbly to work, and established the Priory, one after another joining him, till as many as thirty monks became sheltered beneath our old hills.

The gossiping Chronicler's account of this event, that of William of Malmesbury, translated by the Rev. Dr. Card, is worth transcribing. It runs as follows:—"There was one Aldwin, a monk, who, with a single companion named Guido, lived as a recluse in that very densely wooded chase, which is called Malvern. After long struggles of conscience, Guido considered it absolutely necessary, as the shortest path to glory, to visit Jerusalem, and see the Lord's sepulchre, or meet a blessed death by the hands of the Saracens. Aldwin was disposed to follow his example, but first consulted his spiritual adviser Wolstan. The prelate dissuaded him, and cooled his ardour by saying, 'Do not, I beseech thee,

Aldwin, go any where, but remain in your place: believe me, you would wonder if you knew what I know; how much God is about to perform through you in that place.' The monk having heard this departed, and now remained firm in purpose, and soothed every sorrow by the hope of the prophecy. Nor was it long after that the prophecy hastened to its fulfilment. One after the other successively came to the number of thirty. Abundant were the stores of provision which flowed in upon them from the neighbouring inhabitants, who judged themselves happy in being permitted to minister aught to God's servants; or if there chanced to be need of any thing, they supplied the want by faith, deeming it a little matter to be without carnal food, seeing that they grew fat upon spiritual joys."

To the same venerable writer we are indebted for the following piece of information concerning Swelf, a merchant. The bishop's prediction, in each of these cases, it will be seen seems to have been fulfilled :—"One Swelf, a merchant, had been accustomed to visit him once a year to receive his advice in the healing of his spiritual ailments. Once on a time, after giving the absolution, he observed, 'You often repeat the sins which you have confessed; because, as the proverb goes, opportunity makes the thief. Wherefore I advise you to become a monk, which, if you do, you will not long have the opportunity for those sins.' Upon this the other rejoined, that he could not possibly become a monk, because he found it so difficult to bring his mind to it. 'Go your ways,' said the bishop, in somewhat of a passion; 'a monk you will become, whether you choose it or not, but only when the appliances and means of vice have waxen old in you.' Which fact we afterwards witnessed, because, when now broken down by old age, and warned by disease, he betook himself to our monastery; but though he had many times repented, yet, nevertheless, as often as any one reminded him of the bishop's saying, he still laboured to check his temper, and to soften his disposition."

On carvings underneath the monks' seats occupying the choir of Malvern church, is the representation of a man on his death bed, attended by a physician, disposing of his money bags. This is regarded as pertaining to the merchant Swelf, the implication being, that though he became a monk, for prudential reasons he had concealed some of his hoards of wealth, till, with a view of obtaining pardon and remission for a whole life's sins in the hour of death, the *kept back* portion of his ill-gotten wealth was handed to the monks.

CHAPTER II.

BUILDING OF THE PRIORY.

"Man is a noble animal, splendid in ashes, and pompous in the grave."

SIR THOMAS BROWNE,
"Hydriotaphia or Urn-Burial," 1658.

ALDWIN and his companions under favour of his distinguished bishop, and with the Pope's letters patent in his possession, commenced in the lonely wilds of Malvern the building of his Priory; the sound of the woodman's axe and mason's hammer—wakening for the first time the echoes of its woodland valley—announcing the fact.

The building of the Malvern Priory can have been no light matter. The place was far removed from roads of any kind. The dense forest, on the borders of which the Priory was placed, supplied the requisite timber, and, as far as was practicable, the Malvern Hill stone was used. The cut stones forming the round pillars of the church, and those used in the tower, and other parts of the structure, had to be imported from a distance. How heavy masses of stone were conveyed through the forest, and how a great many other difficulties were got over, must be matter of conjecture.

The building, while in progress, had a strange look. There, far from the haunts of men, where at night the wild boar wandered, and the rapacious wolf sallied forth in quest of prey, religious enthusiasts were erecting a dwelling. Stranger still! the clerical discipline of that day encouraged such seclusion as meritorious.

The church, then built, resembled the present one less than might be imagined; the foundation walls ran in the same direction, in length it was much the same, towards the east it was apsidal, or circular ended. The side aisles, with the exception of the one on the south side of the nave, were much narrower than the present aisles. The tower, nave, transept, and other parts were lower, and the whole structure had a dwarfed and sombre look in comparison with that at present existing. The interior of the church was still less like its present self; instead of the beautiful high painted roof now seen, it had a heavy dome-like stone, or else a flat timbered one; in place of the glorious walls of light now seen, its windows were small and circular headed. The building was for the most part devoid of either ornament or colour, and presented altogether a dark look compared with its present lightness and beauty. Who built the original Norman church? How long was it in building? What were the life and death incidents and vicissitudes attendant thereon? How much of hope and fear commingled in the undertaking? What fraternity of masons laboured thereon? Whose spirit was breathed into its architecture? On these points conjecture may weary itself, but nothing can be known. The style of the Malvern Church was a favourite one in this district, as the cathedrals of Hereford, Gloucester, and Worcester testify; as do also the church of Leominster, and that of the abbey of Tewkesbury.

The Malvern Church, both in its Norman and in its later Perpendicular work, closely resembles Gloucester Cathedral, and there is little doubt somewhat of the same genius presided over it. Let us now suppose the grey Norman minster, and all its appendages, its refectory, dormitories, Prior's-house, and gate-house all completed: let us imagine it all encircled by its high wall; and then let us think what a charmed spot it must have been in that far off wilderness. Need we wonder it appealed powerfully, as it is said to have done, to the blind enthusiasm of those dark times, or that it became famous as the resort of recluses more than usually devout.

What of the monks? Were their labours over when the buildings were finished, and did they all at once become the fat, indolent fellows they are sometimes supposed to have been? It was far otherwise. The Benedictine Order of Monks was perhaps the most distinguished of any. They were directed by sentiments which, if obeyed, would far remove them from both indolence and luxury. Around and within the Malvern Priory, moreover, much had to be done; huge trees in its forests had to be felled, its Priory farm to be enclosed and cleared, its maiden soil to be upturned and cultivated, so as to develop its future harvests of fruit and grain; and the monks had to do it. The domains of conventual institutions in those days were undoubtedly the best cultivated, and monks generally added to their skill in physic, astrology, and science, the best knowledge of agriculture; remembering this, and bearing in mind the fair fame to which the Benedictines of Malvern attained, we have a right to conclude that its monks were amongst the most arduous workers of the period, and that into whatever degree of sensuality they afterwards relapsed, they were, in the Priory's earliest days, amongst the most devout and laborious of ecclesiastics. The Priory garden was well stocked with all kinds of vegetables, savoury and otherwise, to give zest to fasting days, and with herbs famous for their medicinal and healing qualities. The plant vulgarly called "monk's spinage" is still found growing wild in the neighbourhood, and is perhaps a lingering remnant of what the Priory garden contained. The poet thus describes this feature of the ancient monastery:

"When abbeys rose in towered state,
And over wood and dell
Went sounding, with a royal voice—
The stately minster bell.

Then was the abbey garden made
All with the nicest care;
Its little borders nicely cut
In fancies rich and rare.

And there they brought all curious plants.
With sainted names; a flower
For every saint's day of the year—
For every holy hour;
And there was set in pride of place
The noble passion flower.

And there they kept, the joyous monks!
Within a garden small,
All plants that had a healing power,
All herbs medicinal.

And thither came the sick, the maimed,
The moonstruck, and the blind,
For holy flower, for wort of power,
For charmed root and rind."

STONE'S "God's Acre.

Let us take a look at the monks in their monastery. A greater mistake cannot be made than to think that monasticism has ever been an unmixed evil. How ever much that kind of life may be abhorrent to the Christian activity of the 19th century, and how ever much opposed to the plain directions of holy writ such seclusion from active life in able-bodied mortals may be, there was in the conventual institutions of the dark ages much that was adapted to the necessities of those times, and that such institutions did fulfil a most important purpose, and that successive ages have owed much to their labours and fostering care, can never be successfully disputed. For several centuries the monastery was the only home for the studious, the only refuge for the weak,. and almost the only asylum for the unhappy : and there, and there only, was imparted anything worthy of the name of education. The discipline of such institutions was severe, and, it may be, the instruction was barbarous. Still this education, such as it was, saved the world from total ignorance.

The light of knowledge was kept burning in the cloister amidst surrounding darkness; not, like the fabled lamps of the sepulchre, to be extinguished when daylight and pure air were admitted, it was carefully trimmed and preserved for happier generations; and, were the present age divested of all it owes to the patient labour of Benedictine monks, such as those of Malvern, the world would be poorer than it now is. Standing though we do, therefore, upon the vantage ground of the present day's advancement, let us not disdain to follow the poor monk of Malvern's cloister into his seclusion.

I have already intimated that the Order of St. Benedict was one more than usually devout and exemplary. Learning was wisely cherished at Malvern, and, it is probable, in its cloister, the light of a pure Protestant Christianity was enkindled long before the days of Luther.

Let us see how the monks passed their time. They lived, I have said, according to the Rule of St. Benedict. That saint's Rule, by the Council of Douzy, in 876, was declared to be an "inspired work of equal authority with the Canonical Scriptures;" Leo, the Archbishop of Ravenna, calls it "A Divine rule, dictated by the Holy Ghost, and leading infallibly to heaven." This Rule was divided by the founder into seventy-three chapters, or canons, and it enjoined observances such as the following:—

1st. Soon as the Priory clock sounded the hour of two in the morning, the tenor bell of the Convent awoke the echoes of the surrounding forest, and startling, perchance, its wild inhabitants from their security, called the monks of Malvern to their first service. By the aid of their flickering oil lamps which had been burning in their dormitory through the night, they found their way into the church, and for an hour engaged themselves in the "nocturnal," or, as it is sometimes styled, the "cock-crowing." This service was founded on the saying of the psalmist David,—"At midnight will I arise and praise the Lord," and from a tradition that our Saviour rose from the dead at that hour. This duty performed, the monks could return to their dormitory till six o'clock, when 2nd "matins" was said. The hour of six o'clock was chosen for this service from its being the time at which the Jewish sacrifice was offered, and the angels were supposed to have acquainted the women with our Saviour's resurrection at that hour. 3rd. The next service was denominated "tierce," and the time for its performance was nine o'clock, by which was intended a daily commemoration of the Saviour's condemnation and scourging, which was believed to have happened at that hour. 4th. "Sexte" was next said—the hour of twelve at noon being appointed for its celebration—in honour of the time at which our Lord and Saviour was crucified, and when the sun was eclipsed to a total darkness. 5th. At three in the afternoon the monks again met in the choir of the church to sing the service called "none," in remembrance that at that hour our Saviour expired. It was also the time of public service in the Temple. 6th. Three hours later, viz. at six o'clock—the time of the evening sacrifice of the Jews in the Temple, and of our Saviour being taken down from the cross—the service described as "vespers" was said. Lastly, at seven o'clock at night.

"compline" was solemnly sung, this hour being made sacred as the time at which it was believed our "Great High Priest's" agony in the garden began. After "compline" the monks by their "rule" were not permitted to speak to each other. Their duty was to retire in silence at eight o'clock to their hard straw bed, and there engage themselves in sleep or devout meditation till two o'clock, when they were again summoned to begin a new day's devotion by the celebration of "nocturnal."

The monks all slept in separate beds, with their clothes and their girdles on, and a lamp burned beside them. Their beds were formed of a hard mat and a pillow; their covering was a blanket and a piece of serge. Severe punishments were inflicted for disobedience, from simple exclusion from the dinner table, to castigation of the flesh, and total expulsion from the monastery. The monks served weekly in rotation in the kitchen. For be it remembered they were denied altogether, in their home arrangements, the charm of woman's society, and had not power, like the poorest portion of nature's "lords of creation" now, to get a single thing done for them by woman's gentle hand and in her winning way. In cooking, baking, bed-making, washing of pots and basins, and all the thousand and one little etceteras that of necessity have to be done even in monasteries, where monks are to live; in all and everything the monks of Malvern had to help themselves. If in rambling through the forest thickets they rent their black stuff mantles or cowls, they had to mend them, and when sickness came upon them, there was no tender light-handed woman attendant to make that sickness bearable. They were all left to themselves and one another, and though a community of feeling and sameness in desolation, not to speak of higher motives, impelled them to "love one another," the writer cannot help feeling that in such an hour the kindliest of kindly monk-brothers was but a poor compensation for the loss of that other kindly nurse, who has been described as "a ministering angel." The monks not only served in the kitchen by rotation, and at table, but, in exact conformity to the divine injunction, they washed each other's feet, and they had to clean by washing their plates and platters, and—smile not, gentle reader, at the fact—to do their own washing. One object of the rules of St. Benedict was the taming of that unruly member—the tongue. All meals were to be taken in profound silence, the only voice heard being that of a monk, who, in measured tones, read from the Scriptures, or from the law of their founder. The reader, waiters, cooks, &c., dined by themselves after the rest.

Originally no meat whatever was allowed a Benedictine monk, except when sick; but, as monasteries increased inland, and there became a difficulty in procuring a constant supply of fish, some relaxation was made in this restriction. Six hours in each day were devoted to work, and two to reading.

Guests and strangers were admitted to the Prior's table, but without leave of the Prior a monk could not go anywhere, could not receive a letter or a present from a near relative, nor even speak with one, except in the presence of others. The dress of the order, though not fixed by the founder, was afterwards determined to consist of a long loose gown of black stuff, reaching down to the heels, with a cowl or hood of the same material, and a scapulary or low tunic, under that a closer habit of white flannel, and boots or sandals; a leathern girdle completed their costume. One change of dress was allowed.

To represent or symbolise the crown of thorns that encircled the head of the Saviour the tops of their heads were shaved in a circle, called the "corona." From the colour of their outward garment they were usually denominated "black monks." Each of the brotherhood was provided with a knife, a needle, a pen, and tablets for writing upon. Humility and contentment were inculcated; monks were to avoid laughter, were not to speak when unasked, and they were directed generally to bend their eyes downward. In fine, the life of a monk was intended to be a "perpetual Lent."

These were the ordinary rules by which the monks of Malvern were governed, but, as times and seasons demanded it, the variations in dress, ceremonials, eating, and drinking, and in the keeping of fasts and festivals amongst them, were without doubt almost bewildering.

The officers of its Priory consisted of a Prior, who was chief ruler. and whose authority therein was absolute ; under him a Sub-Prior : the "sacrista," who took care of the buildings, vessels, books, &c. ; the "bursar," who acted in all things as treasurer to the monastery ; the "cellarer," who was in all things commissariat officer thereof ; then there was the chamberlain, who provided clothing ; besides these there were the almoner, infirmarer, and other inferior officers.

It will be seen that if there was little of poetry in the daily routine of Malvern's conventual life, there was a good deal of symbolism in it, and that, rigid and hard though the rule was by which the monks were directed, there was considerable meaning in all and everything thereto belonging.

With these facts concerning them threaded together, the reader may, at his leisure, draw as many pictures as may please him of the monks of Malvern in the olden time. He may people as many nooks and corners of our old hills as may suit him with their figures, and, by the same means, he may body them forth anew around the Norman pillars and stately aisles of our noble Priory Church. None will become fascinated with conventual life by this narration. However much such institutions were needed in the past, there was a good deal that was monstrous in them, and they were especially so in their one feature, viz., that in all things a monk had not a bit of free will ; he was tied and bound ; cribbed and confined, both in mind and body ; and, as a fact, dared hardly to say, while living, that his soul was his own.

> "*We* need not bid for cloister'd cell
> Our neighbours and our work farewell,
> Nor strive to wind ourselves *too high*
> For sinful man beneath the sky."
>
> KEBLE.

CHAPTER III.

PRIOR WALCHER OF LORRAINE.

"Whilome each trusty priest at early call
Of matin bell, at prayer was always founde
And eke, a flocke, grey mantled pilgrims alle,
Soughte morninlye the churches hallowed grounde,
And when the vesper's larum 'gan to sounde,
Agen pour'd forth to praise by taper light;
And sacred memorie kept the holie grounde
Of yearlie vigils, for each sainte beside:—
Faythe, hope, and charitie did ever there abide."

ALDWYN is frequently spoken of as the "founder" of the Priory—by which is meant, as stated by Abingdon, that he "begged of the charity of others as much as perfected this foundation." It was by his exertions, mainly, that the work was accomplished; he was the presiding spirit.

The obtaining of Pope Gregory VII.'s letters patent is referred to in Dr. Card's book; and, in Nash's account of the parish of Powick, we have an original grant of a donation from the great Urso D'Abitot to the Malvern brotherhood. This grant is witnessed, among others, by the great magnate's own wife, "Athelissa Vicecomitissa," who is generally believed to have been a Saxon lady, and whose influence had something to do with the grant.

Walcher, the second Prior, was a native of the dukedom of Lorraine, whence came many a distinguished ecclesiastic. He was a person of versatile talents and distinguished attainments. He was deeply versed in the sciences of astronomy, geometry, mathematics, and astrology. He was eminently pious, a man of marked humility, and so truthful, that, says William of Malmesbury, "to disbelieve the words of Walcher was to do an injustice to religion"—"*cujus verbis qui non credit injuriam religioni facit.*" Of the rule of this Prior but scanty accounts have come down to us. William of Malmesbury, however, tells us that he received from Walcher's own lips the following narrative; and, whatever my readers may think, it is evident that the said William regarded that as a reality, which was nothing more than a practical joke with fatal result. It runs thus:—"Not more than fifteen years have elapsed," says Walcher, "since a contagious disease attacked the Abbot of that place, and afterwards destroyed many of the monks. The survivors first began each to fear for himself, and to pray and to give alms more abundantly than usual. In process of time, however—for such is the nature of man—their fears gradually subsiding—they began to omit them. The cellarer more especially, who publicly and laughingly exclaimed that the stock of provisions was not adequate to such a consumption as was going on; that he had lately hoped for some reduction of expense, considering there had been so many funerals, but that his hopes were at an end, if the dead consumed what the living could not. It happened on a certain night, when from some urgent business he had deferred going to rest for a long time, that having at length got rid of the difficulties which delayed him, he went towards his dormitory. Singular is the circumstance now to be related. He saw in the chapter-house the Abbot and all who had died that year sitting in the order they had departed, whereat he was affrighted and endeavoured to escape, but was detained by force. Being reproved and corrected after the monastic manner with the scourge, he heard the Abbot speak precisely to the following effect:—That it was foolish to be ravenously seeking profit by another's death. That he himself should die very shortly; but, that whatever others might do for him, should redound only to the advantage of those whom he had defrauded. That he might now go, and endeavour to correct by his example those whom he had corrupted by his language. He departed, anddemonstrated that he had seen nothing imaginary, as well by the recent marks of the scourging, as by his death, which shortly followed."*

William of Malmesbury was greatly interested in Malvern Priory, and expected great things from it. He concludes his general remarks with these words—"*Ad immortalem spem commemoro dum mortalium rerum penuria monachos trahit et animat,*" which translated means that he hands down the Priory of Malvern to immortal hope, so long as poverty in mortal things attracts monks and inspires their conduct.

Walcher was present, and formed one in what Habbingdon calls the "glorious procession," "intertainment," and "inthronization" of "Simon chancellor of Queene Adelicia, second wife of King Henerie the First," who, he tells us, was "An. Dni 1125, chosen in Normandie Bishop of Worcester and 8 idus maii, being the day of our Lord's ascension, was by the clergie and laitie received at Worcester in solemne procession. He was 20 kal junii by William, Archbishop of Canterbury, made priest at Canterburie, and the next day following, with great honor, consecrated by the same Bishop of Worcester. Simon coming to the Bishops's see was againe with a very great assemblie and multitude of people, and a glorious procession intertained, inthronized, and in him praise celebrated to the highest trinitie. There were present at this solemnitie Roland, Bishop of Hereford, Godefry, Bishop of Bath, David, Bishop of Bangor, the Abbots of Pershore, Gloucester, and Winchcombe, all Abbots of his own diocese; the Prior of Evesham supplying the place of his Abbot, who was detained by infirmite; and Walker, Prior of Malvern, an. 1125."

The tombstone of Prior Walcher, with its inscription, still capable of being deciphered, lies in the recess of St. Ann's Chapel in the Priory Church. It appears to have been buried in the *debris* of the demolished Priory buildings at the dissolutionof the monastery, and

* It is unfortunate that this pretty legend from the monk of Malmesbury does not belong to Malvern; and, though associated by the learned Dr. Card with Malvern *Priory*, had no connection therewith, but referred to an *Abbey* many miles away, viz., that of Fulda. Those who will take the trouble to consult the pages of William of Malmesbury will see that this is so.

was dug up in the year 1711, on the south side of the church, on the site of the cloisters, "a circumstance," says Dr. Card, "which gives a sort of warrant to the conjecture that he was buried in them." The inscription, which is nothing less than a quaint monkish rhyme, is as follows :—

Philosophvs Dignvs bonvs astrologvs, lotheringvs,
Vir pivs ac humilis, monachvs, prior hvivs ovilis,
Hic jacet in cista, geometricvs ac abacista,
Doctor walcherus ; flet, plebs, dolet vndiqve clervs ;
Hvic lux prima mori dedit octobris seniori ;
Vivat vt in coelis exoret qvisqve fidelis. MCXXXV.

which has been thus arranged by Dr. Card :—

"Philosophus bonus dignus
Astrologus lotheringus,
Vir pius et humilis,
Monachus prior hujus ovilis
Hic jacet in cista
Geometricus et Abacista,
Doctor Walcherus.

Flet, plebs, dolet undique clerus,
Huic lux prima mori
Dedit Octobris seniori ;
Vivat ut in coelis
Exhoret quisque fidelis. 1135."

and is translated by Chambers as follows :—

"In this Tomb lies the Body of
DOCTOR WALCHER,
a native of the dukedom of Lorrain, and prior of this Convent ; he was an acute Philosopher, an able Astrologer, a Geometrician and Mathematician, a pious Christian and a humble Monk. His death is universally regretted both by the Clergy and Laity. He died the first of Oct. in the year of our Lord 1135. Let every Christian earnestly pray that his Soul may live in Heaven."

CHAPTER IV.

FOUNDATION GRANTS TO THE PRIORY.

> "And when the hoary Druid race had flown,
> The saintly hermit sought this quiet shade,
> Drank of the rill, and cross'd his shaven crown,
> And kiss'd the relics there devoutly laid :
> Next came the Norman in the Chace exploring,
> And the fat Prior in the convent snoring."

IT is with considerable difficulty that the first benefactions to the Priory of Malvern can be ascertained. There is reason to believe they were considerable.

The foundation is attributed to three several individuals. Tanner tells us it was "endowed by the gift of Edward the Confessor," and the prominence given to the figure of that King in the painted window of the church containing St. Werstan's history affords some ground for the opinion that King Edward had more to do with its foundation than he is generally credited with. He is there painted in gorgeous regal costume, granting to a *minute* monk a charter from which a seal of huge dimensions is suspended. I shall show that the Monks of Westminster, whose convent was specially of King Edward's foundation, manifested regard for the monastery of Malvern by bequeathments thereto. We read in the additions to Dugdale's "Monasticon" (quoted by Chambers) that the "Abbot of Westminster, with consent of Urso D'Abitot, placed there (at Malvern) a Prior and monks, and gave them the manors of Poiwyk,

Newland, and Wortesfield." Powick manor included within it those of Pixham and Priors' Court, with the tythes of Bransford. In an account preserved *in the Pleas*, taken before the King at York, in 1317, the Prior of Malvern of that day is made to express himself in the exact words of Dugdale, supplementing them with the additional piece of information that "King Henry the 1st confirmed and gave them ten pounds worth of land, with appurtenances in Baldenhall, Malvern, Northwood, and Fulford, to hold free from all services.

Bishop Thomas asserts that "Urso D'Abitot was founder before the Conquest." In the "Annales Wigorniensis," "Aldwin," the first Prior is expressly called "the founder," and said to have lived till A.D., 1140. In the register of Godfrey Giffard, who was Bishop of Worcester in 1268, a fourth person is spoken of as having to do with the foundation, in the following words:—"A certain hermit, by name Aldwyn, passed his life in the time of St. Edward the King, in the place where now the Priory of Great Malvern is situated. Also there came a Duke of Gloucester, by name Hudda, and at the request of that hermit granted to him the ground on which the said Priory is situate, together with the wood there as far as Baldgate where the said hermit gathered round him monks, and appointed a sub-prior, Andrew by name, for ruling amongst them according to the order of the blessed Benedict."

It matters little which of these personages is most legitimately entitled to the honour, or whether, as is probable, they all did something to make the undertaking successful; the main fact is evident that by the days of Henry the 1st (the Conqueror's son) the Convent of Malvern was not inadequately endowed.

In the second charter of King Henry I., recorded in the "Monast. Anglic." vol. 1, page 366, all former grants made to the Church are confirmed, and the King adds of his own, Longdon, in Gloucestershire; *Hatfield, in Herefordshire; Quatt, in Shropshire;

* Hatfield in the Holphey Hundred of Herefordshire, situate about midway between the towns of Bromyard and Leominster, was a place anciently of importance. John Colles, High Sheriffe of Hereford, in 1614, lived there. Hatfield Court, a picturesque mansion in the Elizabethan style, now in ruins and mantled with venerable ivy, tells of its former wealth and dignity

Fulford, in Staffordshire; and minor emoluments. From this charter it appears that the several manors and estates which had been granted by the Abbot of Westminster yielded the yearly rent of £24 13s. 4d. It is probable that the King was nothing more than the legal channel through which the donations were made. This was certainly the case with the township of Quatt.

The reader need hardly be reminded that one of the first results of the Norman Conquest was the partitioning of most of the habitable portions of England amongst the chiefs of the Norman soldiery. It was in this way that Urso D'Abitot became possessed of his estates in Worcestershire. The neighbouring county of Shropshire, with trifling exceptions, was given to the Conqueror's kinsman, Roger de Montgomery; and the whole of the country bordering on Wales—for the obvious purpose of repelling a hostile race—was given to chiefs tried and illustrious. These soldier chiefs, in their turn, divided their portions as pleased them amongst their followers. Roger de Montgomery, for his part, gave to one of his retainers, named Helgot, lands in Clee and Stanton, who built in the latter place a castle, which, from its possessor, was named Castle Holgate. To a son of this baron, Herbert Fitz-Helgot, Henry the First granted the manor of Dudmaston, in Shropshire, and ere long he became, by the death of his father, Lord of Castle Holgate.

To a second son, named Wydo Fitz-Helgot, was given, amongst other possessions, the township of Quatt, a domain of considerable extent. Now it was by this Wydo Fitz-Helgot that the township of Quatt thus possessed, together with another estate, became given to the Priory of Great Malvern. It was given, however, *through the King*, and by this means he, so far as Malvern history is concerned, has had the credit of the bequeathment.

The charter of Henry I. to the Malvern brotherhood, dated at Winchester, 1127, is, in substance, as follows:—"I give them" (the monks) says the king, "for the health of my soul, two hides of land, which Wydo Fitz-Helgot surrendered into my hands, whereof one is in Worcestershire, and the other in Staffordshire, by name

Quatt (quit of all guilds and assessments) to hold of me and my successors in Capéte." In 1534-5, the income receivable from Quatt by the Malvern Priory was £3 0s. 9d. The church of Quatt, has been, in times past, sadly neglected. In spite of its modern red brick disfigurements, however, it bears traces of having at one time exhibited both beauty and proportion. In 1255 its income was valued at 12 marks per annum, and it was then in the gift of the Prior of Great Malvern. Pope Nicholas' taxation gave about the same valuation in 1291. In 1534 the preferment of its parsonage was valued at £15 18s. 6d., whereof a pension of 20s. was payable to the Prior of Great Malvern. "I have given them" (the monks of Malvern), continues the King, "the land of Northwood,* to hold quietly and freely for ever." And "I give them 2 solidates of land," "which pertaineth unto Stottensden." This latter bequeathment is that of "Dowles," the supposed "Worcestershire" estate referred to. It adjoins the town and parish of Bewdley. One of the Palatine Earls granted it to Wydo Fitz-Helgot, and its ancient name was "Achescia."

The Prior of Malvern as possessor of Dowles was sued in 1292, for his right of holding *Pleas of the Crown*, of seizing the chattels of men, "fugative," or connected with felony; and having "wayt" in the manor of Dowles. He lost the said suit, and had to pay 6/- damages. The right of holding courts was afterwards conceded to him on the payment of 6/8 annual rent. Ten shillings yearly was received by the convent of Malvern for a weir, at Dowles, with a fishery. In 1534 Dowles and Northwood were collectively valued as a Shropshire estate of the Priory of Malvern, at £9 18s. 9d. per annum. "Heriots" and "amercements" at Court were 10/-. Profit in wood £1 0s. 0d. Total £11 8s. 9d. On the 14th July, 1543, the Dowles estate of "Moch Malverne" was sold for £320.

The township known as Quatt, till the date of its connection with the Priory of Great Malvern, afterwards assumed the additional name of *Malvern*, and in all legal documents is still described as the parish of "Quatt *Malvern*."

* On the east side of the Severn, and opposite Dowles.

It will doubtless be noticed that, though the lands referred to appear to have been all in Shropshire, the charter of King Henry I. speaks of them as being partly in the two counties of Worcestershire and Staffordshire, "a significant hint, that the present territorial divisions of Shropshire were not then settled." (Eyton's Shropshire.)

Hugh, Prior of Malvern in 1304, had a trial to regain possession of a mill, and one acre of land, at "Quatte," which had been taken illegally, and which in consequence had become forfeited to the King. The jury found that a former Prior had made the wrongful acquisition, and allowed possession to be retained on payment of a yearly rent of 10/- The Prior of Malvern in the year following (1206) compounded his predecessors fault by a fine of "one mark paid to the King."

The Priory of Malvern was then very indulgent in the dispensation of holidays to the incumbents of "Quatte Malverne." "Richard de Bristol, clerk in 1304, had license for *two years* non residence for the sake of studye, and respite meanwhile from taking orders." In 1325, Thomas de Leys, Priest, had "a years dispensation of leave." Robert le Hont in 1326 had "three years" dispensation given him for the "sake of studye," being an "alcolyte," and three years more in 1330. Master John Huband, August 1st, 1345, had a year's licence of "non residence," and John Slourtre, Rector of Quatt, had a year's licence for "studye," dated Feb. 7th, 1357.

Possibly there was considerable political sagacity manifested by the Conqueror and those kings who followed him, in their rich endowments of Malvern Priory, and that of other convents immediately adjoining the Welsh border. The unsettled state of the border at that time, consequent upon the fierce incursions of the Welshmen, made necessary the use of every tranquillising means. The power of ecclesiastics over the bodies and souls of men in those dark times is well known; and it is probable that this was one of the means the Conqueror and his followers used, to establish and consolidate their authority in that disrupted part of the country. For whatever the fervour of modern piety may affirm to the contrary :—

> "There was something in that ancient superstition
> Which, erring as it was, the fancy lov'd.
> The spring that with its thousand crystal bubbles
> Bursts from the bosom of some desert rock
> In secret solitude, may well be deem'd
> The hand of something purer, more refined,
> And mightier than ourselves."

And, says Sir Walter Scott, "For several ages abbeys were each a sort of Goshen, enjoying the calm light of peace and immunity, while the rest of the country, occupied by wild clans and marauding barons, was one dark scene of confusion, blood, and unremitted outrage."

No. 1. Obverse.

No. 1. Reverse.

SEAL OF MALVERN PRIORY, TWELFTH CENTURY.

CHAPTER V.

SEALS, CHARTERS, &c.

SEALS OF MALVERN PRIORY.

I.

First Seal. [XLIII, 49, 50.]

12th century. 3 × 2¼ in. The right hand side is imperfect.

Obverse. A figure of the Virgin Mary, with crown, and draped bordered with pearls, sitting on a carved throne, with her feet resting on a footstool ornamented with small arches. In the right hand a sceptre with a lily flower, or fleur-de-lis, at the top. On her lap, the Infant Saviour, with nimbus, lifting up the right hand in the act of pronouncing a blessing, in the left hand an open book.

[+SIGILLVM · SCE · MARIE · [M]ALVERNIE.

Reverse. A smaller pointed oval counterseal, 2 × 1½ in. The half-length figure of St. Michael, the Patron Saint, full face, with open wings, holding before him a crown of three points. The lower part of the seal has wavy lines representing the sea. This refers to Revelation, chapter iv, verses 6—10.

[+] SIGILLUM : S[A N]C[T]I : MICHAEL[IS.]

From an original impression among the Charters of Hereford Cathedral.

II.

Later Seal. [Harl. ch. 83 A. 34].

[A.D. 1287—1300.] Light brown wax, a fine but imperfect impression. About 2⅝ × 2 in. when perfect.

Obverse. A figure of the Virgin Mary, wearing a headdress of unusual form, tunic, girdle, and fur cloak, seated on an elaborately carved throne. The Infant Saviour on her left knee is nearly destroyed, one leg remains.

........................VE]RNI[E].

Reverse. Same as in XLIII, 50.

Charter to which Seal No. 2 is appended.

Sciant presentes et futuri quod nos frater Ricardus Prior Majoris Malvernie et ejusdem loci conventus, dedimus, concessimus et hac presenti carta nostra confirmavimus, Stephano de Lang clerico dicto de Granger, totam terram, et tenementum illud, quod Stephanus quondam vicarius de Lang, Johannes capellanus, de Lang, et Margiria de Gloucestria, quondam de nobis tenuerunt, ad terminum vite eorum in villa de Lang, exceptis inde et retentis nobis, sex selionibus et dimidio terre in littlefeld, apud La Forde, et duobus seylionibus in hacreye super montem, juxta terram Roberti Agu, et uno seylione eodem campo in edberforlong et quatuor seylionibus in fontfeld super lynch, et uno seylione eodem campo apud la Neuwalle, Tenendum et habendum totam predictam terram, et tenementum, cum pratis, pascuis, et pasturis, et omnibus suis pertinentiis, de nobis et successoribus nostris, sibi et heredibus suis, libere, quiete, bene et in pace, in feodo et hereditate in perpetuum. Reddendo inde annuatim nobis et successoribus nostris, ipse et heredes sui, octo solidos argenti ad duos anni terminos, videlicet ad festum beati Michaelis, quatuor solidos, et ad festum Annunciationis beate Marie, quatuor solidos, pro omnimodis serviciis, Wardis, tallagiis, auxiliis, consuetudinibus et secularibus exaccionibus, et demandis, salvis tantum et retentis nobis et successoribus nostris, sectis curie nostre in villa de Lang, herietis et releviis cum acciderint, et regali servicio quantum pertinet ad tantum tenementum in eadem villa. Nos vero predicti frater Ricardus et ejusdem loci conventus et successores nostri, predicto Stephano et heredibus suis, totam terram et tenementum predictum, cum omnibus suis pertinentiis ut predictum est, contra omnes homines et feminas, Warentizabimus, defendemus et acquietabimus in perpetuum. In cujus rei testimonium, presenti carte, sigillum nostrum commune apposuimus, hiis testibus, Willelmo de Parco, Andrea de Bello campo, Roberto de Felde, Symone de Fremelade, Willelmo de de Burthon, et aliis.

British Museum, Harl. ch. 83.A.34.

Let all present and future know that we brother Richard, Prior of Great Malvern and the Convent of the same place, have given, granted, and by this our present charter confirmed, to Stephen de Lang, clerk, called Le Granger, the whole of the land and that tenement which Stephen formerly vicar of Lang, John chaplain of Lang, and Margery de Gloucester, formerly held of us, for term of their lives, in the vill of Lang, except therefrom and retained by us six selions and a half of land in littlefeld, at La forde, and two selions in hacreye-super-montem next to the land of Robert Agu, and one selion in the same plain in Edberforlong, and four selions in fontfeld-super-lynch, and one selion in the same plain at the Neuwalle, To have and to hold the whole land aforesaid, and the tenement with the meadows, feedings, and pastures, and all their appurtenances, of us and our successors to him and his successors, freely, quietly, well, and in peace, in fee and inheritance for ever. Yielding therefor yearly to us and our successors he himself and his heirs eight shillings of silver at the two terms of the year, namely at the feast of the blessed Michael four shillings, and at the feast of the Annunciation of the blessed Mary four shillings for all manner of services, wards, tallages, aids, customs, and secular exactions and demands, saving only and retaining to us and our heirs suits of our court in the vill of Lang, the heriots and reliefs when they may have arisen, and royal service as much as pertains to such a tenement in the same vill. We therefore the aforesaid brother Richard and the convent of the same place and our successors will warrant, defend, and acquit for ever to the aforesaid Stephen and his heirs the whole land and tenement aforesaid, with all its appurtenances as is aforesaid, against all men and women. In witness whereof, we have appended our common seal to the present charter, these being the witnesses, William de Parco, Andrew de Bello Campo (*i.e.*, Beauchamp), Robert de Felde, Simon de Fremelade, William de Burthon, and others.

No. 2. Obverse.
Later Seal. [Harl., ch. 83, A. 20.]

No. 2. Reverse.

No. 3.
Seal of Prior Thomas.
13th Century.

SEALS OF MALVERN PRIORY.

III.

Seal of Thomas, Prior of Malvern, 13th century.

White wax. This is a seal of elegant and interesting design, perhaps that of Prior Thomas de Wick, A.D. 1217. The edge is chipped. 2 × 1⅞ in. [xxxix, 34.]

Pointed oval: In a niche, under an early form of canopy, the Virgin Mary, crowned, seated, holding the Infant Saviour, and a sceptre as before, between St. Michael the Archangel on the right hand, and a Saint on the left hand, above whom is a star. In the base, under a carved arch with tracing at the sides, the Prior, half-length in profile to the left, praying.

Charter to which the above Seal is attached.

[+]SIGILLVM : THOME : PRIORIS : MAIO[RIS : M]ALVERN'

Omnibus Sancte Matris Ecclesie filiis, Simon dei gratia Wigorniensis Episcopus, Salutem. Ex commissi nobis officii solicitudine tenemur ea quæ ecclesiis et divinis locis collatione fidelium mancipantur, ut firmam stabilitatem sorciantur, episcopalis auctoritatis diligentia roborare. Noverit itaque modernorum universitas et in venturis temporibus successura posteritas, quod in dedicatione Ecclesie Sancti Michaelis et beati Martini de Est lech quæ per ministerium nostrum Dei intuitu, et petitione dilectorum filiorum R. prioris, et fratrum Malvernie celebrata est, venerabilis frater noster Gilebertus abbas Gloecestrie donavit eidem Ecclesie unam virgatam terre in campo de Vifhida cum pertinenciis suis in perpetuum libere et quiete possidendam. Concessit etiam cum terra quam dicta Ecclesia ante dedicationem habuerat, omnem libertatem et plenariam communiam totius ville, tam in dominicis pasturis, quam in omnibus aliis rebus, sicut Ricardus filius Puncii fratribus Malvernie concessit, quod ex Carta ejusdem Ricardi quam inspeximus nobis innotuit. Monachi quoque Malvernie dederunt unam hidam terre quam habebant in campo de Sudthropa cum suis pertinenciis et cum omnibus libertatibus et consuetudinibus quas ipsi habebant in villa de Estlech et ejus pertinenciis. Preterea parochiani omnes concesserunt et super altare deposuerunt, cum omnibus decimis suis et obventionibus, universa parochialia quæ Ecclesiis debentur. Hanc siquidem predictorum donationem et concessionem in memorate Ecclesie de Estlech pos-

To all the sons of Holy Mother Church, Simon by the grace of God Bishop of Worcester, greeting. By the anxious care of the office which has been committed to us we are bound to corroborate with the diligence of episcopal authority those things which are delivered to churches and divine places by the gift of the faithful, in order that they may acquire firm stability. Therefore let the whole body of those who now exist, and posterity which is about to succeed in future times, know that in the dedication of the church of Saint Michael and of the Blessed Martin of East Lech, which was celebrated by our ministration at God's disposition and by the petition of our beloved children R——, the prior and the brethren of Malvern, our venerable brother Gilbert the abbot of Gloucester gave to the same church a virgate of land in the territory of Vifhida with its appurtenances to be held for ever freely and quietly. He granted also with the land which the said church held before the dedication, all the liberty and plenary common of the whole of the vill, as well in demesne pastures, as in all other things, as Richard the son of Puncius granted to the brethren of Malvern, which is declared in the Charter of the same Richard which we have inspected. The monks, also, of Malvern gave a hide of land which they held in the territory of Sudthrop with its appurtenances and with all liberties and customs which they themselves held in the vill of East Lech and its appurtenances. Moreover all the parishioners have granted and deposited upon the altar with all

sessione in perpetuum habendam auctoritati pontificali confirmantes, omnes qui de prelibatis aliquid subtrahere vel inde quicquam infringere attentaverint, publice excommunicavimus. Ut igitur ratum in perpetuum et inconvulsum perseveret, presentis scripti seriem sigilli nostri impressione communimus et publice notioni commendamus. Testibus Gileberto abbate Gloecestrie, Ricardo Archidiacano Gloecestrie, Patricio et Radulfo monachis Gloecestrie, Ernisio et Hugone monachis Malvernie, Johanne filio Frecher', Pagano, Magistro Willelmo clericis episcopi, Osberto capellano, Rogero janitore Malvernie, Aldred.

British Museum, L.F.C. xviii 2*
A.D. 1139—1149.

heir tithes and offerings all the parochial things which are due to churches. Confirming therefore this grant of the things aforesaid and this gift for ever to be held in the possession of the aforesaid Church of East Lech, by pontifical authority, we have publicly excommunicated all those who shall have attempted to subtract anything from what has been appointed or to infringe anything thereof. Therefore, to the end that it may stand settled for ever and unassailed, we fortify with the impression of our seal the text of this present document and commend it to public knowledge. These being witnesses:—Gilbert, Abbot of Gloucester, Richard Archdeacon of Gloucester, Patrick and Ralph, monks of Gloucester, Ernisius and Hugh, monks of Malvern, John the son of Frecher, Paganus, Master William, Clerks of the Bishop, Osbert the Chaplain, Roger the porter of Malvern (? keeper of the key of the Town Gate), Aldred.

Deed referred to in the above document, Photograph of which has been taken by permission of the authorities of the British Museum (see Frontispiece).

Sciant omnes presentes et futuri, quod ego Ricardus filius Puncii pro anima mea, et uxoris méé Mathildis, et liberorum meorum, et pro animabus patris et matris méé, atque omnium parentum meorum, concessi et in perpetuam elemosinam libere et quiete dedi Deo et Sancte Marie et Sancto Michaeli Malvernie, et Monachis ibidem Deo servientibus, ecclesiam de Lecha cum quinque virgatis terre liberis et quietis et absolutis ab omni servicio, et cum tota decimatione de dominio meo, et de curia mea ejusdem ville, et cum omnibus pertinentibus ad jam dictam ecclesiam de Lech. Concessi etiam predictis monachis et clericis eorum ad deserviendum ecclesie eorum de Lech constitutis plenariam communiam totius ville et terre méé, in aquis, in viis et semitis, et pasturis, et in omnibus aliis rebus, et in dominica pastura mea, scilicet bobus ipsorum cum meis, et aliis overiis eorum cum aliis overiis meis, quiete et absque omni vexatione in perpetuam elemosinam habendam. Testes sunt, Simon et Osbernus fratres mei, Willelmo Bras, Richardo de la Wastine, et alii.

British Museum, L.F.C. xviii, 2.
12th century.

Let all present and future know that I Richard son of Puncius, for my soul and that of my wife Mathildis and of my children, and for the souls of my father and of my mother and of all my parents, have granted and in perpetual alms freely and quietly have given to God and to Saint Mary and to Saint Michael of Malvern and to the Monks there serving God, the church of Lech with five virgates of land free and quit and absolved from all service and with the whole tithing of my demesne and of my court of the same vill, and with all the things appertaining to the already mentioned church of Lech. I have also granted to the aforesaid monks and to their clerks for service of their church of Lech appointed full common of the whole my vill and land, in waters, in ways and paths, and in pastures, and in all other things and in my demesne pasture, to wit in their oxen with mine, and their other flocks and herds with my other flocks and herds quietly and without any vexation to be held in perpetual alms. The witnesses are, Simon and Osbern my brothers, William Bras, Richard de la Wastine, and others.

IV.

The following is the grant of Henry I., as to *assarts* in the forest of Malvern :—

CARTÆ ANTIQUÆ IN ARCE LONDINENSI.

Brit. Mus., M.S. Harl. 85, f. 132b.
II., 29.

Henricus Rex Anglorum et Dux Normannorum concessit ecclesie beate Marie Malvernie et Monachis ibidem quietanciam de assartis que a fratribus ejusdem Monasterii vel eorum sumptu in foresta Malvernie facta sunt vel futuris temporibus in bosco suo de Malvernie facere voluerint pront ad utilitatem ecclesie sue expedire viderint cum una virgata terre in Badenhale de feodo de Hanle quam rex Edwardus dedit et pater predicti regis Henrici videlicet Willielmus concessit et predicta assarta libera esse precepit et prohibuit quod inter assarta non computentur. Et etiam donavit eis terram de Northwode ad sartandum inter Haukebroke et Lyndrugesich ab Hevedweye in Sabrina quiete et libere in perpetuum possidendum. Et est datum Carte ipsius Regis Anno Verbi incarnati MCXXVIII. Indictione quinta. Wynton.

Henry King of England and Duke of Normandy has granted to the church of the blessed Mary of Malvern and the monks therein the quittance of the essarts which have been made by the Brethren of the same Monastery or which they shall have wished to make in future times in his wood of Malvern, as they shall have considered expedient for the use of their church, together with a virgate of land in Badenhale of the fee of Hanle, which King Edward gave, and the father of the aforesaid King Henry, namely William, granted, and ordered the aforesaid essarts to be free and forbade that they should be reckoned among the essarts. And also he has given them the land of Northwode for essarting between Hawkebrook and Lyndrugesich from Henedwye in the Severn to be possessed quietly and freely for ever. And the date of the Charter of the said King is in the year of the Incarnate word 1128, in the fifth indiction, at Winchester.

Lindrigesith, N.N. No. 18, another copy, at f. 179b.

CHAPTER VI.

A PIOUS BARON AND TYRANNICAL ABBOT.

"I love these ancient ruins;
We never tread upon them but we set
Our foot upon some reverend history."

WEBSTER.

"How all things glow with life and thought
Where'er our faithful fathers trod:
The very ground with speech is fraught,
The air is eloquent of God.

In vain would doubt or mockery hide
The buried echoes of the past;
A voice of strength, a voice of pride,
Here dwells amid the storm and blast."

IN the fifth year of the reign of Henry II., 1151, William Burdet assigned to Roger, or Rogerus, the Prior of Malvern, lands on which to build a monastery, and mill, with its appurtenances, in Warwickshire—by name "Avercote," or "Aucote,"—as a cell to the Priory of Malvern, and endowed the same. The assignment runs thus:—"I, William Burdet, give to God and Saint Mary, at Malvern, and to the monks serving God there, all the lands I have at Aucote, with the mill and Schetinton, with all its appurtenances." The grant was made on the condition that the monks should send two of their convent to serve in the church there, from the "feast of St. Michael's" till that time "twelve months." The next year, there were to be two monks more, and as the capacity of the convent became enlarged others were to be added. To Malvern Aucote was to be a cell, and its Priors were from time to time to be constituted out of the brethern at Malvern. The agreement "betwixt" William Burdet and Roger the Prior was set in exact legal-monastic form, and was signed at Westminster in the presence of Lawrence, Abbot of Westminster, Gregory, Abbot of Malmesbury, and the Abbot of St. Albans. Robert, Earl of Leicester, was one amongst other witnesses.

The monks of Malvern had another cell at Brockbury, in the parish of Colwall, Herefordshire, in which two monks were located. Brockbury was situate in a thickly wooded district. It was formerly entirely surrounded by forest, and must have been sufficiently desolate and unprotected to have satisfied the longings of the most devout ascetic.

A path therefrom still exists across the mountain, called the "Pig's Path"—a corruption of "Pix's Path," it being the way by which the newly consecrated holy wafer was sent from the Priory of Malvern to the monks domiciled in that lonely cell.

Over both these cells the Prior of Malvern had jurisdiction. In appointing the officers for each he had to get the consent of the Abbot of Westminster; but the said Abbot exercised no control whatever in the disposal of their revenues; and, in reference to the grant of Aucote, it was stipulated that neither of them was to "diminish the substance of the place."

The circumstance which led to the foundation of the little Priory of Aucote is of a somewhat dramatic character. It is strikingly illustrative of the spirit of adventure of those times—of its summary way of settling difficulties by an appeal to the sword, and of the little regard then paid to the life of even the most loved amongst them. The event, in all its simplicity and directness, as narrated by Dugdale, runs as follows:—"William Burdet, being both a valiant and devout man, made a journey to the Holy Land for subduing of the infidels of those parts, and his steward, whilst he was thus absent, solicited the chastity of his lady, who resisted those his uncivil attempts with much scorn. Whereupon he grew so full of envy towards her, that so soon as he had advertisement of his master's arrival in England, he went to meet him; and, to shadow his own foul crime, complained to him of her looseness with others, which false accusation so enraged her husband, that when he came home, and she approached to receive him with joyful embraces, he forthwith mortally stabbed her; and, to expiate the same unhappy act, after he understood the truth, he built this monastery." Who Burdet was, where he lived, or why he came to the altar of Malvern Priory, in particular, to offer a penitent's atonement for the shedding of innocent blood; on all these points both reader and writer must content themselves to remain in ignorance.

A recumbent figure from the tomb of Lady Burdet is engraved by Dugdale, who says, "She had her hands cut off as she held them up in a supplicating posture." He also reports "Her statue is with her hands cut off in the middle." "Of this storie," continues he, "though I have nothing but tradition, yet that he was founder hereoff is most certain."—*Dugdale's Warwickshire.*

William Burdet, grandchild of the founder, gave the rent, which was 12/-, of a tenement for the maintenance of a "lampe to burne before the altar of our Lady in the Church there," and a "water mill being in Radcliffe in the County of Leicester."

Sometime near the end of the reign of Henry II., and, so far as can be seen, during the rule of Prior Walter first or second,—for there were two Prior Walters in succession after the death of Roger,—a considerable addition was made to the Priory church of Malvern, in the building of a Lady Chapel.

Very faint traces of this building now exist above ground; but remains of the crypt may still be seen immediately beneath the east doorway of the church, and also the Semi-Norman shaft which formerly supported the roof.

Some years since, at the expense of the late Rev. F. Dyson, the ground was searched, and foundations were discovered that proved conclusively that a Lady Chapel of very considerable dimensions once existed on the spot. The remains thus discovered belong to what is known as "Semi-Norman," of which the east end of Worcester Cathedral affords a good illustration.

This Chapel has been represented in restored views as a copy, on a small scale, of the Lady Chapel of Gloucester Cathedral, which is late "Perpendicular" work. This theory is unsupported by evidence of any kind, while on the other hand the fact that underneath the east window "Decorated" bosses and tracery have been discovered affords distinct evidence of the existence at some period of a structure in this style; and I have little doubt that this was the Lady Chapel, built in the "Decorated" or "Middle Pointed" style, at the time when that style was in vogue, over the "Semi-Norman" crypt.

During the reign of Henry II. a dispute arose between the Bishop of Worcester and the Abbot of Westminster, as to which of them should have the jurisdiction of Malvern Priory. This dispute seems to have been of a more acrimonious character than became persons of so sacred a calling. The monks of Malvern desired to be exempt from episcopal jurisdiction, and preferred that of the Abbot. On a vacancy in the office of Prior occurring in the Monastery of Malvern, the monks chose Walter or "Walterus," and they persuaded the Abbot of Westminster to induct him into it. This indignity the Bishop of Worcester successfully resented: he suspended the new Prior and eventually succeeded in regaining his jurisdiction. A patched up peace between the disputing brethren was made, and so during the short rule of some three Priors all went on with that heavenly-mindedness so desirable in spiritual affairs. In the year 1279, William de Ledburg, or "Ledburie." was elected Prior, duly approved by the Abbot. and instituted without any demur by the Bishop. But Prior Ledburg was not a man of inflexible virtue; and crimes altogether derogatory to his monkish vows were laid to his charge. His manner of life became known to Godfrey, Bishop of Worcester, a man of sterling piety and rigid discipline. The Bishop first severely admonished the Prior, and in the end, for his "soul's health and reformation of his morals," held a regular visitation, at which the "serious charges" made were proved. Upon this the Bishop at once deposed the Prior. Richard de Eston, or, as some say, Wm. de Wykewan, was elected in his place. This election, though approved of by Worcester, was resented by Westminster, whose Abbot refused to accede to it, upon which war was again proclaimed. and the old dispute was carried on with increased violence. Long and angry controversies ensued. A well-known writer on Malvern subjects in a letter dated Feb. 22, 1867, gave the following summary of this dispute as described by Bishop Thomas in his *Antiquitates Prioratus Malverne* :—"A deputation of monks went up to London, under the hope of appeasing and making terms with the Abbot; but instead of receiving the deputation courteously, the wrathful and tyrannical priest treated them as mutineers, threw them, on his own authority, into prison, and, as stated by Thomas, on I presume reliable authority, loaded the newly elected Prior with chains in his dungeon." "The Abbot then insisted on the restoration of the wicked de Ledebury, spite of his alleged immoralities, nor would he release de Wickewan till this was done, and his authority firmly re-established in Malvern. The Bishop was obliged to succumb in the end." In his *Survey of Worcester Cathedral*, Thomas says "The cause was hotly controverted in the courts of Canterbury, and at Rome, and in that of the King, and ended not till Nov. 1283, when the monks of Malvern and the Abbot of Westminster, to make him" (the Bishop) "amends for the expenses he had been at in defending his lawful jurisdiction over that Priory, released unto him the manor of Knightwick, in which the King granted him free warren." The arrangement consisted in the manor aforesaid, with all its emoluments, being given up to the Bishop of Worcester's use, the Malvern Priory being declared entirely exempt from his jurisdiction, and remaining only nominally dependent upon that of the Abbot of Westminster.

William de Wykewan, after being released from the prison-house of the Abbot of Westminster, returned to Malvern, and was directed to bear rule at the cell or Priory of Aucote. At times doubtless he revisited Malvern, and it is probable that he died there. Somewhat corroborative of this is a tombstone, found underneath the blocked up Norman doorway of the Church formerly leading to the Cloisters of Malvern. This fragment, of 13th century date, was found in the year 1863, and refers without doubt to a "Willelmus de Wickwana." The following is a suggested restoration of the inscription :—

> (Hac jacet in cista Wil)lelmus de Wikwana ;
> (Spiritus in coelis cum) Christo nunc requiescat ;
> (Corpus ut in terr) a lector sta : perlege : plora ;
> (In cinerem redii) t : prior hic : eris ipse quod exstat.

TRANSLATION.

> *In this tomb lies Wil* liam de Wikewan ;
> May *his spirit* now rest *in heaven with* Christ ;
> *As his body in earth* : reader, stand, read through : bewail ;
> *He has returned to ashes* ; prior was this man : you yourself shall be what he is.

One third of the stone is broken off, and consequently all conclusions respecting the inscription must remain conjectural. The part supplied in the Latin verses is in brackets, and in the translation in italics. The name "De Wikewan" occurs twice in a document quoted in Nash's "Worcestershire," vol. 2, page 17. Whoever this De Wykewan was, the stone in question was intended to do the double duty of honouring the departed and admonishing those who survived him. The inscription is boldly engraven in Lombardic characters.

The loss of the manor of Knightwick, with others that befel them, rendered the monks of Malvern unable for a time fully to discharge their accustomed functions of almsgiving.

The following Extracts relating to Great Malvern Priory, from the Cotton MSS in the British Museum, Faustina A. III. *(Registrum Cartarum Ecclesiæ Beati Petri Westmonasteriensis)*, translated from the original text, refer to these transactions, and will be read with interest.

Privilege of Pope Adrian IV., concerning the cell of Saint Mary of Malvern :

> Adrian the Bishop, servant of the servants of God, to his beloved sons Gervase, Abbot of the church of St. Peter, Westminster, and his brethren, greeting and apostolical benediction. As often as such things are desired by ecclesiastics which agree with justice and do not deviate from the path of reason, with willing mind we ought to grant them, and we ought to accomplish the wishes of those who ask them, with a furthering effect. To this object, beloved sons in the Lord, we, willing to give an agreeable assent to your just requirements, and to preserve to the church of the blessed Peter of Westminster, in which ye are devoted to his divine worship, all his rights and possessions whole and intact, do confirm the cell of St. Mary of Malvern, which is known to belong rightfully to your monastery and to be subject to it, with all its appurtenances, to you, and, through you, to your church, by apostolic authority, and we establish this by the virtue of this present charter. Ordering that no man ever at any future time be allowed to infringe this page of our confirmation,

nor even in the least degree to contradict it. But if any one presume to attempt it, let him know that he will incur the indignation of Almighty God and of the blessed Peter and Paul his apostles.

Dated at the Lateran Palace, 8 kalends of June. [25th May.]

Adrian IV., Pope from A.D. 1154 to 1159.

Charter of Godfrey, Bishop of Worcester, that he has no jurisdiction in the cell of Great Malvern :

To all the faithful of Christ to whom the present letter shall come, Godfrey, by divine permission Bishop of the Church of Worcester, greeting in the Lord. We have inspected apostolic letters, not cancelled, nor abolished, nor vitiated in any part, containing that the Abbot and Convent of Westminster, in the Diocese of London, with all their cells and Priories and especially with the Priory of Great Malvern and the Monks of the same cells and Priories, belong to the Church of Rome, with no one's intervention, and are exempt from all Diocesan law and ordinary jurisdiction. We therefore truly acknowledging for us and our successors the aforesaid exemption in the same Priory of Great Malvern in our Diocese, admit that the aforesaid Priory and monks of the same place are exempt and free from all episcopal jurisdiction and ordinary jurisdiction; moreover that they ought to be subject to the Abbot and Convent of Westminster only, according to that which is more fully contained in Privileges of divers former Roman Pontiffs granted to the same. Furthermore whereas between the aforesaid Abbot and Convent of Westminster and the Prior and Monks of Great Malvern aforesaid on the one part and us on the other, a matter of question had arisen concerning the right of patronage of the said Priory, also concerning possession or, as it were, the right of visiting the said Priory and Monks of the same, and of correcting things needing correction, and of removing those who should be removed, and of seeking, demanding, and receiving from the same, procurations by reason of the visitation, we acknowledge for ourselves and our successors that the right of patronage or the advowson in that Priory and also all manner of jurisdiction, lawful, Diocesan, and ordinary, in the aforesaid Priory and Monks of the same, rightfully appertains to the same Abbot and Convent of Westminster; and we of our own accord purely and absolutely yield all right and claim which we have or could have had hereafter, or possession of, as it were, lawful Diocesan or ordinary jurisdiction by us or our predecessors at any time or in any manner acquired, and we grant them for ourselves and our successors to the same Abbot and Convent of Westminster by these presents. And let not the Priors for the same Priory for the time being, nor the Monks, be bound to proffer obedience to us or our successors in any way for that Priory or for the things appertaining to the same, excepting only the parish churches, portions, and pensions ecclesiastical appertaining to the said Priory which they acquire for their own uses, in the which churches indeed, portions, and pensions ecclesiastical, we reserve to us and our successors canonical jurisdiction. So, however, that we may not demand any procurations from the same churches, portions, and pensions, or parsons, by reason of the same. In witness whereof our seal has been appended to these presents.

Dated at Westminster, Friday, the Vigil of St. Leonard the Abbot, in the year of grace, MCCLXXXIII.

Agreement between Westminster and Malvern :

To all the faithful of Christ about to inspect the present writing, Thomas de Wych, Prior of Great Malvern and the Convent of the same place, greeting in the Lord. Let the whole of you know that, whereas by grant of our venerable father William, by the grace of God the Abbot, and our brethren of Westminster, it is lawful for us to elect for ourselves a Prior out of our own or their congregation when our Priorship is vacant, lest their liberality be irksome to them, we grant and profess that we are subject to them after this manner, namely that we will present our elected [Prior] to our Abbot and our brethren at Westminster, desiring their assent, and his election having been approved by them on condition only that he be fit, the same our elect shall in that same place make to our Abbot obedience of submitting to him according to the Rule of the Blessed Benedict, saving this, that he shall not be maliciously amoved by the Abbot. Moreover our Abbot of Westminster shall visit for ever our house once only every year, with ten of his own horses, and we will honourably admit him as is becoming, and in the same place he shall make his stay for two days and two nights at our cost, and shall enter our

Chapter as an Abbot and freely correct things that should be corrected as well in the Person of our Prior as of our Monks, according to the Rule of St. Benedict, provided he shall attempt nothing maliciously without reason; so also that it shall not be permitted to him to amove a Monk from Malvern, or to send one thither from Westminster without our assent. We will also that the monks of our house make their profession to the Abbot at Westminster according to the ancient custom and freely return to Malvern after having made their profession. Moreover, the same our Abbot shall receive his household in the Manor of Powick according to the ancient custom once every year, with this arrangement however, that he will not exceed in the number of horsemen twenty horses of his own, nor maliciously to the injury of our house bring strangers with him. Suit, also, of the hundred, and view of frank pledge, and all other customs which hitherto the Abbot and Monks of Westminster have been accustomed to have of the Manor of Powick, so henceforth they may have notwithstanding a charter of any Abbot of Westminster obtained respecting the suit of the same hundred, provided that no prejudice be produced against us respecting other articles contained in the same charter. And in order that all these things may obtain the effect of perpetual establishment, we confirm them by the present writing, and corroborate them by the impression of our seals. These being the witnesses, &c.

King Edward* [I] confirms the form of peace made between the Lord G[odfrey Gifford] Bishop of Worcester, and Westminster, respecting the Cell of Malvern:

Edward, by the grace of God King of England, Lord of Ireland, and Duke of Aquitaine, to all whom the present letters shall have come, greeting.

We have inspected the letters patent which the venerable father Godfrey, Bishop of Worcester, made to our Beloved in Christ the Abbot and Convent of the Church of St. Peter, Westminster, and the Prior and Convent of the Cell of Great Malvern, concerning the form of peace, respecting certain contentions and discords had between them, entered into and confirmed by friendly composition in these words:—

To all the faithful in Christ, &c., As is written in the second preceding leaf [See pages 7-10 of this transcript].

And because the form of peace aforesaid, in the presence of us and our council mediating, ordained by the assent and will of the parties aforesaid, has been entered upon and confirmed, in order that continual remembrance of the matter thus concluded may be held more fully and certainly, we by the tenor of these presents attest the form and composition aforesaid thus entered upon and confirmed, and also we grant and confirm them for ourselves and our heirs, as much as in us lies, as the letters patent aforesaid reasonably testify. In witness whereof we have caused these our letters to be made patent.

Witness me myself at Hereford, the fifteenth day of November, in the eleventh year of our reign. [A.D. 1283.]

Also: The Ratification by the same King of the Peace made between the Abbot and Convent of Westminster and the Prior and Convent of Malvern:

Edward, by the grace of God King of England, &c., to all whom the present letters shall have come, greeting.

We have inspected the letters patent, which our Beloved in Christ Brother William de Ledebury, Prior of Great Malvern, and the Convent of the same place, made to our Beloved in Christ Brother Richard, Abbot of Westminster, and the Convent of the same place, of the ratification of peace between the same Abbot and Prior and Convents aforesaid on the one part and the venerable Father Godfrey, Bishop of Worcester, and his Chapter, respecting certain contentions and discords between them moved, before us and our council entered upon and confirmed, at our mediation, in these words:—

Let it be patent to all by these presents that we, Brother William de Ledebyri, Prior of Great Malvern, and the Convent of the same place, do

* Edward I. was at Rothelan, near Denbigh, on 13th November, 11th year, but at Hereford on 15th November, 12th year, A.D. 1283. See "Close Rolls" and Hartshorne's *Itinerary of Edward I.* in *Collectanea Archæologica*, vol ii, page 129. It is probable that the scribe of the Cotton M.S. wrote xi instead of xii by error.

ratify and hold valid the peace made by the Lord Edward, by the grace of God King of England, and his council, between the venerable father Lord Godfrey, by the same grace Bishop of Worcester, and his Chapter, on the one part, and Richard, by the same permission Abbot of Westminster, and the Convent and us on the other, being willing to fulfil and confirm it and in future times firmly to observe it. We will also that if we contravene it, which God forbid, that the Lord King and his heirs compel us to observe it by any of his and their ministers under any penalty they please to inflict on us of losing any of our goods whatever, or distraining on them, moveable and immoveable, and assigning them to whomsoever they please. In witness whereof to these present letters we have caused the seal of our Chapter to be appended. Dated at Malvern, 7th of the ides of October [9th], at the close of the eleventh year of the same King. [A.D. 1283.]

We therefore, holding valid and agreeable the ratification aforesaid made in the aforesaid form, grant and confirm it for ourselves and our heirs as much as in us lies, as the letters patent aforesaid reasonably testify. In witness whereof we have caused these our letters to be made patent.

Witness me myself at Hereford, the fifteenth day of November, in the eleventh year of our Reign. [A.D. 1283.]

As some compensation, gifts of property from other sources were made to the Malvern monks, Gilbert de Clare, son-in-law of Edward II., Lord of Malvern Forest, being among the donors.

I beg the reader to cast his eye back in imagination to the lonely haunts of Malvern in that far off time. Let him think of the monks between the hours of their constantly recurring services; rambling along our fine old hills: let him picture them with their black serge dresses, turned up cowls, and shaven crowns, now meditating on this science, and then on that; now lifting up their voices in pious song, and now vexing themselves with petty disputes and "carking care." Think of them looking deep down, with troubled brow, into the subtle mazes of theology, and unfathomable mysteries of Providence, and anon see them straining beneath a burden on the Priory farm, or, with a toiler's earnestness, industriously cultivating the neighbouring grange of Newland. Or picture them in the cloister cell, with ready pen, multiplying copies of the sacred page; or engaged in illuminating a missal that should be the marvel of future ages. See them soaring into the delectabilities of literature, or solacing their leisure moments with exaggerated narrations of saintly martyrs' sufferings, or legendary lore. Think of them thus, and multiply the picture, but do not think of them as being so very different from any of us. Men they were of "like passions" and like frailty, and like fluctuations of hope and fear commingled with them, and though removed so many years away, and surrounded by circumstances so differing, they were made like us; and in more respects than we think we are akin to them.

"Monks," says a recent writer, "had a great mission and they fulfilled it, and the more we become acquainted with their history and inner life, the more inclined shall we be to put a charitable construction on both."

The labours of men who sheltered sacred truths as within an ark for so many generations, and who, in the midst of all their errors and corruptions, kept the embers of pure religion burning, should never be despised; with all their faults they taught many a noble House of God to rise as it were from the dust, and point its tapering spire to Heaven, and exhibited in the rearing of such buildings, an expansiveness of thought and breadth of purpose that at least will bear to be put in comparison with anything later generations have done.

"Huge, mighty, massive, hard and strong,
Were the choice stones they lifted then:
The vision of their life was long,
They knew their God—those faithful men.

They pitched no tent for change or death,
No home to man's last shadowy day;
There! there! the everlasting breath,
Would breathe *whole centuries away*."

CHAPTER VII.

KNIGHTS AND BISHOPS.

A chase for Royale deere
  Rounde doth besette thee,
Too manie I do fear
  For aught theye gette thee;
Yette though theye eat away
  They corne and grasse and haye,
Doe not forgette I say,
    To prayse the Lorde.—*Old Song.*

"The very nature of the place was peculiarly fitted to draw the mind aloft. Religion found here a temple erected by nature which does not yield to the figurative temples raised of old by serene philosophy."—*Reflections relative to the Malvern Hills.*

"THE Chase of Malverne," wrote Leland, in the reign of Henry VIII., "is bigger than either Wire of Feckenham, and occupieth a great part of Malverne Hilles. Much Malverne and Little also is set in the Chase of Malverne. Malverne Chase (as I hear say) is in length in some places a twenty miles; but Malverne Chase doth not occupie all Malverne Hilles." This ample domain was a royal hunting ground, and as such bore the dignified name of a "forest," from the time of the Conquest till some time in the reign of Edward I. Then, with other possessions, it became bequeathed as a marriage dowry to a subject in the person of the gallant Gilbert de Clare, "the Red Knight," who was Earl of Gloucester and son-in-law to the King, having married Joan de Acres, Edward I.'s daughter. Becoming the property of a subject, it henceforward bore the title of "The Malvern Chase." Gilbert de Clare's father was famous on account of being foremost amongst those distinguished individuals who wrung from the hand of King John that bulwark of English liberty, the "Magna Charta," the first baron whose name was affixed thereto being none other than the said Richard de Clare, Earl of Hertford. His son Gilbert was an equally distinguished patriot, and it is no little honour to Malvern Priory that endowments from such a source should have been made to it.

Gilbert de Clare's bounty was considerable, and is frequently referred to; we have not any particular account thereof, and it is probable his munificence consisted greatly in contributions to the Priory of liberal supplies of wood, game, &c., from his hunting grounds in the surrounding forest. Like most of his compeers Gilbert de Clare greatly delighted in field sports, and particularly in hunting, and did not always permit his enthusiasm to keep him within legitimate bounds. His manor extended to the top of the Malvern Hill, beyond which the Bishop of Hereford had hunting rights. Over this boundary the noble "antler bearer" and other game would sometimes go, followed by Gilbert's dogs, himself, and attendants. This the Bishop of Hereford determined, if possible, to prevent.

As to the propriety of priests engaging in the chase, as early as the reign of King Edgar ecclesiastical canons made it improper for them to do so, or to engage in other secular sports; as to hunting it was enjoined "that no priest be a hunter, or fowler, or player at tables, but let him play on his books as becometh his calling;" and though in the reign of Richard I. monks in some cases had special license to "hunt hares, foxes, and the wild cat," all other game being reserved for the King, hunting generally on the part of ecclesiastics was strictly prohibited on pain of excommunication, and the very "permission" granted to some only shows the strict rule in the case.

Still, in defiance of all rule, monks and other ecclesiastics often delighted in hunting. Peter de Blois records of Walter, Bishop of Rochester, that, at the age of 80 years, he followed the chase with such perseverance and spirit, that he totally neglected the affairs of his diocese. And we have the authority of Malvern's monk, that in the 14th century so little did persons of that sacred calling heed injunctions to the contrary that, in his day, "religion" had become—

> A ryder and romer aboute,
> A leader of love-days (or merry meetings),
> And a land buyer;

that he was continually seen going

> From manor to manor
> With a *heap of hounds at his heels;*

and that the haughty spirit of such men taught them to despise even the "kneeling" courtesies of their tenant dependants.

Whatever may have been the case elsewhere, it appears certain that at the period referred to the saintly Bishop of Hereford, Thomas de Cantelupe* did enjoy the pleasures of the chase. His residence at Colwall was in the midst of the forest, and was an extensive one. His fish-ponds there were ample, and by whatever name such a residence was then called, it answered the purpose, at some periods of the year, of the bishop's "hunting-box." During the reign of Edward I., on the question of "hunting rights" a "great controversy" arose between the said Bishop and Gilbert de Clare.†

This controversy may well be termed "great," both because of the intensity with which it was conducted, and of its costly manner of settlement. The "Annals of Worcester Church" inform us that a "suit at law was commenced," and judges, or arbitrators, were appointed to decide between the contending parties. The court of adjudication was held within the boundaries of "the chase," and the award was anythirg but favourable to the Red Knight. A writer in the "Magna Britannia," page 249, says, "to whom they determined it we have no account." Another authority says, "because the beasts of the wood often passed the boundaries of

* "Thomas de Cantelupe was of a very noble and ancient family, but of a much more noble and excellent mind, being not only extreamly witty, but even from a child very studious and peaceful."—PRICE's *History of Hereford.*

According to Fuller, Bishop Cantelupe "was the last Englishman that was canonized, and was the only Saint that the church of Hereford afforded."

† "Concerning a free chace which the bishop claimed in the Manors of Colwall and Eastnor."—PRICE.

Herefordshire, and did not return, Gilbert, Earl of Gloucester, had a foss made on Malvern hill;" and the great controversy resulted in Gilbert de Clare being compelled to keep upon the eastern side of the hill, and entailed upon him the necessity of his causing a deep ditch to be dug along the whole length of the Malvern Hill. This ditch, after a period of six hundred years is still visible over most of its extent, and must formerly have been an immense work. In places, the hard rock is cut through, and the trench is said to have been wide and deep; enough, in the first instance, to have prevented game from passing from manor to manor.

Such a work, in a place that was described as a "bald hill," with a forest wilderness on each side, was certainly no light matter. It is probable that it would have been impossible but for the co-operation of the Malvern monks. The writer has little doubt that Malvern Priory was the head quarters of the working gang, and that it was in return for favours thus conferred by its monks that Gilbert de Clare became so prominent a benefactor to the Malvern Priory.

Let the reader, with pilgrim staff, pace that ditch from end to end; let him look into it, through the dark vista of the six centuries that have intervened since its formation; and people his mind with the busy scene that trench once assumed, and the "Duke of Gloucester's Ditch," as it is called, will have an interest for him it may not have had aforetime. And whatever of folly he may see in the digging of such a trench, he will behold it as a work of no ordinary dimensions.*

Gilbert de Clare's troubles with Bishops were not destined to be all at once at an end. Consequent upon the digging of the trench a new trouble arose, this time with Godfrey Giffard, Bishop of Worcester, who had "assart" in the Malvern Forest, and upon whose territory the Earl encroached in the formation of his ditch.

* In the orders made by the law-day and court of Hanley, there holden the 23rd day of June in the 31st year of Henry VIII., 1540, concerning the preservation and maintenance of the Chace of Malvern, it is ordered, among many other things,—"To wit, that none of the inhabitants of Colwall or Mathon, do from henceforth staff-drive any kind of their cattle into the chace, further than *the shire ditch*, after the old custom, on pain of 20 shillings; and that none of the said inhabitants do cross any of the chace-wood growing on this side of *the shire ditch* over the hill on payment of 20 shillings."

This new difficulty was settled in the following manner:—The Earl of Gloucester and his wife Joan and their heirs agreed to pay the Bishop and his successors, at their manor house of Kempsey, two brace of good bucks and does, at different times of the year, and during the vacancy in the see, the said tribute was to be paid to the monastery of St. Mary, Worcester. Abingdon tells us that this agreement was long after complied with, and it would appear that such a rich contribution to the pleasures of the Bishop's table was too good a thing to be lost sight of, or to be allowed to fall into arrear.

Till the establishment of its Priory, Malvern was a place inhabited only by the denizens of the forest. Its establishment, however, soon caused, as in other places, a little community to assemble round it, and by the middle of the 13th century, a company of some twenty or thirty "poor men" lived in the neighbourhood, and daily presented themselves at the gate of the Priory to be supported with their families by alms there distributed. Many of these assisted the monks in the cultivation of the Priory domain.

The neighbourhood of Malvern had other inhabitants. As early as 1229 a church, other than that of the Priory, was built, and an incumbent appointed. This church stood at the corner of the churchyard. The Prior of Malvern appointed the incumbent, Randolphus de Pidele being the first, followed by Garland de Sedebury in 1237. The church continued in the patronage of the Priory till the dissolution of the monastery, when the building was taken down. We know nothing of the character of the early incumbents of Malvern, but, as they did not make themselves notorious for contrary conduct, we may charitably hope they were akin to the very "poore parsons" spoken of a little later by Chaucer, that—

"Rich were of holie thought and work,"

and who

"Sette not their benefice to hire,
And left their sheepe accumbered in the mire,
And ran to London unto St. Poule's:
To seeken them a chantery for souls.
Or with a brotherhood to be withold:
But dwelt at home and kepte well their fold,
So that the wolf he made it not miscarrie;
They were shepherds but not mercenarie."

Amongst the noble dust, reposing within the consecrated domain of Malvern Priory, is that of distinguished heads of the noble family of Brian de Brompton, who were Lords of Clun in Shropshire, and from whom the little town of Brampton Brian takes its name. The parish of Stow, situate two miles north east of Kington, belonged to that family, and as early as the year 1291 the advowson of the church, and "an estate" had been given to the Priory of Gre t Malvern. The revenues of this church were given to augment the "pittance" of the monks. The value was £6, a considerable sum in those days; £4 went to the Vicar of Stow and the rest belonged to the monks. In 1341 great poverty overtook the neighbourhood of Stow in consequence of continual wars, the lands were trodden down, laid waste, and left untilled, and there was pressure from both "taxation" and "poverty." At this time nine vills in Wales, belonging to Stow, were reported "unassessable." In the same century the Prior of Great Malvern held "half a hide in La Stow, under John Fitz-Alan, by service of doing suit to his court at Clun." "The Prior also at his own cost did *ward* at Clun Castle, for 20 days in wartime, sending a *serviens* and horse for that purpose."* In 1534 the Rectory of Stow, with the annexed Chapelry of Kington, as appropriated by the Prior of Great Malvern, was valued at £8 13 4.

In the sacred enclosure of Malvern, as has been said, the house of Brompton de Brian sought burial places, and in connection therewith the following curious will has come down to us.

Extract from the will of Sir Brian de Brompton, dated Nov 27th, 1262 :

> "In nomine patris et filii, et spiritus sancti Ego Briannus de Brampton Senior, Anno dom. 1262, in vigilia apostolorum Simonis, et Judæ condo testamentum meum. Volo corpus meum sepeliri in Prioratu majoris Malvernie inter predecessores meos, et cum corpore palefridum meum cum harnesio, et equum summarium cum lecto meo. Lego Agneti Lannath nepti meæ marcum, Briano nepoti meo quem nutrivi 100s ad terram emendam, Herberto nepoti meo 3 marcas, hujus autem testamenti mei executores constituo dominum Johannem de Turberville nepotem meum et dominum Briannum filium meum primogenitum."

This will is sealed with the testator's arms "2 Lions pass."

TRANSLATION.

In the name of the Father, and of the Son, and of the Holy Ghost. I Brian de Brompton Senior, in the year of our Lord 1262, on the Vigil of the

* Hundred Rolls.

Apostles Simon and Jude, make my will. I wish my body to be buried in the Priory of Great Malvern, amongst my predecessors, and with the body, my palfrey and its harness, and my sumptuary horse with my couch.
I bequeath to my grand daughter Agnes Lannath one mark. To Brian my grandson whom I brought up, one hundred shillings to buy land. To Herbert my grandson three marks.
Of this my will I appoint as executors Lord John Turberville my grandson, and Lord Brian my first born son.

In Eyton's History of Shropshire this will is quoted, at page 249, vol. 4, with the following note:—

"Dugdale's transcript (*Ashmole Library, vol. 39*) seems to be an extract rather than the whole. Nevertheless I give it as the original is destroyed. I think that the Knight's bequest was of his *districr*, his sumpter-horse and bed, to the monks of Malvern, together with his body. A literal construction of the above would imply that the whole were to be buried with the deceased."

The statue of the knight in old armour, now reposing on the north side of the chancel of Malvern Church, usually attributed to the family of Corbet, most probably belongs to the distinguished house of Brompton.

CHAPTER VIII.

MALVERN IN THE THIRTEENTH CENTURY.

> "They had been the almshouses where the aged dependants of more opulent families retired as to a home, neither uncomfortable nor humiliating. They had been inns to the wayfaring man, who heard from afar the vesper bell at once inviting him to repose and devotion, and who might sing his matins with the morning star, and go on his way rejoicing."—*Ancient Religious Houses*, by PROFESSOR BLOUNT.

THE thirteenth century was a most important one for the civil liberties of England, and there was no part of the country which did more to conserve and develop those of a political character than the famed "Marches of Wales," within whose borders the Priory of Malvern was placed. There existed, two miles southward, the Priory of Little Malvern, belonging to the Church of Worcester, in which there were ten Benedictine monks. This Priory, like that of the greater Malvern, was resorted to by persons more than usually devout, and was specially distinguished because of its remoteness and "wilderness" character. With the brethren of Malvern these no doubt fraternised, and the existence of a second religious house helped to do away with the desolateness of the Malvern situation.

There were at Colwall, not only the Bishop of Hereford's country residence, but the Malvern cell of Brockbury, situated in the midst of a dense forest.

At Ledbury there was a church of considerable dimensions, and we have the authority of the famed "Doomsday Book" for asserting that from the time of the Conquest a priest had dwelt there. Ledbury's existence as a town is of later date, and its famous legend of "Catherine Audley" belongs to a century later. The old castle of "Bronsil," on the western slope of the Holly-bush Hill, then existed, and its owner, whose very name is now matter of conjecture, majestically lorded it over a somewhat extensive domain. The frowning Gothic tower of Hanley Castle was a prominent object from Malvern Hill. And though history is silent in reference to a spot now denominated "The Moat," and situate a mile and a half down the valley, as far as observation can inform us, and a deep moat and other things can speak, it does appear that in the midst of that thickly wooded chase, there was, even thus early, a residence of some importance, with chapel adjoining, at which place, probably, some of the forest lord's retainers were located.

Other places of minor character existed, the very names of which are forgotten. Those mentioned, however, with the Priory Grange of Newland, were about all with which the Malvern Priory was immediately surrounded. Along the Welsh border, then, and for some time previously, warfare of no ordinary character was continually being carried on, and the surrounding country to the banks of the Severn was overrun year after year by fierce contending hosts, and we may be sure Malvern was not exempt from the cares and trials such a state of things involved.

The troubles of the reign of King John brought that monarch into this immediate neighbourhood. He frequently passed from Ledbury to Worcester, and returned over a like course, and it is probable the Priory of Great Malvern sometimes sheltered him. In the month of October, 1200, King John was at Hereford. In November of the same year he was at Ledbury, whence he made his way to Worcestershire, being at Feckenham on the 8th and 9th of that month. This would put Malvern Priory in his path. Four years later he was at Worcester, from 11th to 20th of August. The year 1206 found him at Worcester, Tewkesbury, and Ledbury; and in 1211, on the 16th and 17th March, he was at Ledbury, whence he proceeded, by way of Worcester, to London. In 1212 we find him at both Tewkesbury and Worcester, and on the 22nd of November of that year he resided for one night at Hanley Castle. 1214 found King John again in the neighbourhood, proceeding from Hereford, by way of Ledbury, towards Worcester, where he arrived on the 27th December.

Such things as inns did not then exist, and religious houses were made to supply their place. The Priory of Malvern, as was common in that day, entertained the wayfarer. Abingdon, speaking in immediate connection therewith says :—"It is certaine yt abbies and priories covenanted yn theyer foundacion to have theyer gates ever open to receive the poor;" and he continues, "we see what Great Malverne did in sustayninge theyer necessities."

We have the authority of the good Latimer for asserting that till the end of the chapter Malvern Priory was famous for being given to the "vertu of hosptalyte," for its "good howskeeping," and for "feeding many and that daily."

Rambling minstrels or "jongleours" formed important visitants at our monastery. During the middle ages no festival of the nobility was complete without them, and all great gatherings of the clergy abounded with them. They travelled singly and in parties, not only from house to house and convent to convent, but from one country to another. When their audience was of serious mood they chanted from the old romances of chivalry, or repeated satirical poems; at other times scandalous love tales were narrated by them, and frequently they brought with them the last new song or sensational tale; to these methods of entertainment they afterwards added that of the mountebank, posture maker, and conjurer. The halls of the barons and guest chambers of the monks continually abounded with these, and though their jests and acting were not of a refined character, their visits did not appear on that account to have been less welcome.

After the commencement of the Crusades the wandering minstrel added to his other professions that of an Eastern storyteller. It was by this means that Eastern fable in all its luxuriance was first taught to blossom on English soil. To Malvern Priory the minstrel came, and here, as elsewhere, rehearsed his wild narrations, and its monks listened to alleged wholesale depredations of fabulous monsters, of many headed dragons, griffins, and their like. The wandering minstrel had other themes, and as of most interest he frequently told of the fierce onslaughts of the Saracenic hosts, and of the mighty valour of the conquering Crusaders. These were magnified with all due poetic license, added to which he rehearsed "golden legends of saints and martyrs," and fascinated the imagination of his hearers by narratives of the splendour of Oriental palaces.

Let the reader convey himself back for a moment to that far off time, and picture the reflective monk of Malvern's quiet cloister listening to such things; multiplied a hundredfold, as minstrel after minstrel visited the Priory, and as tidings of the mingled reverses and successes of the crusading hosts reached the monastery, partly supported, as that monk was, by hopes of holy scripture, and partly inspired as he was by the belief in some such marvellous interposition helping them as holy legends spoke of; let him think how deeply mysterious all must have appeared; how he must have pondered thereon, and wondered whereto it would lead, and what would be the end thereof.

CHAPTER IX.

THE HALL OF THE PRIORY.

> "Hadst thou a tongue thou couldest well
> Of olden times and grandeur tell,
> When thou wert young and fair.
> Thou could'st relate of feudal day,
> Of hoary minstrel's roundelay,
> Of monk with beads; and prayer."

SOME time in the early part of the reign of Edward III., a very considerable addition was made to Malvern monastic buildings in the shape of a timbered hall. This building stood on the south side of the Priory Church, near where "Knotsford Lodge" now stands; it was 76 feet in length and 14 feet broad, and existed as late as 1841, when it was taken down to make way for modern, but less interesting structures. The chief interesting features belonging to it as a building consisted in the very elegant tracery of its windows, and its high pitched and handsomely ornamented roof. Before the Society of Antiquaries, March 28th, 1844, this hall was thus described by Edward Blore, Esq., who exhibited exterior and interior views thereof, taken by him two years previous to its ruthless demolition. After describing the beautiful roof, above mentioned, he went on to say "that it formed a very interesting illustration of the monastic architecture of the fourteenth century; that it consisted of a hall with the usual partition, and two doors at one extremity adjoining the butteries; the general character of the construction and ornaments showed that it was built in the early part of the reign of Edward III. It was constructed entirely of timber, which was in a very sound state ; the hall was divided into four bays, by three principals to give support to the purlins. In each bay, except in that which contained a plain door of entrance, were two tiers of square-headed traceried windows, the pattern of the tracery being varied, as was usual in works of that kind." It stood north and south, and was manifestly of late Decorated character. In form it was a parallelogram. The heads of its windows exhibited an instance of the application of very bold wood tracery, of which there were several varieties (see plates). The windows were fourteen in number. In the entire length of the roof were five sets of principals, resting on a chamfered wall-plate. John H. Parker, Esq., F.S.A., says, "Timbered roofs of this period are comparatively scarce;" "It is lamentable to observe how fast they are disappearing;" "That of the hall of Great Malvern, the finest example that existed in this country, or any other, has been wantonly destroyed." In April, 1844, after noticing Mr. Blore's paper, the *Gentleman's Magazine* says, "This very curious structure was wantonly demolished in 1841 by a speculative tradesman."

It is some satisfaction that the window carvings of this building, after being worked into a barn to fill up the space that otherwise would have been occupied by bricks, and remaining there for many years, have lately been taken out, and are now preserved in the Malvern Museum. Wood engravings of some of these window headings are given on the pages adjoining.

An artist writing in 1835 thus notices this structure: "We visited the venerable church, with its richly ornamented porch, its battlements and pinnacles—its windows glowing with the brilliant hues of the amethyst and topaz, the sapphire and the ruby—its quaint carvings and its sculptured tombs—a miniature cathedral. Passing under an antique gateway coeval with the church, we entered a farm-yard in which stands a long building formerly the refectory, but now resounding with the thresher's flail."

An interior view of this old Hall will be found facing page 11, as also a sketch, taken from the painted windows of the church, of the monk St. Werstan there referred to.

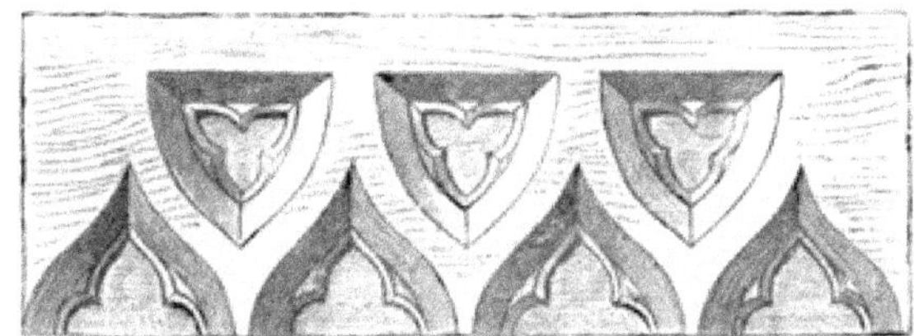

WINDOW HEADINGS OF QUESTEN HALL, CARVED IN WOOD.

Engraved to scale, 1-18th of inch to the inch.

CHAPTER X.

VISION OF PIERS' PLOUGHMAN.

"I cannot but believe that within that church and its precincts lies the dust of many a holy brother, who has often experienced, amid all the errors of his creed, a lofty piety; who shed a sanctity over the place of his retreat with which his heart and life corresponded."—*Reflections Relative to Malvern Hills.*

SOME time not far distant from the date of the building of the "Hall of the Priory," referred to in the last chapter, Malvern becomes associated with a literary work which constitutes one of the most famous and interesting of its antiquities. I refer to the "Vision of Piers' Ploughman," one of England's earliest national poems.* In the list of Priors lately obtained from the British Museum, and which will be found on a subsequent page, the name occurs amongst the Priors elect, of one for whom I have claimed the honour of being the author of the poem in question. No place other than Malvern can be, I venture to say, so clearly connected with the poem, and to none other person can such honour so fairly belong. It has long been felt that if composed at Malvern, a person in, and not under, authority in its Priory, must have been the writer; and

---

* An early-printed copy, bearing date 1550, went through three editions in one year. The second edition was entitled "The Vision of Pierce Ploughman, now the second time imprinted by Roberte Crowley, dwellynge in Ely rentes in Holburne. Whereunto are added certayne notes and cotations in the mergyne, gevynge light to the Reader." Another addition was published by Owen Rogers, in 1562, and was described as "The Vision of Pierce Ploughman, newly imprynted after the author's olde copy, with a brefe summary of the principall matters sett before every part called passus. Imprynted at London, by Owen Rogers, dwellynge near vnto great Saint Bartelmewes gate at the sygne of the Spred Egle." For two hundred years the work was circulated in manuscript.

this I think is now made clear. Thomas Wright, Esq., F.S.A., says of this work :—" Independent of its historical and literary importance it contains many beauties, and, as one of the purest works in the English tongue as it existed during the century in which it was composed, it is to be hoped that ere long the work of the 'monk of Malvern,' as a link between the poetry and language of the Anglo-Saxons and those of modern England, will be made a prominent text-book."

Its composition is neither that of rhyme nor blank verse, nor is it at all comparable with that of any prevalent amongst us. It is written in a kind of melodious rhythm, borrowed from the Anglo-Saxons, and known as "alliteration," of which the opening lines of the poem afford a fair specimen :—

> In a *somer season*
> When *softe* was the *sonne*,
> I *shoop* me into *shroudes*
> As I a *sheep* weere.
> * * * * *
> Ac on a *May morwenynge*
> On *Malverne* hilles.

The "vision" is made up of a series of graphic allegorical paintings, reminding most readers of those of the divine dreamer, John Bunyan, some persons even supposing that the idea of the "Pilgrim's Progress" originated in "the vision."

Both in its name and style of composition the poem commended itself to an oppressed race. Ploughmen and common labourers gladly welcomed a work whose hero was chosen from amongst them, especially when that hero was made the possessor of wisdom and exalted piety, and was contrasted so favourably with their oppressors. In its composition also the poem became directed to the same end. The Anglo-Saxon poetry was written as prose: with them metre was unknown; it, however, became displaced by the rhyme of the Anglo-Normans, who, three centuries before our poem's date, had become the dominant race; but, during the whole time of this displacement, alliterative verse was used in the rustic songs of the working classes, and they, at the date of its composition, were perfectly familiar therewith. In choosing this channel of communication, therefore, our author addressed himself to these despised people in a language of their own.

The poem opens in the manner following:—In the summer season of the year, when the sun was "softly" shining, its hero dressed in sheepskins, like an unholy hermit

> Went wide in this worlde
> Wonderes to here.

On a May "morwenynge" (morning) he finds himself on "Malverne Hilles," and there great marvels befel him. Worn out with wandering he rests himself on a broad bank in one of its valleys, by a stream's side, whose waters so merrily murmured, that he fell asleep, and there in a dream the people of the world appear to him, gathered in a fair meadow. On the east side was a tower on an eminence choicely made; a deep dale was beneath it, and a dungeon therein, with deep ditches, and dark and dreadful of sight. In the fair meadow were gathered—

> All manner of men
> The meene and the riche,
> Werchynge (working) and wandrynge
> As the world asketh.

These are severally described. Ploughmen in setting and sowing laboured full hard, and won what wasters with "glotonye" destroyed. Some in that field in pride's clothing disguised themselves. In prayers and penances put them many—

> Al for love of our Lorde
> They lived full strait
> In hope to have after
> Heaven's rich blessing.

Some by "chaffare" (merchandise) sought to thrive, and some as "minstrals conned" and got gold for their glee. As "japeres" and "jangeleres," others "fooles" made of themselves, and by feigning "fantasies," and showing dislike of work, manifested their their kin to Judas's children, and their love of the Devil's service. Begging friars had their bags and their "belies" of bread "fully crammed," they drunk, went to bed, and with loose talkings rose. Pilgrims and palmers there were seen; profligate hermits, that "lothe were to swynke" (work), friars of the four orders who sought riches for their "copes," and whose calling was to work "mischief on this mold" (earth). Pardoners, with Bishop's seals, who of falsehood, of fasting, and of broken vows, pardoned all who paid. Parsons and parish priests, Bishops and bachelors, barons and burgesses, all were there. Sergeants-of-law, who "for poundes" served the bar, but who for God's love would not

Unclose their lips once.

And says our poet—thou mightest better meet "myst on Malverne Hilles," than expect anything from men of "*hire* mouths" till "money be showed." Cooks and their knaves cried, "Hot pies, hot! Good geese and 'grays,' go dine! go." Taverners told a like tale—

White wine of "Oseye,"
And red wine of "Gascoigne,"
Of the Ryne and the "Rochel."

All this he saw "sleeping," and seven times more.

As the poem proceeds we are again and again introduced to the field "full of folk," and are made to listen to "Reason" lifting up his voice in the character of a preacher. The sermon attributed to Reason is an earnest appeal to the common people; he proved that the pestilences* that had visited the earth were for "pure synne," that the south-western wind on the Saturday evening,† in which "Pyries" (pear trees), plum trees, "beches" (beeches), and "brodeokes" (broad oaks) were "blowen" to the "grounde," occurred because of "pure pride" and no point "ellis" (else). He then appealed to "Wastor" to go to work; idlers at the "wyne pyn" (public-house) were to be beaten if they would not labour. Fathers were to correct their children while young, nor spare the rod under penalty of "spilling" the child. Prelates and priests were warned to prove on themselves, and do it in "dede" that they "prechen" to the people. The King was admonished to love the common people, and to be just to them; to keep the laws, not to be covetous, nor do anything contrary to the truth, if he would God please; telling him, if he did otherwise, God would not know him, nor any "Seynt of hevene." The Pope he prayed to have pity on "holi chirche," and ere he gave grace to others to

"Governe first hymselve."

Pilgrims that sought "Seynt James"

"And seyntes of Rome,"

he urged to seek "Seynt Truthe."

* Several dreadful pestilences visited the country in the 14th century.
† The great wind supposed to be alluded to occurred in 1362.

Not the least amongst the charms of the poem are its constant allusions to the customs and habits of the times in which it was written; every character seems to have had a similitude to personages moving before the author's eyes. Monks of the four orders, pilgrims, austere barons, rambling minstrels, and great feudal lords continually appear and disappear before the vision of an appreciative reader.

The poem contains references to the state of the country at that time, its great forests find a place in its pages, and the ploughing with cows yolked together, and the fenceless state of the fields; and the generally forlorn condition of the labourer and small farmer often manifests itself. Mention is made of the hunting of boars, wolves, foxes, and brocks (badgers).

The luxury of the higher classes is frequently complained of; one mark of refinement mentioned is curious. From the earliest times the hall of the house had been regarded as the common place for meals both for master and servants; indeed, the hall, as its name imports, was at first the entire house, and formed the resting place by night as well as living place by day. The first deviation from this rule was for the accommodation of the lady, who had her "bower" or room separated from the hall by a door; to this was added, as refinement progressed, a private parlour; but down as far as the fourteenth century it was considered a mark of pride for any one to take their meals out of the common hall; this will enable the reader to understand our author's complaint that in his day—

> "The hall was in mourning
> Each day in the week,"

and that there the lord nor the lady delighted not to sit, each having a rule to "eaten" by himself in a "pryvee" parlour, or in a chamber with a "chymnee."

The author was a man full of truth and love. He had the fathers at his fingers' ends, and his familiarity with holy writ was most perfect. He was, moreover, a people's man; his was amongst the first, if not the very first, of successful attempts to speak to the masses by written composition. He was, moreover, the first popular assailant of the corruptions of the Romish Church, and, as a resident of Malvern, identifies the place thus early with our country's struggles for religious freedom. It is impossible now to estimate the effect of this poem. Evidence of its extensive circulation in MS. is found in the fact that more original copies have come down to us than that of any similar work. Some of these copies show that unskilful hands aided in their multiplication; and it is believed that, through the length and breadth of the land, the common people who were unable to read had it upon their tongues. The poem is full of holy sentiments. and breathes so much common-place, evangelical truth, that a reader can hardly fancy it the work of a monk five hundred years ago. The royal domain of religious truth is there made common ground; the fountain of knowledge is opened; and, without the interposition of Pope or Priesthood, the common people are invited to walk within the enclosure of holy scripture. The sublimest and most vital of truths are mirrored in its pages, and it is impossible to over-estimate its leavening and elevating power.

CHAPTER XI.

MALVERN PRIORY CHURCH.

"Time, foe alike to weak and strong,
Has batter'd, noble relic, long,
Thy walls and tower grey."

"Hail, time-worn structure, happily transformed
From what thou wert." BOOKER.

LATE in the thirteenth, or early in the fourteenth century, considerable benefactions were made to Malvern Priory. Amongst them Bishop Godfrey Giffard gave thereto "two mills in Wicke, situated on the river Teme, and one mill on the brook of Lawern adjoining, where it runs into the Teme*;" and Walter de Maydenston, Bishop of Worcester, "appropriated to them the church of Powyke, to make them amends for their loss of several churches and manors during the wars between England and Wales, to enable them to pay their debts, and to support them in the maintenance of twenty-six monks, and thirty poor men living therein."† The losses in question consisted of the manor of Canterbanham, and the parish church of Laugh Mayn, in the diocese of St. David, together with a prebend in the said church, the manor of Fuleford, in the diocese of Lichfield, and the parish church of Pichcot in Lincoln diocese, all of which had been taken from them. Abingdon says, "The Priorie of Malverne, which

* Thomas' Survey of Worcester Cathedral.
† Ibid.

was neverthelesse but a littel religious house, yt maintained 26 monks and 30 poor men continually, besides their hospitallitie, loosing theyer manors and churches in Wales, Fuleford, in the bishopric of Coventrie, and Lichfield, and Knightwyke, in the countie of Worcester, ruinated thus by civill warrs and powerfull adversaries, obtained of Walter, Bishop of Worcester, an. 1314, the appropriation of their church of Powike, whereof they were patrons."

In former chapters mention has been made of the original dimensions of Malvern Church, and of additions afterwards made. A large portion is Norman; there are remains of Transition, and also of Decorated work; and some have thought that at one time it contained considerable portions in the First Pointed or Early English style. In the year 1239, according to "Thomas' Survey of Worcester Cathedral," Walter de Cantelupe, Bishop of Worcester, did newly consecrate "the conventual church of Great Malvern."* It would appear that from the foundation of the monastery the monks were never long at rest, but that buildings of some kind were continually being carried on, and that but for the decaying hand of time and the ruthless spoliations of the past, we should have before us represented in Malvern Church portions of every period of ecclesiastical architecture.

The fifteenth century saw great changes wrought in Malvern Church. The changes, indeed, of that period amounted to a reconstruction of the whole building; and, since it is to them that in the main it owes its present glory and beauty, it becomes me, as far as practicable, to make an examination of the works then carried out.

We have no record of the changes of that period, other than that presented by the walls of the church. These, however, now that the "churchwardens' whitewash" has been taken from them, speak plainly of what was done, and it is to these evidences that I address myself.

* The fact of this consecration has puzzled many; it was in obedience to a constitution made in London in 1237 by the Papal Legate, the inference being that Malvern Church, as well as many others, had not before been consecrated.

Let the reader follow me into our noble Church, let us pass together under the beautiful porch built during the Perpendicular period, and having shut out the outside world by means of the massive lock and quaint key committed to our keeping, let us take our stand beside the ancient font at the extreme west end of the building. The view of the church from that point is very beautiful; the eye should first be permitted to run along the very chastely painted roof; by that means the striking height of the building becomes perceptible, and as the eye stretches along past the vaulting under the tower, towards the great east window, something akin to a feeling of wonder must possess the beholder. Yet it must be owned the long walls over the Norman arches of the nave look plain and bare from this point, and the total absence of ornamentation or arcade upon them becomes painfully felt. They are heavy looking, their great height and length giving them an appearance that is anything but pleasing; and it is a relief to the eye to rest in turn upon the stately Norman pillars and the massive arches by which they are supported.

Having taken from the stand-point referred to a general view of the building, we next proceed to examine the church a little in detail. And first there is the font belonging to the Norman period. Its bowl is large, and if it was intended to be used for infants, whatever opinions may be held on the question of baptism, it is evident that nothing less than immersion was contemplated. It does not at first sight clearly appear what necessity there was for a font in a Benedictine monastery, especially when it is remembered that Malvern had a parish church closely adjoining. But that parish church did not exist till many years after the convent's establishment, and, as in the monastery's early days the church bore a strong resemblance to that of one specially devoted to missionary work, in a country that from its desolated aspect was denominated the "Wilderness of Malvern," it is probable that in the baptism of converts to Christianity that font had a work to do that was both charitable and meritorious.

The Norman pillars of the nave are massive; though devoid

of ornament, the masonry in them is far from being uncouth, and they bear evidence of skill in their construction. They do not run up to the immense height of the Norman pillars of either Gloucester Cathedral or Tewkesbury Abbey Church, nor have they the lightness or beauty of those which support the nave of Hereford Cathedral; still, they are in fair proportion, and their dimensions accord better with the size of the arches that spring from them than do either those of Gloucester or Tewkesbury. In great part they are as firm and exact as when they were first erected, and, when their venerable age of nearly eight hundred years is remembered, with all their plainness, considerable interest attaches to them. Plain though they are, there appears to have been at some period an intention to ornament them, as will be seen from the respond of the north-east pillar adjoining the tower. There a beginning at ornamentation was made, and on the third arch westward traces of zig-zag ornament are faintly marked out. This shows that ornamentation was in progress in the Norman portions of the church, and it may be, that in the chancel and other parts of the old church, which were taken down at the Perpendicular reconstruction, ornamentation did exist, and had reached as far as the nave arches, when circumstances occurred, of which I shall have to speak, which induced the monks to take down the old Norman church as far as the nave, and to re-construct the whole building in the Perpendicular style.

Presuming for a moment that the reader has duly feasted his eyes on the painted roof, and that he has taken in careful review the arches and pillars of the nave, I bid him in the next place to look above the nave arches on each side of the church; he will find that the walls there are composed partly of Malvern Hill stone rubble, and partly of square stones of a sandstone character. The latter are of various sizes and lengths; some are of such large dimensions as to make it hard to understand how they were lifted to their present position, and it would appear that great difficulty must have been experienced in dragging such masses of stone through the forest tracks, as they must have been in that far off time.

A careful examination of these nave walls will show us what was done to them at the reconstruction of the church in the fifteenth century. The Malvern Hill stone therein evidently marks the height of the nave walls of the original Norman church, and it would appear that the builders of the Perpendicular period in the first place took off the old roof, and then, using these walls of Malvern Hill rubble as a substructure, ran up those of the red sandstone character to their present great height, upon which they placed a flat wooden roof, painted and panelled much in its present fashion. The old Norman nave must have been hardly half the height of the present one, and, owing to this and its small windows, it must have had, as already noticed, a dark and sombre aspect, and the change produced by the alterations referred to must have been great, and the contrast remarkable.

The reader having duly pondered the remarks made concerning the nave of our Church, I now ask him to move from the old font, the point of view from which former observations were made, and to come with me to the examination of the nave aisles. Comparing the north aisle with that on the south side, he will perceive that the former is as near as possible double the width of the latter; he will also see that the arch of entrance from the former into the transept is of a purely Perpendicular character, showing it to have been built at the Third Pointed period (that of the fifteenth century). The south aisle evidently retains the width it had in the original Norman Church (that of the twelfth century). It would appear, therefore, that while the builders of the Perpendicular period were greatly influenced in all their operations by the structure they found existing, in this case, at least, they took down the walls of the north aisle entirely, and, building the one at present existing from its foundations, made an aisle on that side of twice its former width. The walls of the south aisle were not interfered with, as is evident from the existence therein, near its east end, of a blocked-up doorway belonging to the Norman period, as well as from an arch remaining of that period at the end of the aisle over the entrance to the present vestry. The reason for this is obvious.

F

The domestic buildings of the Priory were on the south side of the church, as were also the monks' cloisters. To have widened the aisle therefore on that side, would have necessitated the taking down and removal of some of these, and this being found inexpedient, the aisle in question—notwithstanding that its opposite neighbour was so enlarged—was allowed to retain its former width. The south wall—thus left untouched—till within this fifty years retained its small circular-headed windows belonging to the Norman period, the last of which, that over the blocked-up doorway, was only stopped up during the late restorations. The Perpendicular windows in the north aisle of the nave, and the small Norman ones in the south aisle, as well as the great west window, were filled during the 15th century with stained glass of a most interesting character, portions only of which now remain.

The reader having strolled leisurely up and down the nave and along its aisles, and having made his spirit as attentive as needs be to the histories revealed by its hoar pillars and grey stone walls, before leaving this part of the church, should just take a glance at the "mason's marks" of the Norman period. The first and second pillars on the north side of the nave contain many of these; they are very rude cyphers, and unlike anything seen elsewhere by the writer; it may be however, that some reader may find in them an analogy to symbols of the kind elsewhere existing, and as such they may not be devoid of interest. Passing on to opposite the pulpit, the reader is next directed to observe that the walls supporting the tower are raised upon the remains of the old Norman tower, the layers composing which are all considerably out of place; and it is evident that in consequence of the former tower's great weight, a "settlement" had at some time taken place. This settlement, over its whole extent, inclines in an easterly direction, and has evidently been so great that it would seem as if the old tower must have fallen; indeed, if the original tower was of the usual weight and bulk of Norman towers generally, it would appear to have been impossible for it to have stood with its foundations in the position we see them; and I am about to propound a theory that the tower in question *did fall*, that in its fall it did considerable damage, that thereby the eastern portion of the church was all but destroyed; and I am of opinion that it was in consequence of the ruin thus wrought that it became a matter of necessity for the monks to rebuild the church in the fifteenth century. This they did much in the fashion we now see it. The devastations made by the falls of towers of Norman churches are matters of considerable notoriety, so much so that a great archæological authority remarks that it is some "proof that a tower is not Norman if it has not fallen;" and Professor Willis tells us that "in examining the history of Norman cathedrals, it would be found that falls were the characteristics of several of them—in short, that this falling was a way they had got into, and they could not help it." In proof of the truth of Dr. Willis's remarks, the following facts concerning Norman towers may be cited. Referring to the Norman tower of Gloucester Cathedral, Mr. Parker writes:—"These early towers must have been too hastily built, or inadequately constructed, for frequent mention of falling towers occurs in the annals of the times. It is recorded of Roger, natural son of Henry I., and Bishop of Worcester from 1163 to 1180, that while celebrating mass in St. Peter's church, Gloucester, one of the great towers at the west end of the church fell down with such a terrible noise and dust, that the multitude present all ran out in confusion, but the undaunted bishop still went on with the service, with one or two monks, wondering why the people ran away!"

The following is a list of the Norman towers, with the dates at which some of them fell:—Winchester Cathedral, tower fell in 1107; Ely Cathedral, tower fell suddenly in 1331 or 1341; Gloucester Cathedral, tower fell suddenly in 1160; Worcester Cathedral, tower fell in 1175—two towers fell in 1222; Lincoln Cathedral, tower fell in 1240; Norwich Cathedral, spire and tower fell in 1361, destroying the choir; Hereford Cathedral, western towers and front fell within the last century; Wells Cathedral, prevented from falling in 1321, by inverts and buttresses, "in gross violation of all taste and architectural propriety" (see Dr. Willis's paper);

Chichester Cathedral, tower and spire in 1861; Dunstable Priory Church, two towers fell in 1221; Evesham Abbey Church, one tower fell in 1213; Canterbury Cathedral, tower saved from destruction, in Dr. Willis's opinion, by means similar to those at Wells; Salisbury Cathedral, the spire 23 inches out of the perpendicular—its fall predicted in the *Builder*, April, 1861; St. Nicholas, Hereford, St. Mary's Redcliff, Bristol—both truncated spires, owing either to their upper part having fallen, or to their being left incomplete in apprehension of a fall. These facts help to support the theory of the fall of Malvern's Norman tower, and though there are no other evidences than that of the walls themselves, a careful examination of the works carried on during the 15th century will give considerable support to the theory. The whole of the church eastward from the tower was then rebuilt from the ground—a likely circumstance to have occurred had that part of it been destroyed by the fall of the tower in the way suggested.

PRIORY CHURCH, MALVERN.

PRIORY GATEWAY, MALVERN.

CHAPTER XII.

FIFTEENTH CENTURY.

"Even such is time, that takes on trust
 Our youth, our joys, our all we have
And pays us with but age and dust :
 Who in the dark and silent grave,
When we have wandered all our ways,
 Shuts up the story of our days."

SIR WALTER RALEIGH.

"*Now* is seen the *passion for utility* when all things are accounted by their price,
And the wisdom of the wise is busied in hatching golden eggs."

TUPPER.

HAVING thrown out suggestions as to the probable necessity for the 15th century reconstruction of the church, and having briefly noticed what was done during that period both in the nave and its aisles, I proceed to point out the works then carried on in the choir, transept, and their surroundings. The transept, of which only the north portion now remains, was then considerably altered and enlarged. The transept arches under the tower, though changed in style, do not appear to have been materially raised. The transept was not much heightened, and the part of it remaining is still much lower than other parts of the church. What was done appears to be this, the tower was built on the ruined remains of the old one, and was carried up to its present great height so as to give a clear interior view of the great east window. The north transept was widened, and its present beautiful windows inserted. A like work was probably done in the south transept, but all remarks respecting it must be conjectural, as it has long since ceased to exist. The north and south aisles of the choir were formed during the same period. The present beautiful tower was then entirely constructed, the space underneath it was vaulted, and bosses and shields inserted. The aisles of the choir on either side were also vaulted, and, though the vaulting in each case is somewhat plain, it has a pleasing effect when viewed in its entirety.

There was evidently an intention to vault the whole choir; shafts are run for this purpose between the clerestory windows, and, as the walls of the chancel are panelled after the purest fashion of the period, it may be that this panelling was meant to be finished with a roof of fan tracery vaulting, after the style of the cloisters of Gloucester Cathedral, which it will be remembered Malvern church a good deal resembles, especially in its Third Pointed work. Had such a design been present in the mind of the architect, regret can but be expressed that it was not carried into execution, since, beautiful as the present painted ceiling is, the addition of vaulting in the manner referred to would have added much to the beauty and effectiveness of the building.

Sir Reginald Bray, the architect of St. George's, Windsor, and of Henry VII.'s chapel in Westminster Abbey, was architect to the alterations of the period under consideration, and the ornamentation and taste displayed without curtailment at Westminster and Windsor may give some clue to the intentions of the same architect at Malvern. St. George's Hall, Windsor, has a beautiful painted roof, to which the original one of Malvern may have had some resemblance. Henry VII.'s chapel at Westminster is elaborately vaulted, and it may be that it was with the view of displaying something akin thereto that shafts were built and other preparations were made for vaulting the chancel of the conventual church of Great Malvern.

The great east window, it will be observed, is filled with stained glass, the prevailing colours of which are yellow and white, giving it an air of great lightness. The other windows of the choir are merely panels pierced to admit light. This gives them on the outside a somewhat awkward appearance, with which that of the nave windows contrasts favourably; the outside effect in this case is sacrificed to the inside beauty. Behind the reredos is a small semi-circular wall, the space between it and the reredos forming a small vestry or sacristy, access to which is obtained by means of doorways on each side of the communion table. In the top of this semi-circular wall are squint-holes or "hagioscopes." The squint-holes in each case turn to a common centre, and were apparently designed to give to attendants at the high altar views of the altars in the Lady Chapel as well as in the chapels of the north and south aisles. In the ancient Norman church an apsidal wall beyond the present semi-circular one formerly existed, foundations of which were recently discovered. Between this and the one now existing, there was a procession path, as at Hereford, Durham, and other places. At Durham there exists behind the altar a seat or throne for the officiating priest, and it may be there was formerly a like arrangement at Malvern. The wall of the present reredos was built at the Perpendicular period, and consequently is of later date than the semi-circular one above referred to.

Before leaving the inside of the church the reader is directed to the south chapel, traditionally denominated the "Chapel of St. Anne." He will perceive that the semi-circular wall under the east window is fitted with large quantities of the old tiles, but as these will be referred to in a subsequent volume he is only asked to take passing notice of them. There is a recess in the south chapel under the Knotsford tomb, the former use of which is a matter of conjecture. It has sometimes been regarded as a confessional. This, however, is improbable. In addition to the tombstone of Prior Walcher—which has only been recently placed there—and that of another monk, on the furthest side there are two stone coffins, probably containing the remains of persons distinguished in the annals of the church. The roof of this recess is panelled after a Perpendicular fashion, showing it to have been formed at that period, and something akin to fan-tracery vaulting appears. That the recess was in existence before the Knotsford tomb is evidenced by the fact that, whilst in the

battlement, or wall, that fences the south side of the tomb, there are openings to give a view of the former high altar, the said tomb now comes between and effectually blocks this view. Only those parts of the wall are pierced from which a view of the former high altar could be obtained. This recess, with its surroundings, looks like a small chauntry chapel.

The alterations of this period, which amounted as has been said to a complete reconstruction, became sufficiently complete in the year 1460 for the Rev. "Father in Christ and Lord, Lord John by divine permission Bishop of Worcester," to consecrate the same. Bishop Carpenter's Register preserved in Edgar Tower, Worcester, informs us that the said Bishop was received into the Malvern Convent on the last day but one of the month of July in that year, with great pomp and ceremony : the bells of the convent rang out joyful peals in honour of the occasion, and a host of ministering clergy and their servants were in attendance, who, the register informs us, were duly feasted at the expense of the "house," and lodged in the monastery. On the day following (31st July) these all took part in the solemnities of the consecration, and then in gorgeous processions they with the monks again and again paraded through the building ; singing, chanting, and bowing as they went with all the attendant pomp and circumstance that in those days, with a mitred bishop presiding, was wont to attend such a solemnity. The record of the event as preserved in Bishop Carpenter's register, runs as follows :—

Registrum Carpenter, vol. i. f. 155. Consecracio altarium in prioratu majoris Malvernie. Penultimo die mensis Julii Anno Domini millesimo CCCC sexagesimo, Reverendus in Christo pater et dominus, dominus Johannes, permissione divinâ Wigorniensis Episcopus, erat receptus in monasterium sive prioratum majoris Malvernie per priorem et Conventum ejusdem, cum pulsacione campanarum, et ibidem pernoctavit, cum clericis, ministris, et servientibus suis, sumptibus domus. Et in crastino die sequente consecravit ibidem altaria, videlicet, primum et summum altare, in honore beate Marie virginis, Sancti Michaelis Archangeli, Sanctorum Johannis Evangeliste, Petri et Pauli Apostolorum, et Benedicti Abbatis. Aliud

Translation.

Consecration of altars in Priory of Great Malvern on the last day but one of the month of July in the year of the Lord 1460. The Rev. Father in Christ and Lord, Lord John, by divine permission Bishop of (Wigorn) Worcester, was received into the Monastery or Priory of Great Malvern by the prior and convent of the same, with the ringing of bells, and passed the night there with the ministering clergy and their servants at the expense of the house. And on the day following he consecrated altars there, viz., the first and great or high altar in honour of the Blessed Virgin Mary, St. Michael the Archangel, St. John the Evangelist, Peter and Paul the Apostles

altare in choro, a dextris, in honore Sanctorum Wolstani et Thome Herfordensis. Aliud in choro, a sinistris, in honore Santorum Edwardi Regis et Confessoris, et Egidii Abbatis. Quartvm, in honore Petri et Pauli, et omnium Apostolorum, Sancte Katerine et omnium virginum. Quintum, in honore Sancti Laurentii, et omnium martirum, et Sancti Nicholai, et omnium confessorum. Sextum, in honore beate Marie virginis, et Sancte Anne, matris ejusdem. Et septimum, in honore Jesu Christi, Sancte Ursule, et undecim milia virginum.

and Benedict Abbot. Another altar in the choir, on the right hand, in honour of Saints Wulstan and Thomas of Hereford, another in the choir on the left, in honour of Saints Edward King and Confessor and Egidius Abbot. Fourth, in honour of Peter and Paul and all Apostles, St. Katharine and all Virgins. Fifth, in honour of St. Lawrence and all martyrs, and St. Nicholas and all Confessors. Sixth, in honour of the blessed Virgin Mary and St. Anne her mother, and seventh, in honour of Jesus Christ, Saint Ursule, and the eleven thousand Virgins.

CHAPTER XIII.

ROYAL FAVOUR.

"What marvel, that a scene so rich, so fair,
Should admiration, e'en in *Royal* breasts,
Awaken? Admiration, that inspired
Of old, for yonder venerable pile,
Devotion, and munificence, and zeal,
To rear those richly tinted windows." BOOKER.

GREAT object of ambition with the monks of Malvern in the 15th century was to make their church unrivalled, especially in the extent and beauty of its stained glass windows. Only a small quantity of painted glass was in existence in their church before its reconstruction and rebuilding at the date referred to, and those portions were carefully fitted into its 15th century windows, as may be seen on examination. Soon as possible other glass of much beauty, of great extent, and of infinite variety, was added. And whereas at first probably only one window was so distinguished, as time went on nearly every window of the church was made to glow in the sun-light with rich pictorial representations. Fresh painted glass windows began to be added about 1450, and these continued to be multiplied till the beginning of the 16th century; the year 1505 marking the date of the last additions.

How funds were raised by the monks for these artistic works, the cost of which must have been nearly as great as all the other alterations to their church, the windows themselves help to explain. Not only

KING EDWARD THE CONFESSOR GIVING A GRANT TO MALVERN MONK.

From the painted windows of the Priory Church.

are those stained glass windows "A Mirror wherein wee may see how to believe, how to live, how to die, how to passe through Temporalitie to eternitie," but they are a portrait gallery of its distinguished benefactors. It would seem to have been the wont and intention of the monks of Malvern to strive to immortalise in pictorial representation all great contributors to their monastic institution, as well as to pourtray events of more than usual import. The miraculous interposition of angels, in the foundation of St. Michael's oratory, in Saxon times, and the martyrdom of the saint, are shown in the delineation of St. Werstan's legend, as well as in the pictures of the uprearing of their Norman church. In like manner they have left behind them the portrait of their earliest benefactor, *St. Edward*, the Confessor. They did honour to him in a full length picture, in which he is seen delivering to one of Malvern's first monks a ponderously sealed charter, legally entitling them to certain lands given them by that king. Next to him stands the saintly Wulstan, Bishop of Worcester, handing over his benefactions in the shape of a sealed document, and with it affording to the monk kneeling at his feet his gracious benedictions. Near thereto is Henry I. in kingly robes, and with crowned head, bequeathing, out of his royal beneficence, lands to the Priory.

The gifts of these high personages all refer to the foundation grants of the Priory. Other benefactors of a later period are depicted. In the clerestory window of the choir Ecclesiastics of high degree, as Bishops and Archbishops, are shown; and with them Prior John of Malvern, who helped to make the church in 1450; to whose labours and influence most of the 15th century work in the church is due. The whole of these personages without doubt in some way contributed to the monastic funds.

As Lord of Malvern Chace and Duke of Gloucester, King Richard III. was a benefactor to Malvern Priory and is honoured accordingly. Abingdon says, "I conclude with the large west window, which hath presented the Last Judgment, unto the which King Richard III. was (as it seemeth) a benefactor, though in his life he feared not so much as he should that seat of infinite justice, here is on the right hand, France and England quartered without difference, supported with 2 boars argent and covered with a Duke's crown. On the other side are the arms of his wife, and after Queen," "and covered with the crown of a Dutchess." And according to the same writer in almost every window some portrait notice of benefactors is given, generally with some heraldic sign or device.

But of all the windows of the church thus distinguished, the north window of Jesus Chapel was the most richly adorned with portrait memorials. "In that large and stately window," says Abingdon, "is set out in a glass, first, The lively Picture of that wise and devout King, Henry the Seventh, praying, all armed saving his hands and head, whereon he weareth an Imperial crown, and his Royal Taberd, France and England quartered; behind him kneeleth his Queen Elizabeth, the undoubted heir of the house of York, and of all England, crowned also: and on her mantle France and and England quartered; and next to her Arthur, Prince of Wales, their son, compleate in armour (saving his Hands) and head covered with a princely crown: and on his taberd France and England, with a label of 3 argent. *Their heads are all bent to Heaven*: after him kneeleth Sir Reginald Bray, Henry the Seventh's faithful servant in adversity, and counsellor in prosperitie, as the former, bearing on his coat armour argent, a cheveron between 3 Eagles legs erazed sable, and so offereth himself on his knees to God in this church, whereunto he was a benefactor." "Next is in like sort to be seen Sir John Savage, with his arms being argent, a pale Fusille sable; and last Sir Thomas Lovel being as the former of the Privy Counsel to this King, and bearing on his coat armour argent, a chevron between 3 squirrels gules." An inscription in the window represents the whole of these august benefactors as *alive* at the time.

Not without some good reason were these portraits placed in the church, the principal one probably being that the King and his distinguished suite were benefactors thereto. A document known as the Lichfield MS says that "the situation of Malvern was so much admired by Henry VII., his Queen and her two sons, Prince Arthur and Prince Henry, that they were induced to beautify the Church with stained glass windows to a degree of magnificence that made it one of the proudest ornaments of the nation." This document has without sufficient reason been considered as somewhat apochryphal, and but little reliance has been placed on its statements; I am inclined to think that full credence should be given to it. Abingdon says, "The windowes show the Royal munificence of *Henry VII.*, *his Queen*, and Prince Arthur, the Duke of Gloster, after King, with many Lords Knights and gentlemen, and Sir Reginald Bray, most eminent among the re-edifyers of that beautiful church." There has always been a tradition that Henry VII., his Queen, and his two sons, paid a visit to Malvern, and that the King had his abode in the room over the gateway of the Priory. These considerations, and others that might be urged, lead to the belief that the distinguished personages mentioned did visit Malvern, that much of the magnificence of the Priory Church was owing to them, that they *did* adorn it with much of the beautiful glass for which it has become famous, and that it was in honour of their benefactions and visit, that such beautiful portraits (two of which only remain) were bequeathed to posterity.

That King Henry VII., with Prince Arthur and others, visited Worcester towards the end of the fifteenth century is beyond doubt. Provision for them at Worcester monastery was as follows:—

"Bred viii li; floure xl s viii d; three and halfe tunns ale cs; one tun wyne xli; spyce, pepur, saforn, clowse, synemond, gyngyr xij p'd; small reysons viij p'ds; datys, sugyr, waxe; bevys lx s; xx motons xl s; iij dozen capons; ij capons of geese for ye Kinge ij s viij; iij dozen chyckense; iij signettys; ij pekoks; iij feysons; w't a dozen and a halff of lappwyngs; plovers iiiij; harviesowys; couple of connyngs; viii dozen pegynes; ccccc eggs, iiij s; vi q'ts buttur, xii d; xx galons mylke xx d; xij Loodes wood; xxx dozen of horsebred, xxx s; iiij Loode hey xxvi s, viij d; ertherne potts; fyve and halfe desen iiij s, vi d; in rewardys by my lord xi li, vii s; in rewordes by th celerar cv s, vi d; in mustart xv d; vynegur xvi d. Sum tot. lxij li, ij s, v d."*

* Noake's "Monastery and Cathedral."

CHAPTER XIV.

INSIDE THE MONASTERY.

"Perchance from its seclusion oft might stray
Some pensive monk, who, thoughtless of his way,
Sought contemplation in the distant glade,
'Till night had veil'd its varied hues in shade."
THE ABBEY GARDEN.

BEYOND the gatehouse was the Priory close, a charmed and secluded spot, walled in from the outer world, and inspiring such religious awe as afforded the monks protection and security. When once within the gate, it was the duty of the "hostelarius" to take possession of strangers of whatever kind, religious or secular. If they came on horseback, he had their steeds in charge. It was his office to conduct strangers into the cloister, and through whatever offices of the convent they had liberty to go. He had to see they were properly apparelled, that none were barefoot, and that the spurs on the feet of knights and others had been removed. It was his office to conduct into the Chapter house those who wished, and had liberty to fraternise with the brethren, as well as those whom religion or the claims of business permitted to enter.

Two sites that can still be identified enable us to fix the position of the domestic buildings of the Priory. The guesten hall of the Priory, sometimes denominated the refectory, stood on a portion of ground now occupied by Knotsford Lodge, and on the *western* side of the former cloister. This guesten hall remained till about forty years since, and was taken down to make way for less pretentious structures. A description of the building has been given at page 61. The north east point of the same cloister is quite as certainly identified by the position of the south transept of the church, the site of which transept may be easily determined, and may be seen by the ground plan.

Near the guesten hall stood the Prior's house, probably on the site of the present "Abbey boarding house." There were other apartments near it, devoted, as occasion required, to the reception of visitors. The guesten hall was still in existence when Dr. Card wrote his account of Malvern Priory in 1834, and is thus referred to by him: "If one of the monks who lived in the 12th or 14th centuries could now revisit Malvern, he would find its fine acres sold, and if he awoke from his slumbers, and turned his eyes toward the monastic refectory, have as much difficulty in recognising it as the wayfaring man in discovering a safe tread between shifting sands and *mirages*, so different an aspect has it assumed in the lapse of ages. That hall where he held high festivals with his Prior and brethren is now converted into a barn; and the oaken board on which he partook of his meals changed into mangers for horses and oxen."

The refectory proper probably stood in the usual place, viz,, in the south cloister; as at Worcester and most other Benedictine houses. Be this as it may, it would have windows opening into the kitchen which adjoined it, through which meats were served; and there would be a desk or pulpit for reading during dinner-time. Most likely it was wainscoted with oak, and had in some conspicuous place a painting of the crucifixion. A dresser, heavy oaken benches, almonries, cupboards, &c., would complete its furniture.

It is clear that the south transept of the church, which at the north east corner, as has been said, joined the cloisters, was not identical in position, or arrangement, with the north transept. Dr. Thomas, in his Latin account of Malvern Priory, gives a ground plan of the church, showing the run of the walls both of the Lady

Chapel, at the east end, and this south transept (see plan of church), and it would seem that in his day the walls, though "in ruins," were above ground. It appears too that the south transept was shorter, and was not in line with the one in the north, but was removed further toward the east. This transept was a chapel dedicated to St. Ursula and the eleven thousand virgins, and had a large east window. Side mullions, and the spring of the arch of such window may still be seen, and the fact is beyond question. The cloister and domestic buildings, coming as they would do against this chapel, made the window in question a necessity, and it is possible that it had no south window, or, if there was one, it was high up, and of small dimensions.

The cloister of Malvern Priory was, as elsewhere, a rectangular yard or enclosure on the south side of the church, embracing the buildings I have mentioned. It was a paved arcade, and probably, considering the prevalence of wood in the neighbourhood, covered with a timber penthouse roof. This is rendered still more likely by what we know of the hall above referred to, which was of open timber work. This covered arcade served to unite the various buildings of the monastery with the church, while at the same time it secured a secluded ambulatory, or walk, sheltered from the inconvenience of the weather. On the south side was the *scriptorium*, or writing-place, furnished with desks, in which the art of writing manuscripts and illuminating them was carried on. The lavatory would probably have been at the south-west corner, the nearest point to the *Hay-well*, from which, as already intimated, plentiful supplies of water were obtained.

Adjoining the church at the north east was the sacristy containing the ecclesiastical robes, hangings, service books, thuribles, and such other articles as were required for the celebration of divine service. Over this the dormitories, from which there may have been an entrance by staircase into the church, for the convenience of the monks at their constantly recurring services, by night as well as by day. One of the most important features of the eastern side of the cloister remains to be particularised, viz., the Chapter house: it

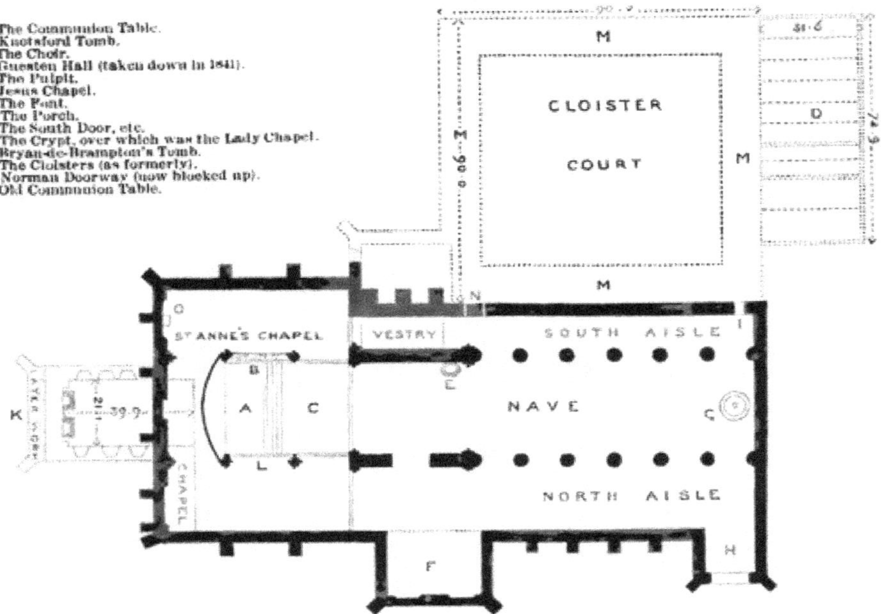

A. The Communion Table.
B. Knotsford Tomb.
C. The Choir.
D. Guesten Hall (taken down in 1841).
E. The Pulpit.
F. Jesus Chapel.
G. The Font.
H. The Porch.
I. The South Door, etc.
K. The Crypt, over which was the Lady Chapel.
L. Bryan-de-Brampton's Tomb.
M. The Cloisters (as formerly).
N. Norman Doorway (now blocked up).
O. Old Communion Table.
CLOISTER
COURT
M
D
VESTRY
SOUTH AISLE
NAVE
NORTH AISLE
ST ANNE'S CHAPEL
CHAPEL
F
H
K
90·0
39·9
SCALE OF 10 5 0 10 20 30 40 50 60 70 80 90 100 FEET

is likely that it was of Norman architecture, and as such the reader may think of it, as either square in form, oblong, or circular. The greater proportion of early specimens are square with a raised seat for the Prior, and a stone bench all round for the monks. Here councils were held, and transgressors against the monastic rules were tried, and the general secular business of the Priory was done. There were besides those I have mentioned several minor offices.

Such was Malvern's cloister, such its principal offices, in the olden time, the location let us hope, and believe, of many self-denying, studious, laborious, and devout men, who for a while did good service to the community. As riches poured in upon them, luxury with all its concomitants of vice and immorality without doubt had come with them. There were always some bad men in monasteries, as there are now in all professions and callings, in spite of the restraints which modern life and civilization afford. With growing wealth it became more difficult to maintain that self-denial, purity, and prayerfulness, to which monks were so solemnly pledged. There were dark sides to Malvern's Convent dwellers. Let us hope there were many bright ones, times of growth in righteousness as well as decadence, times of origin as well as extinction. Little did the monks of Malvern think as the 15th century drew towards its close, as they looked with delight upon their re-edified church and lately consecrated *seven* altars, that early in the next decade the doom of monkery would be sealed; that then their beautiful church would betake itself to new offices; that their altars would be thrown down as abhorred things, and the domestic buildings in which they had feasted, fasted, joyed, and wept, would be levelled with the ground.

The following translation of a document in the British Museum, the original text of which is in the author's possession, shows that till the end the Abbot of Westminster insisted upon exercising his jurisdiction over the Malvern monks. The missive is dated 1st October, 1511. (British Museum, Harley MS).

Letter of the Visitation of our Cell at Malvern:

John by Divine permission Abbot of the exempt Monastery of St. Peter of Westminster belonging, with no intermediary, to the Court of Rome, to our well beloved in Christ the Prior of the house or cell of Great Malvern, greeting in the author of our health.

Anxiety for the duties which we have undertaken equally persuades and compels us to visit you and your said house or cell both in its head and in its members for certain lawful reasons at this monastery actually as (with God's permission) we do so intend and purpose to visit you. We therefore warn and strictly charge you, and we will and command that by you all and singular your fellow monks and fellow brethren of your said house or cell be cited to appear, both you and they, on the eighteenth day of this present month of October in your chapter house at the accustomed hour, with continuation and adjournment of days then following, if it be necessary, until the final settlement of this manner of our visitation inclusive, in the presence of us or of our commissary or commissaries, on this behalf lawfully and sufficiently appointed, to undergo duly and lawfully this manner of our visitation in accordance with the requirements of the law and the custom of past time, and moreover to perform and to receive that which befits the sacred ordinances and the precepts of our religion of Saint Benedict. And concerning the day of the receiving of these present letters, and also of all that ye shall do in the premises ye are to certify, clearly and openly, us or our commissary or commissaries aforesaid at the said time and place by your letters patent containing an account thereof, together with the names and cognizances of those who are thereby to be cited, in a certain schedule which is to be attached to your said letters certificatory.

Given under our seal, on the first day of the month of October, in the year of our Lord fifteen hundred and eleven.

CHAPTER XV.

OUTSIDE THE MONASTERY.

"The holy fathers here were wont to stray,
And oft they traversed this secluded dell,
They saw the summer sun's retiring ray
And heard in echo Hanley's castle bell.

And often here, by adverse fortune driven
Some lonely mourner sought the cloister's shades
To weep in solitude his way to heaven,
And praise his God amid these verdant glades."

THE last chapter concerned itself exclusively with the inside of the monastery. I propose in the present one to take in review some of the convent's surroundings, as they were presented in the 15th century.

Near the top of Church street at the junction of three roads, and opposite the old parochial church of St. Thomas, which was then standing, stood a road-way cross. The only relic left of this once venerated object is its shaft, which many years ago was removed out of its place in the middle of the roads, and was set up on the side of the terrace. The arms of the cross are gone, and a round ball has been placed on the head of the shaft We have no means of knowing what its base was like, but it was most probably surrounded by steps. Around this cross, in ancient times, the scattered inhabitants of Malvern were often gathered to hear the preaching of friars, or Wickliffians, many of whom traversed this neighbourhood and would there often exhort to reformation of manners, and preach the doctrines of the cross. There also country people came with various commodities for sale, under the shadow of the cross to bargain and traffic with the monks. A local poet whilst this cross was standing in the roadway thus apostrophised it :—

> "Four hundred years have pass'd away
> Since thy foundation stones were laid,
> And many a pageant, grave and gay,
> Has dwelt beneath thy cross's shade.
> In time's dark days, old monks and friars
> Have stood and preached thy steps upon,
> And knights, and barons proud, and squires,
> And serfs,—have mix'd thy guests among.
>
> And oft the gladsome village maid
> And swains in dance have paced the round,
> And some have pass'd in joy array'd
> But many more in sorrow bound.
> Thy church's bells, in sadness speaking,
> Have toll'd death's knell, and call'd to prayer!
> And many a time, in gladness breaking,
> Joy's nuptial notes have fill'd thy air."

In the churchyard, near its western entrance, at a point where formerly was the only way to the church from the outside of the convent, stood another cross of larger dimensions, the shaft and base of which cross still remain. Its extended arms met the gaze of all as they entered into the ancient graveyard, perhaps by a lich-gate. Steps surrounded this cross, and an image of Saint Mary was fitted into its shaft. Britton tells us that "crosses were erected at the entrance of churches to throw the mind into an attitude of solemn thought and reverence." Here as they approached the church worshippers had to pass beneath its shadow. Next came the church porch, in the centre niche of which was a larger image of the Virgin Mary, and devout worshippers of that period, as they entered the church, thought it a duty to ejaculate an "Ave Maria" as their upward glance caught the venerated object.

Below the Priory, not far from the railway, was the mill of the monks. There their corn was ground, and in the mill-dam fish for fasting days were preserved. The Priory farm extended all round the Priory close, but in greatest extent southward of the church, It was without doubt well tilled and cultivated. Benedictine monks were generally the best of farmers and gardeners, and there is every reason to think those of Malvern formed no exception to the rule.

From the "Hay-well" (High-well) supplies of fresh water in great abundance ran into the Priory domain, and for those who aspired to greater sanctity in beverage the waters of St. Ann's well were available.

The entrance to the Priory was by the gateway, parts of which still exist, for there are reasons for believing that this gate-house is now not more than half its original size. It is next to certain that formerly buildings of some kind were continued between it and the west window of the church, against which there are evidences of an apartment existing. It is probable also that communication therewith existed with the room, or Parvice, over the church porch. Rooms over gate-houses had various uses. Sometimes they were chapels, where visitors and travellers on arrival and departure offered up their devotions to Almighty God. At other times and places they formed the *Hospitium*, or guest chamber, for the reception of distinguished visitors, and sometimes they were the muniment house of the monastery, where, under the triple keys of the superior, the treasures were kept. Whatever use the rooms were applied to in Malvern monastery must remain matter of conjecture. A tradition is extant that the author of Piers' Ploughman there composed his remarkable poem. It is likely in, or somewhere near that building, a small chapel did exist. The posts of the Priory gate are still remaining, halfway within the building; they are strong and very massive and show where its great hinges were inserted.

The gates, or doors, of the monastery were closed by day and night except for the brethren or their guests to pass in and out. On the right hand side of entrance was the porter's lodge, with a small window, still to be seen, on the outside of the gate, so as to enable the monk-porter to see the guest before admittance, and to hold converse, if necessary, with him. It is possible that a round tower stair gave access from this chamber to the room above, as at other places. Henry VIII.'s general surveyors thus describe this arrangement at a like gate-house elsewhere: "A Porter's lodge w^{t} a chymnee, a round stayre leding up to a high chamber." The north front of this Priory gateway is still very beautiful; its general features remain as they were left by the builders in the 15th century. It is "a genuine and interesting piece of antiquity. The front is composed of two divisions; the arch has a square head, and the spandrels are filled with quarter-foils enclosed in circular ribs. Springing from the apex of the arch, on a moulded corbel, is a highly enriched oriel window, having its angular mullions relieved with delicately carved pinnacles." On the east wall near the roof are a quantity of tiles, ornamented like those in the church. Formerly it probably formed the interior of an apartment. It is easy to imagine the look of this gateway, with its ponderous doors swinging upon hinges of great strength and laced hither and thither with ornamental iron work and studded with knobs of the same material.

CHAPTER XVI.

THE PRIORS.

> " Names that shall sink not in oblivion's flood,
> But with clear music, like a church bells chime,
> Sound through the river's sweep of onward time."

I AM able to give two catalogue accounts of the Priors of Great Malvern. The first is the one generally found in histories of Malvern. It has several omissions, and has always been known to be imperfect.

Aldwinus tempore Willelmi Conquestoris	
Walcherus ob. 1st October ..	1135
Rogerus 5 Henry II ..	1159
Walterus ..	1165
Walterus	1191
Willielmus Normannus	1222
Thomas ob.	1242
Johannes de Wigornia 1242 presentatus per Abbatem Westm. in vigilia beati Johannis Baptiste, anno gratie 1242 resignavit die Lune proxima post festum beati Luce Evangeliste 1259.	
Thomas de Bredone	1259
Frater Will'us de Ledbury ..	1279
Ricardus de Estone, ob. 3 non. martii	1300
Hugo, circa	1314
Frater Johannes Malvern	1435
Johannes Benet	1449
Ricardus Dene ..	1462
Ricardus Bone ..	
Ricardus Frewen ..	
Masculinus Ledbury 2nd Feb.	1503
Frater Thomas Kegworth 20 Jany.	1511
Richard Whitbourne, alias Bedyll, the last prior, had a pension of 66£ 13s 4 assigned to him at the dissolution.	

The account following is now for the first time published, being copied from MS in the British Museum, and has obligingly been sent me by W. de Gray Birch, Esq., of that institution. It gives a much fuller account of Malvern Priors, and by its aid a fairly complete catalogue can be made. The antiquarian Cole visited

Malvern in 1744, and I shall be able in a later chapter to give fully the results of his inspection.

Cole writes: In Mr. Browne Willis's copy of Mr. Abingdon's Survey of Worcester, he has entered, before the account of Great Malvern Priory, printed in that book, a list of the Priors of that house, and, as I had the use of that book by the permission of his grandson and executor, I have entered them here:—

Priors of Great Malverne, 1744:

Alwinus primus Prior 1085.
Walcherus Lotharingus occurs 1125 and died 1135.
Rogerus 1151 and 1159.
Walter 1165.
Roger Malebargh 1177.
Tho: de Wicke occurs 1217.
Will: Normannus 1222.
Thomas died 1242.
I.... succeeded 1242 as in Anglia Sacra, vol. 1, p. 491.
Thomas resigned 1266.
Will; de Wikewan succeeded 1266.
Will: de Ledbury 1279 usurpavit, occurs 1277, was deposed 1287.
Will: de Wikewan 1288, durante lite
Richard de Eston succeeded 1287, died 1300.
Hugo de Wyke presided 1314 and resigned 1340.
Tho; de Legh succeeded 1340, died 1349.
John de Painswick elected June 27, 1349, died 1361.
Symon Rysley elected Sept: 4, 1361. Byscheley, MS. Widmore, v. vol.: 40, p. 87.
Richard Rolle elected May 17, 1397. Polle, MS. Widmore, ut supra.
John Malverne occurs 1349.
J. Bennet occurs 1449.
Richard Mathern or Mathon resigned 1457.
Richard Dene succeeded elected in July 1457, and occurs 1463.
Richard Frewen 1480 and 1483.
Masculinus Ledbury 1503, died 1506.
Tho: Kegworth elected Jan: 5, 1506, and 1516.
Tho: Dereham 1533 and 1537.
Richard Whitborn alias Bedyl, last Prior, had a Pension 1541 of £66 ,, 8 ,, 4. which was vacated before 1552.

(British Museum, Cole's Various Parochial Antiquities, vol. x. Add. MS. 5811, f. 118*b*.)

"Prior John of Malvern" is a title given to three different persons distinguished in connection with monastic institutions of this neighbourhood. A Prior "John of Malvern" succeeded John Green as Prior of St. Mary's monastery at Worcester in the year 1395. "He was" according to Noake, "one of the English divines who were sent to the Council of Constance in 1414," and was a witness against John Badley, a poor tailor of Worcester, against whom a charge of denying "transubstantiation" was made, and who was tried and found guilty in the "carnarie chapel" at Worcester, and was afterwards burnt at Smithfield.

In the Malvern Priory windows a second "Prior John of Malvern" is mentioned, who helped to make the church in 1435, thus: "Orate pro anima domini Johannis Malverne, qui istam fenestram fieri fecit." To this Prior credit is generally given for much of the Perpendicular work in the church.

In the list of Priors from Cole's MS, there are supplied the names of five Priors not mentioned elsewhere, occurring between the years 1349 and 1397, and amongst them a third *Prior John of Malvern* "occurs 1349," and according to the same authority a John de Painswick became Prior in that year. How can this be reconciled? About the year 1362 that remarkable poem "The Vision of Pier's Plowman" is believed to have been written, and writers have generally attributed the composition of it to the Malvern Priory, and have esteemed a Robert Langland to be the author. Who was he? "Among the learned men of that age (Edward III) was Robert Langland, a secular priest, born Salopshire in Mortimers Clebury." (Holinshed vol. 2, p. 1003). "This year John Malverne, a Fellow of Oriel College in Oxford, made, and finished his book entitled the Vision of Piers Plowman," (Stow's ann. p. 238) and Wood in his Hist. and Antiq. Univ. Oxon says "Robertus Langland Johannes Malverne nonnullis appellatur: fertur autem inter sui saeculi poetas maxime facetos excelluise" *(Robert Langland is called by some John of Malvern, he is moreover reported to have excelled amongst the most elegant of poets of his time).* This shows us pretty clearly that Robert Langland and John de Malvern of the years following 1349 were not two, but one and the same person, the first being his secular name, the last the one he was known by as a monk. This change of name on joining a religious community was common; Abingdon says, "mislead with curriositie I was a while desirous to know ye names of ye most ancient monkes till I perceaved yt in former ages when the Englishe were only known by singell or Christian names they followed yt use, but when they came to surnames for distinction of families, the religious obscured them-selfs under straigne surnames and most often assumed the names of the Places where they were borne."

How John of Malvern could have been Prior, and John de

Painswick at the same time, is a difficulty that there is but one way of solving. Thus :—John of Malvern was elected Prior, but for some reason he permitted the honour to fall on another. Assuming that he was the writer of the poem, the reason for this might have been that he was desirous to be relieved of the cares and duties of such office so as to be able to devote himself fully to the composition of his poem. As prior he had none to control him. The poem in question is scathing in its character to monks themselves, as well as to the religious orders generally, and it is probable that Langland did not allow his office to fall on any one of different mind from himself, and who would be a hindrance to him. The history of this remarkable man may be easily computed. Robert Langland was a native of Cleobury Mortimer, on the borders of Wales,—a line of country then so full of disquietude and excitement, especially on religious questions, as to give prominence to many of its inhabitants as followers of Wickliffe. There Robert Langland became associated with rural habits and country occupations. Gentleman, as he must have been, and probably ambitious, he went to Oxford. There the dead languages revealed to him deep mines of ancient thought. The mighty tomes of the Christian Fathers were opened before him. In its original tongue he drank in the inspiration of holy scripture. The invisible things of "the Kingdom" became revealed to him, and something of what is known as Calvinistic doctrines possessed him. Of this the poem itself is evidence. Thus inspired, he longed to tell what he knew and felt to *ploughmen and common labourers*,—a class whom he had known in their neglect, and loved because of their simplicity,—and he sought the seclusion of Great Malvern Priory for the prosecution of his purpose. As a scholar and Fellow of Oxford he was without doubt revered by the monks, and they thrust upon him the robe of Prior. Malvern's quiet cloister saw him slowly accomplishing his work, and by the year 1362 the poem went forth. The work is written in the exact idiomatic expression of the common people of that day: the sublimest verities of holy church are there given utterance to in a kind of composition that the common people could comprehend, and in a language that belonged to them alone.

CHAPTER XVII.

THE DISSOLUTION.

"The earth where abbeys stood
Is layman's land, the glebe, the stream, the wood:
His oxen low where monks retired to eat,
His cows repose upon the Prior's seat,
And wanton doves within the cloister bill,
Where the chaste votary warr'd with wanton will."

CRABBE.

THE church of the monks had begun to lose somewhat of the glitter of its 15th century's re-edification. Its patron and late benefactor Henry VII. was dead, and Henry VIII. was on the throne of England, when the dissolution of monastic houses became imminent. Come it did and that speedily. It was an age of change. The church generally by the corruption and greed of the clergy and monastic orders had become a bye-word and reproach. The ill-living of monks was matter of notoriety. The conventual system had outlived its primitive simplicity and usefulness, and there did not appear to be necessity for its longer existence. Such writings as that of Malvern's own monk "The Vision of Piers Plowman," and others of like character, had exposed the system unmercifully, added to which there were frightful accounts unfolded at the visitations of abbeys of "detestable crimes practised in the cloisters of iniquity and impurity." Independence of thought began to be manifested as well as desires for religious reform, and emancipation from abject superstitions. Against Malvern's monks at the time no charge was made beyond that of their veneration for miserable relics. But above and beyond everything else the great wealth absorbed by religious communities, and the austere way in which they were lording it over their heritages, made their extinction a *pecuniary* necessity to King and Commons alike. We learn from Spelman (History of Sacrilege) that on the part of the Commons "sympathy was felt for nuns and monks," but that Henry VIII. declared to them in his usual bluff manner, that if the bill were not passed which put him in possession of all monastic establishments, with the property belonging to them, both real and personal, he would cause some of their heads to be struck off. The dissolution of the monasteries, when once contemplated, for various reasons became an event of more easy and speedy accomplishment than had been anticipated. The lesser monasteries had already been dissolved, when a final fiat was issued; and amongst other houses of even more wealth and greater magnificence, in the year 1538, the Priory of Much Malvern, with all its faults, benefits, and shortcomings, was doomed to come to an end. The monks' last midnight mass had to be offered, their last vigil to be chanted, their last matin to be sung. Their time-honoured doles of bread and meat, given to the many poor constantly surrounding their gate, would have to cease.

The change wrought by the dissolution of the monasteries was a momentous one. Some were shocked at the proposal. For though sick of the conventual system, and though monks themselves were desirous to vacate their cells,* few persons were prepared to acquiesce in the devotion of monastic riches to secular purposes, or to admit that anything so ancient and time-honoured could be in everything wrong. Differences of opinion existed. Those who approved of the extinction of monasteries felt regard for the stately domestic and ecclesiastical buildings which the monks had upreared. Was all to be sold, sacred and profane alike? Was nothing to be spared? Nothing thought worth keeping? Was it right that endowments, which had been solemnly

* Many monks were found by the visitors "Whiche instantly knelyng on ther knees houldyng up ther hands, desyred to be delyvered of such relygyon."

bequeathed by the faithful for holy purposes, that all these should be disposed of, and the proceeds given to worldly uses? Such questionings agitated many. Amongst others the good Bishop of Worcester, the saintly Protestant Latimer, thought some good could come out of monasteries, and the continuance of Malvern Priory had the distinguished honour of being pleaded for by him. In a letter to Cromwell he asked that in every county two or three monasteries might be preserved and kept. "Natt in monkrye he mayneth natt so," but to "mayntayne tochynge," and for other good and devout purposes. For Malvern he interceded in the following words:

"But now syre another thynge, that by your favour I myght be a motionare unto you, at the request of an honeste man, the Prior of Grett Malverne, in my dioc. referrying the successe of the hooll matter to your ownly approvyed wissdom and benynge goodnesse in every case ffor I knoo that I doo play the ffowll, but yett with my foolysshnesse I somewhatt qwiette and unqwiette man, and mytygatt hys heuynesse, which I am bold to doo with you, ffor that I kno by experience your gooodnesse, that you wyll bear with ffowlls in their freylnesse. Thys man both heryth and feryth (as he sayth) the suppressione of hys Howse, wich thowgh he wyll be conformable in all poyntts to the kyngs hynesse plesewre and yours ons knoyn, as both I advertysed him, ande also his bowndon dewtye ys to be, yett neuerthelesse yf ye thowght hys interprysse shuld natt be mystake nor turn to ony displesewr he wold be an humble sewtere to your lord shyp, and by the same to the kyngs good grace for the upstandynge of his forsayd howse, and contynuance of the same to many good perpassesse, nat in Monkrye, he mayneth natt so, God forbyd, but ony other ways, as shuld be thought ande seyme good to the kyng's majestye, as to mayntayne tochynge, prechynge, studye, with prayynge, and (to the which he is much gevyne) good howskepynge; for to the vertu of hospitalyte he hathe byn grettly inclynyd from hys begynnynge, and ys very much commendyd in thes partees for the same; so that if c c c c c marks to the kyngs hynesse, with c c marks to yourselffe for your good wyll might occasione the promotione of hys intentt, att leste way for the tyme of hys lyffe, he doubyth natt to make hys frends for the same, yf so lytull cold bringe soo much to passe. The man ys old, a good howskepere, fedyth many, and that dayly, for the contreth ys poore and full of penurye: and, alas my good Lord, shall we not see ij. or iij. in every shyre changyd to such remedye?

Thus to thys honeste man is importuyte hath browght me to beyounde my dewte, savyng for the confydence any truste that I have always in your benignytye. As he hath knolege froom you, soo he wyll prepare for you, ever obednentt to your aduertyessmentt. Syr Wlliam Kyngston can make reportt of the man."

"13 *Decemb.* "H. L.
"*Hart.*" "WIGORN""

What effect this letter had on Cromwell's mind, or the king's, we know not; that it did not have the desired effect is clear, for, in the year of the destruction of all the greater monasteries, Malvern's Priory was dissolved and had to share the common doom. Very shortly the place could not be found.

"Where priests 'mid tapers dim
Breath'd the warm prayer, or tun'd the midnight hymn,
Where trembling penitents their guilt confessed,
Where want had succour, and contrition rest,
Where weary men from trouble found relief,
And men in sorrow found repose from grief."

Such things were no more to be seen, except in the poor memorials that thought should devise, or painter's pencil might portray.

The monks of Malvern had large estates and possessions. They had revenues accruing to them from manors near and distant, including those of Newland, Powick, and Woodfield, near Malvern, Longley-on-Severn, and some in the Welsh principality. They had estates of greater or less extent in the counties of Worcester, Hereford, Brecknock, Salop, and Warwick. They had three corn mills on Lawrn brook, one at Powick, and another at Aucot, large property in lands at Quatt in Shropshire, with its church. Churches belonged to them in Wales, Longden, Upton-on-Severn, and at Dowles near Bewdley, churches in the diocese of St. David's, at Pitchcote in Lincoln diocese, Hanley Castle in Worcestershire, East leach in the deanery of Fairford, and the tythes of Archesfonte in Sarum diocese, cells in which were some of their monks, at Colwall, Herefordshire, and at Aucot in Warwickshire. The secular business involved by this large inheritance gave the monks no small amount of occupation. Their ledger entries were large, and their accounts, books, and general archives considerable. The disposal of these estates and the settlement of the various interests involved in them, required from the commissioners of the king, no little skill, labour, or pains. The annual revenue of the monastery at the dissolution, according to Speed, was £375 0 0. This in present money might be reckoned in thousands in the place of hundreds, and even then the reckoning would afford no exact criterion of the convent's wealth and resources.

The following summary of persons connected with the Malvern monastery at its dissolution will give some idea of the extent of its sway, and of the vastness of its interests.

Richard Whitbourne, alias Bedyell, was the last Prior. He was most likely a native of the village whose name he bore; a family of Beddles dwelt there till recently. Others of the monks were William Umbersley, William Ffrome, Richard Webley, Richard Poll or Poole, Richard Suckley, Christopher More, William

Bennet, Reynolds Werstan, Hugh Lychefeild, Thomas Powyck, Maculyne Coleman, Richard Stretton, Maculyne Malvern, and Gylbert Alford. The whole of these afterwards bore the prefix of "Sir;" and the Prior was called a "*clerk*." Amongst others the following clerks, or clergymen, were dependent upon the monastic funds:—Sir Wm. Robyns "Curatt" of Newland, Sir Richard Gyllham, Vicar of Malvern, and Sir Roger Matthew, Vicar of Longley. The Bishop of Worcester was entitled to fees, viz., 6/8 for Upton Snodsbury and 2/- for Woodesfeild. The following *lay* men and gentlemen had pecuniary interests in, or claims upon, the monastery as "corrodyes, annuities, and ffees:" Sir Richard Lygon, Knight, William Lygon, Esq., and Roger Lygon, Gent., (these and others after the dissolution received their annuities by "*thands of their Servants*") Richard Lycham, Gent., John Knyll, Gent., William Cokesay, Gent., Sir Anthony Kingston, Knight, Richard Warnecomb, Esq., John ap Rece, Esq., Rowland Morton, Esq., John Burghyll, Esq., Robert Wyneby, Yoman, John Lylle, John Gough, Thomas Byrd, John Gor, Thomas Bennet, Philip Baxter, Richard Blon, Richard Alen, William Sharpe, William Nevelle, Richard Glover, and others. Sir John Russell, Knight, was "chyeff stuard," and Thomas Rock, Gent., had the "understuardshypp," and both were entitled to fees accordingly, as were also George Blount, Esq., "Stuard of Dowles and Metton," and Sir Humphrey Fferrers, Knight, "Stuard of Abecott," &c.

A "corrady," mentioned above, was such provision as we should now call board and lodging. For such consideration as had been agreed upon, an ordinary layman entered a monastery and lived therein. Sometimes he had a horse in the convent stables, and, more rarely, a servant to attend upon him. Such men were not bound by vows, but, under certain regulations, had liberty to go out and return again to the monastery at their own will and pleasure. During the visitations of religious houses which preceded the dissolution, many complaints were made that "corradys" had been sold to the damage of the institution, i.e., the money received was put into the Abbot's or Prior's pockets, or spent, and the "corrady" left an incumbrance upon the house. Other complaints were that men, sometimes with wives, so placed at the mercy of the monks in their old age, were treated in manner so cruel as to shorten their lives, that in their dying hours their friends were not permitted to see them, or were "put owt thens," and that when death did come their private "coffers wer broke" and their little wealth stolen. Nothing of this kind was, however, charged against the Malvern monks. Speaking of this lay element in convents, Coke, in his "Institutes," says:—"Monks were bound to deal almesse to the poore, and to keep hospitality; and, as touching the almesse that they dealt, and the hospitality that they kept, every man knoweth that many thousands were well received of them, and might have been better if they had not had so many great men's horses to feed, and had not been overcharged with such idle gentlemen as were never *out* of the abbeys."

CHAPTER XVIII.

"SCUDAMORE PAPERS."

"Time hath, my lord, a wallet at his back
Wherein he puts alms for oblivion."

SHAKESPEARE.

JOHN Scudamore and Robert Burgoyn, Esquires, were the king's receivers of the monasteries in the border counties in his highness's court of augmentation. Their accounts are contained in the "*Scudamore Papers,*" a voluminous MS. in the British Museum, the parts concerning Malvern monastery alone occupying eighty pages of foolscap. The whole MS. is interesting even to its remotest "item;" and valuable as being a literal transcript from those times. I have found difficulty in making selections, and have had to exclude much of curious detail; but to have printed all relating to Malvern would have been to exceed reasonable limits. The accounts begin with 32nd Henry VIII. and are continued, with quaint variations in spelling and *items*, through succeeding years.

The multitude of persons to whom "Peneyons, corrodes, anuytes" and "ffees" were paid will astonish those who have regarded convents as only concerning their regular and proper inmates.

Payments were made for convenience, or otherwise, at various places; in 33rd Henry VIII. at "Malvern Major," both in the term of the Annunciation (Lady Day) and in that of St. Michael. Atother times London was the place of payment, and payments were also dated in the several years from Hereford, Ludlow, Lichfield, Worcester, and "Beawdeley."

The following are letters concerning Malvern monastery. The first from John ap Rice, an over civil Welshman, who, with many holiday terms, excuses himself from immediate payment of rent. The second is from Edward North who, in the king's name, writes to his "very Louyng ffrend John Scudamore Esquyre" giving him authority to cause the "sea walles and decayed places" of Longley on Severne to be "well and sufficiently repayred" out of the funds of the dissolved Priory.

After my moste hartye com'endacion's unto you. Where as I have receyved of late a p'cept to be afore you at Worcester for the payme't of the re't of Malv'ne that I have in lease at Brecknoke, ffor as moche as I am com'e but v'y lately ffrom' above hether that I am not only wery but also so letted with busynes here that I can' not con'eniently come unto you myself at this tyme for the said purpose, these shalbe hartely to desire you to holde me excused at this tyme, and because my payme't for thole year is four and fyftye poundes viij.s. viij.d. by the teno'r of my lease the counterpayne whereof you mr. burgoyne haue, or els ye sha'll see my lease at yo'r pleasure, It maye please you to make my debent'r therafter, and you Mr. Scudamore receyuyng the same at yo'r com'yng hether ye shall haue the said rent of me foorthwi'th. In which doing ye sha'll doo me very thankefu'll plesure to be as thankefully reme'bred agein if I may or can' haue the occasion' thereto. Thus our lorde haue you in his keping. ffrom Hereford the xvith of January.

Yours adsuredly to his powr.
John ap Rice.

Endorsed:—To the right worshipfull Mr. Scudamore and Mr. Burgoyne Esquiers at Worcester.

British Museum, Add. MS. 11041, f. 62, (*Scudamore Papers*, vol. 1.)

After hartie commendac'ons fforasmoche as the seea walles wt. in the p'isshe of Longney in the countie of Gloucest'r being p'cell of the possessions of the late monastery of Moche Malvern in the countie of Worceyto'r is in grete decaye very nedefull to be repayred and amended wth. all expedic'on as I am credyblye enformed, and albeit ye have been slack heretofore in forseing the repayring therof, which will be a meanes to dymynysshe the kinges ma'tes possessions there wth. other detryment and inconuenyence to the countrey if spedye remedye be not p'uyded for the same as I am enformed, In considerac'on whereof thiese shalbe to requyre you and on the kinges ma'tes behalf to commaunde you ymmedyatly upon' receipt herof to repayre to the said p'isshe of Longney eyther by yo'r self or yo'r sufficient Deputie, and to su'ey the said sea Walles and decayed places, in what ruyne they be. And therupon': to cause the same to be well and sufficientlly repayred and amended in all suche places where nedefull repa'c'ons ar to be made and done, on the kinges ma'tes behalf. And further that you cause all other p'sons whiche ben or ought to be contrybutory to the Repayring therof to amende and Repayre the same so far as by teno'r of their' landes or by appointment and assignement of the Commissions of Sewers in these p'ties they shalbe bounden and called thereunto. to thentent the said Repa'c'ons may p'cede instely and sufficiently according to right and equytie as well for p'suac'on of the countrey there as other the better mayntenance of the kinges ma'tes enheritaunce and possessions in the same p'ties. Desiering you further to use yo'r discrec'on herein as may be for the kinges ma'tes most aduantage and commodytee. Wherof I doubte not And so bydde you hartylye farewell ffrom London' the xvith of August. And of all suche som'es of money as you shall disburse for the same on the kinges ma'tes behalf you shall have due allowance accordinglye by vertue hereof. Your asswyrd ffrynd Edward North.(*)

* Afterwards first Baron North.

Endorsed:—To the Right Worshipfull and my very Louyng ffrend John Scudamore Esquyre one of the Kinges ma'tes Receyuors of his highne's court of Augmentac'.

British Museum, Add. MS. 11041, f. 41, (*Scudamore Papers*, vol. 1.)

Scudamore Papers, Vol. xvii.

"Pensions and Annuities to the Religions of Dissolved Monasteries, co. Worc., Salop, Staff., and Heref.—32–34 Henry VIII."

British Museum, Add. MS. 11057.

Fo. 6.—"Pensions of Moche Malvern. Termino Annunciationis dominice, Ao. xxxijdo. R. Henr. VIIIvi."

Malverne major	Item payd the ffyrst day of Apriell' ao. xxxij. do. R. Hen. VIIIvi., to Richard Webley late monk ther, the som'e of ffyve markes sterl. for hys half yeres penc'on due at our lady day last.	lxvj s. viij d.
Malverne	Item payd the last day of Apriell ao. xxxiijtio., R. H. viij vi. to Sir William Umbersley late mon'ck the som'e of ffyve markes sterl. for hys half yeres penc'on due at our lady day last	lxviij s. viij d.
Malverne	Item payd the same day and yere to Sir Richard Poll' the som'e of thre poundes sterl., for the half yeres penc'on due ut supra	lx s.
Malverne	Item payd the same day and year to Sir Richard Suckeley the som'e of foure poundes sterl. for hys half yeres penc'on due ut supra	iiij li.
Malverne	Item payd the iijde. day of May anno predicto to Sir Christopher More alias Aldyne the som'e of ffyve poundes sterl., for the half yeres penc'on due ut supra.	c s.
Malverne	Item payd the same day and yere to Sir William Bennett the som'e of ffyve markes sterl. for hys half yeres penc'on due ut supra	lxvi s. viij d.
Malverne	Item payd ye ijde. day of May anno predicto to Sir Richard Whytebourne alias Bedyll late prior ye som'e of ffyftye markes sterling for his half yeres penc'on due ut supra	xxxiij l. vj s. viij d.
Malverne	Item payd the viijth day of May anno predicto to Sir Reynold Werstane the som'e of three poundes sterling for hys half yeres penc'on due ut supra	lx s.
Malverne	Item payd the xvijth day of May anno predicto to Sir Hugh Lychefeld the som'e of thre poundes thre shillynges ffoure pens sterl for hys half yeres penc on due ut supra	lxiij s. iiij d.
Malverne	Item payd the iiijth day of June anno predicto to Sir Thomas Powyck late monck' yer the som'e of three poundes sterl. for hys half yeres penc'on due ut supra	lx s.
Malverne	Item payd the xth day of June anno predicto to Sir Maculyn' Colman' the som'e of ffyve markes sterl. for hys halfe yeres penc'on due ut supra	lxvj s. viij d.
Malverne	Item payd the same day and yere to Roger ffrome, late monck ther, the som'e of tenne markes sterl. for hys half yers penc'on due ut supra	vj l. xiij s. iiij d.

Termino Sancti Michaelis, Ao. xxxiijtio. R. Henr. viij vi.

Malverne	Item payd the ffyrst day of November anno xxxiij cio. R. Hen. viij vi., to Sir Maculyn' Malvern, by thandes of Richard Skelton, thre poundes syxe shillynges eyght pens sterl. for hys half yeres penc'on due at Michaelmas last	lxvj s. viij d.

Fo. 7b.—"Annuities, Corrodyes, ffees, Smaye, and Proxys of Moche Malverne."

Malverne S.	Item payd the last day of Apriell anno xxxiij cio. R. Hen. viij vi., to Sir William Robyns, Curatt of Newlond the som'e of ffoure merkes, half yeres stipend due at our lady day last..	liij s. iiij d.
Malverne A.	Item payd the xvijth day of May anno predicto to John' Iyll' the som'e of thyrtene shyllynges ffour pens sterl. for hys half yeres annuitie due at our lady day last. &c..................	xiij s. iiij d.
Malverne A.	Item payd the same day and yere to Thomas Byrd the som'e of tenne shyllynges sterl. for hys half yeres annuitie due ut supra.	x. s.
Malverne A.	Item payd the same day and yere to John Gor the som'e of Tenne shyllynges sterl. for hys half yeres annuitie due ut supra	x s.
Malverne A.	Item payd the vith day of August anno xxxiij cio. R. Hen. viij vi. to Phelyp' Baxter the som'e of tenne shillynges sterl. for hys halfe yeres annuitie due at our lady day last	x s.
Malverne A.	Item payd the xith day of October anno xxxiij cio. R. Hen. viij vi. to John Burghyll' Esquyer the som'e of twentye syxe shyllynges eyght pens sterl. for hys hole yeres annuitie or corrodye due at Michaelmas last	xxvi s. viij d.
Malverne ff.	Item payd the xxviijth day of November anno xxxiij cio. R. Hen. viij vi. to Sir John Russell Knyght Chyffe Stuard there by thandes of Thomas Rock the som'e of ffoure markes sterl. for hys hole yeres ffee due unto hym at Michaelmas last	liij s. iiij d.
Malverne ff.	Item payd the xxviijth day of November anno xxxiij cio. R. Hen. viij vi. to Thomas Rocke gent. the som'e of ffoure markes sterl. for hys hole yeres ffee for the understuardshyp yer due at Michaelmas last	liij s. iiij d.
Malverne A.	Item payd the xxixth day of November anno xxxiij cio. R. Hen. viij vi. to Richard Blon' by thandes of William More gent the som'e of ffortye shillynges sterl. for hys annuitie for too hole yeres endyd at Michaelmas last as apperyth by mr. auditor debenturs	xl s.
ff. Malverne	Item payd the ij de. day of December anno xxxiij cio. R. Hen. viij vi. to Richard Skelton the som'e of Twenty shelynges sterl. for hys hole yeres ffee due at Michaellmas last as it apperyth by a debentur &c	xx s.
A. Malverne	Item payd the ij de. day of December anno xxxiij cio. R. Hen. viij vi. to Roberte Wyneby yoman' the som'e of twenty shelynges sterl for hys hole yeres annuyte due at Michaelmas last as it apperyth by a debentur	xx s.
A. Malverne	Item payd the iij de. day of December anno xxxiij cio. R. Hen. viij vi. to John Gough the som'e of Ten' shelynges sterl. for his half yeres annuyte due at Michellmas last	x s.
A. Malverne	Item payd the vth day of December anno xxxiij cio. R. Hen. viij vi. to Richard Warnecombe Escuyer the som'e of thirtene shelynges ffoure pence sterl. for hys hole yere annuyte due at Michaellmas last	xiij s. iiij d.

Post audit' apud London'.

Malverne	Item payd the xixth day of february anno xxxiij cio. R. Hen. viij vi. to William Cokesey gent the som'e of thirtene shelynges foure pence sterl. for his hole yeres annuyte due at Michelmas last as it appereth by master audytours debentur by thandes of Robert Wyxton', armiger	xiij s. iiij d.	
Malverne	Item payd the xxvith day of ffebruary anno xxxiij cio. R. Hen viij vi. to John ap Rece Escuyer the som'e of Ten powndes sterl. for his annuyte for a yere and a half endyd at the ffeast of the natyvyte of Seynt John Baptist due unto hym as it appereth by mr. auditours debentur, &c................	xli.	
Malverne	Item payd the ij de. of March anno xxxiij cio. R. Hen. viij vi. to Sir Richard Lygon', Knight, by thandes of Roberte Burgoyn' Escuyer the som'e of ffoure powndes sterl. ffor his annyte for ij hole yeres endyd at Michelmas last	iiij li.	
Malverne	Item payd the ij de. day of March anno xxxiij cio. R. Hen. viij vi. to William Nevelle by thandes of Roberte Burgoyn' Escuyer the som'e of ffortye shelynges sterl for his hole yeres annyte due at Michelmas last.............	xl s.	

Repara'cons.

Malverne major	Item delivered the xvijth day of November anno xxxiij cio. R. Hen. viij vi. to Sir Roger Mathewe vicar of Longney and Richard Parke in prest towardes the beyng of Stuff for thamendyng of the See Wall at Longney three poundes sterl.	lx s.	
Malverne major	Item delivered the same day and yere to William Grenyng and John Spycer in prest for ther Workemanshyp upon the sayd Wall ffortye shelynges sterl.	xl s.	

*　　*　　*　　*　　*

post audit'.

Malverne major	Item payd the xxviijth day of December anno xxxviij cio. R. Hen. viij vi. to Thomas Body by thandes of John Heswyn' his servaunte the som'e of thurtene shelynges foure pence sterl. for reparacyon' etc. as it appereth by a byll of particulars assigned with mr. audytours hand..........................	xiij s. iiij d.	
A. Moche Malverne	Item payd ihe ffyrst day of Julye anno xxxiiij to. R. Hen. viij vi. to William Sharpe by thandes of John Himckes gent. the som'e of ffortye shyllynges sterl. for hys hole yeres annuitie due unto hym at Michaelmas last as apperyth by a debentur	xl s	exa.
A. Moche Malverne	Item payd the iiijth day of Julye anno xxxiiij cio. R. Hen. viij vi. to Roger Lygon' gent. by thandes of Richard Morrys hys servaunt the som'e of ffyftye shillynyes sterl. for hys annuitie for too yeres and a halfe endyd at our lady day last	l s.	exa.

A Herefford'.

Malverne	Item payd the xxvjth day of October anno xxxiiij to. R. Hen. viij vi. to John Burghille Escuyer the somme of twentye and syx shelynges and eight pence sterlyng for his hole years anuyte or corrodye due unto hym at the ffeast of Saynt Michell last	xxvi s. viij d.	exa.
Malverne	Item payd the xxith day of November anno xxxiiij to. R. Hen. viij vi. to Sir John Russhell, Knyght Stuard ther by thandes of Conand Richardson the som'e of ffoure markes sterlyng for his hole yeres ffee due at Michelmas last past, &c	liij s. iiij d.	exa.
Malverne	Item payd the xxijth day of November anno xxxiiij to. R. Hen. viij vi. to Robert Burgoyn' Esquyer to and for thuse of William Nevell' gent. by the handes of John Dodyngton gent. the som'e of ffortye shyllynges sterl. for hys hole yeres anuytie due vnto hym at Michaelmas last, &c	xl s.	exa.

post audit'.

Malverne	Item payd the iij de. day of December anno xxxiij to. R. Hen. viij vi. to the Busshopp of Wigorn' by thandes of John Smyth the some of eight shelynges and eight pence sterl. for a yearly pencyon or proxy goyng out of the Churchee of Snodesbury (vj s. viij d.) and Woodresfeld (ij s.) &c. due unto hym for one hole yere at Michaelmas last past as it apperith by a debentur ...	viij s. viij d. exa.
Malverne	Item payd the xvith day of January anno xxxiiij to. R. Hen. viij vi. to Sir Richard Lygon Knyght and William Lygon Esquyer by thandes of John Chapman servaunt to the seyd Sir Richard the some of Twentye shyllynges sterling for one half yeres annytie due vnto them at Michaelmas last, &c	xx s. exa.

Reparacons.

Moche Malverne	Item delivered the xxviijth day of May anno xxxiiij to. R. Hen. viij vi. to Sir Roger Mathewe vicar of Longney John Bray and John Bullock the some of ffyve markes sterl. in parte of paymente towardes the makyng of the See Wall at Longney vpon there accompt.	lxvi s. viij d. exa.

A Hereff'.

Malverne	Item payd the xxvijth day of October anno xxxiiij to. R. Hen. viij vi. to Sir Roger Mathew vicar of Longney the som'e of foure powndes nyne shelynges and thre pence sterl. for so much money by hym payd over that he received, etc., as it apperith by a byll of partie assigned with Mr. Auditours hand, &c	iiij li. ix s. iij d. exa.

*   *   *   *   *

Payment of Dettes.

Malverne major.	Item payd the xijth day of August anno xxxiiij to. R. Hen. viij vi. to Humfrey Wathall' the som'e of ten powndes sterling yn full recompens of a certen dett to hym owed by the late howse of Much Malverne as it appereth by a decre under the Seale of the Courte of Augmentations &c	x li. exa.
ff. Moche Malverne	Item payd the ffyrst day of November anno xxxv to. R. Hen. viij vi. to George Blount Esquier Stuard of Dowles and Metton by the handes of Thomas Wen' the som'e of twentye shillynges sterl. for hys anuitie for one yere and halfe endyd at Michaelmas in anno xxxiiij to. R. Hen. viij vi.	xx s. exa.

Lytch'feld.

ff. Moche Malverne	Item payd the sixth day of November anno xxxv to. R. Hen. viij vi. to Sir Humfrey fferrers Knight' per nomen Humfridi fferrers gent Stuard of Abecott &c. by thandes of ffrancis Thyrlewall' the som'e of twentye shelynges sterl. for his hole yeres ffee endyd at Michellmas last past as it apperith by a debentur, &c	xx s. exa.

Reparac'ons.

Malverne major	Item payd the vth day of ffebruary anno xxxv to. R. Hen. viij vi. to Sir Roger Mathewe vicar of Longney Thomas feld and Richard park the som'e of three poundes eleven pence sterl. whearof lviij s. iiij d. for a nue bote made by Robert Symons for the repare of ye Seewall at Longney and ij s. for the laughyng of the seyd bote and vij d. for the mendyng of the old Cheyn that was upon the olde bote the wiche was don by the othe of the aforenamed persons.....	lx s. xj d.

Beawdeley.

ff. Malverne major.	Item payd the xxvjth day of October anno xxxvij mo. R. Hen. viij vi. to William More gent. understuard of the Courte of Moche Malverne the som'e of ffoure markes sterl. for hys hole yeres ffee due at Michaelmas last......	liij s. iiij d. exa.

ff. Malverne major.	Item payd the xxvijth day of October anno xxxvij mo. R. Hen. viij vi. to Sir John Russell Knight by thandes of Thomas Pope the some of ffyve poundes syxe shillynges and eyght pens sterl. for hys ffee for the Stuardshyp of moche Malverne due for too yeres endyd at Michaelmas last	cvj s. viij d. exa.
Malverne major.	Item payd the vth day of December anno xxxvij mo. R. Hen. viij vi. to Roger Lygon Esquyer the som'e of three poundes sterl. for so much money owyng vnto hym for hys annuitie due vnto hym for three yeres endyd at Michaelmas last	lx s. exa.
Malverne major.	Item payd the ijde. day of Januarye anno xxxvij mo. R. Hen. viij vi. to Anne Burghyile Wydowe Executryx of the testament of John Burghyll deceassed the som'e of thyrtene shillynges and foure pens sterl. for the half yeres Corrodye or annuitie due unto hym at Michaelmas last	xiij s. iiij d. exa.

Receipts on account of dissolved Monastries, etc., 35-38 Hen. VIII. Brit. Mus., Add. 11,059.

Malverne major.

Brekenock	Item received the xxviijth day of January anno xxxiiij to. R. Hen. viij of John a prees Esquyer by thandes of phelyp' a pricherd his servaunte the som'e of twentye three poundes sterl.	xxiij li exa.
Brekenock	Item received the xxviijth day of March anno xxxiiij to. R. Hen. viij vi. of John a prees esquyer the some of thirty and syx shelynges and a peny sterl.	xxxvj s. id. arr. exa.

Malverne major.

Newland	Item received the xxvth day of October anno xxxv to. R. Hen. viij vi. of Sir Richard Cale the som'e of Twentye Sevyn poundes ffoure shyllynges and ffoure pens sterl. vpon hys debt'	xxvij l. iiij s. iiij d. exa.

* * * * *

Receptus fforinsecus.

Moche Malverne	Item received the same day and yere [i.e. 25 oct., 33 H. 8.] of W.... Geffrys for a lytle bell' containing in weyght xlviij poundes beyng .... chappell' the som'e of tenne shillynges sterling	....

* * * * *

Malverne major.

sm. de Abecott	Item received the xviijth day of ffebruary anno xxxv to. R. Hen. viij. of Johane Robynson wedow by thandes of William Hegnkes the some of ffortye ffoure shelynges and syx pence half peny sterl. yn partye of payment of hur tenthes etc......	xliiij s. vj d. ob. exa.
	Item received the xixth day of Apiell anno xxxv to. R. Hen. viij vi. of ...... by thandes of LLewellyn Thomas the som'e of twentye and three poundes..........................	xxiij li exa.
	Item received the .... anno xxxvj to. R. Hen. viij vi. of Th.. . Knottysford sen........ Richard Laycockes the [some of] Nynetene poundes sevyn ......ges and syxe pens........	xix li ..
Longney	Item received the xvth day of August anno xxxvi to. R. Hen. viij vi. of Thomas Knottysford the som'e of Twentye poundes ffoure shillynges and ffoure pens sterl........................	xx li. iiij s. iiij d. ex.
Terra in Com Breckon	Item received the xxviijth day of August anno xxxviij R. Hen. viij of Thomas ap Gwillim Wever the somm of thertye three shyllnges and foure pens in part payment of his charges	xxxiij s. iiij d.

Pyxam &c. { Item received the xvith day of August anno xxxvi to. R. Hen. viij vi. of Richard Cave the som'e of Twentye poundes ...... } xx li exa.

Malverne { Item received the xvith day of October anno xxxvi to. R. Hen. viij vi. of John Grene the som'e of Twentie one shillynges and two pens upon a debt' [debenture] .... } xxj s. ij d. exa.

{ Item received the xvijth day of October anno xxxvi to. R. Hen. viij vi. of Roger ....ward by thandes of Sir William Robyns the sum of three poundes sevyntene shillyngs three pens ob. sterl. upon a debt. .... } lxxvij s. iij d. ob. exa.

Longney { Item received the xvijth day of October anno xxxvi to. R. Hen. viij vi. of Thomas Knottysford the som'e of Twentie one poundes thurtene shillynges ffyve pens qa. sterl. upon a debt' } xxj li. xiij s. vd. q. exa

post audit'.

Malverne { Item received the .... day of ....ember anno xxxvjto. R. Hen. viij vi. of William Sheldon' Esquyer the som'e of Syxe shillynges nyne pens ob. sterl. for hys xths. .... for Suckeley v s. v d. and for Kempster .... } vj s. ix d. ob. ex.

* * * *

Haughmond and Malverne major { Item received the xxijth day of October anno xxxvi to. R. Hen. viij vi. of Thomas Acton Esquyer by thandes of Richard Lane the som'e of three shillynges eyght pens ob. sterl. for xthes. .... } iij s. viij d. ob. ex.

.... { Item .... October anno xxxvij mo. R. Hen. viij vi. of .... Thomas Knottysford the some of ffortye three...... upon a debt' .... } xliij li viij d. qa.

(Other entries follow, too fragmentary to be of value.)

(Many entries destroyed by damp, but the marginal names remain) Breknock, Pyxam and Nueland, Hillympton (?), Malverne major, Alecott, Longney.

CHAPTER XIX.

SUNDRY DOCUMENTS.

"Books that have the rime of age
And chronicles of eld."

THE following interesting remains of the dissolved monastery I think worth preserving:

(From a book of pensions in the Augmentation Office.)

Moche Malv'ne in ye Contie of Worcestr. Surrenduryd and Dyssolved.

Penc'ons assygnyd to the late Prior & Monks yt by Robert Sowthewell Esquyr, and other the Kyngs Com'yssion's appoyntyd to take surrendyr of the religious house wt. in the Countie of Worcetr. to be payd unto the seyd late prior and monks at the ffeasts of thanunciat'on of or. Blessyd Lady the Virgyn and Seynt Michall tharchangell yerely Duryon theyr naturall lyffe by equall porc'ons the fyrst yerely payment to begyn at the Ffeast of thannunciation of or. lady next ensuyng thys day viz the XII.th day January in the XXXI.th yere of the reign of Sov'aign lord King Henry the VIII. viz. to

Richarde Whythorne, Prior	lxvi*ll.*	viiis.	ivd.
Roger Ffrome Sub Prior	xiii*ll.*	vis.	viiid.
Richarde Suceley, Sexton	viii*ll.*	,,	,,
Richarde Webley	vi*ll.*	xiiis.	ivd.
William Umbersley	vi*ll.*	xiiis.	ivd.
Maculyne Malv'ne	vi*ll.*	xiiis.	ivd.
William Benet	vi*ll.*	xiiis.	ivd.
Thomas Powyck	vi*ll.*	,,	,,
Richard Pole	vi*ll.*	,,	,,
Renold Werstan	vi*ll.*	,,	,,
Hugh Lychfyld	vi*ll.*	vis.	viiid.
X Tofer Aldwyn, als More Scoler in Oxford ..	x*ll.*	,,	,,

Pr. Nos. ROBERTE SOUTHWELL.
RI. GWENT.
JOHANNE LONDON.
ROBT. BURGOYNE.
JOHN AP RICE.

MINISTERS' ACCOUNTS.

Brit. Mus. Add. MS. 24832, f. 44, (Extract from Minister's Accounts in the Record Office, London.)

Com. Wigorn.

Terræ et possessiones nuper monasteriorum et Prioratuum de Bordesley Majore Malverne Okehylle et Pershore in comitatu Wigornie predicto sursumredditorum.

Compota omnium et singulorum Ballivorum Collectorum prepositorum ffirmariorum et aliorum officiariorum Ministrorum et occupatorum dominiorum Maneriorum Terrarum et Tenementorum Rectoriarum decimarum porcionum et pencionum ac aliarum terrarum et tenementorum ac possessionum et hereditamentorum tam spiritualium quam temporalium dictis nuper Monasteriis et Prioratibus ac Domibus religiosis pertinentium et spectantium modo in manu et possessionem metuendissimi et illustrissimi Principis Domini Domini Henrici viij vi. Dei gratia Anglie et Francie Regis fidei defensoris Domini Hibernie et in terra sub Deo supremi capitis anglicane ecclesie devenientium et existentium ratione separalium sursumredditionum sive libere resignationis tam eorundem nuper monasteriorum et Prioratuum quam omnium et omnimoda terrarum et possessionum eorundem ubicunque jacentium et existentium infra hunc regnum Anglie et alibi infra dominium sive Regimen dicti Domini Regis per nuper Abbates et Priores ac alios Gubernatores et conventus antedictorum nuper domorum Religiosorum in manus supradicti domini regis ad usum suum proprium heredum et successorum suorum imperpetuum prout in separalibus actis hujus modi sursumredditionis sive resignationis sub sigillo Conventuali predictorum nuper monasteriorum et domorum Religiosorum inde Retornatur (?) per commissionarios domini Regis ad id assignatos et per ipsos in Cancellario ejusdem Regis certificatur et ibidem sub eisdem sigillis Remanet de Recordo plenius liquere et apparere poterit videlicet a ffesto Sancti Michaelis Archangeli anno xxxii do. Regni dicti domini Regis nunc Henrici viij vi. usque idem ffestum Sancti Michaelis archangeli extunc proxime sequentem anno regni ejusdem domini Regis xxxiij scilicet per unum annum integrum.

ut inferius.

County of Worcester.

Lands and possessions of the late monasteries and Priories of Bordesley, Great Malverne, Okehylle, and Pershore in the aforesaid County of Worcester, surrendered.

The accounts of all and singular the Bailiffs, Collectors, Provosts, Farmers, and other Officers, Ministers, and occupiers of the demesnes, Manors, Lands, and Tenements, Rectories, Tithes of Porcions and Pensions, and other lands and Tenements and possessions and hereditaments as well spiritual as temporal pertaining and belonging to the said late Monasteries and Priories now come and being in the hands and possession of the most dread and most illustrious Prince the Lord Lord Henry the VIII.th by the grace of God King of England and France, Defender of the Faith Lord of Ireland and on earth under God supreme head of the English Church, by reason of the separate surrenders or free resignation as well of the same late monasteries and Priories as also of all and all manner of lands and possessions of the same wheresoever lying and being within this kingdom of England and elsewhere within the demesne or Realm of the said Lord King by the late Abbots and Priors and other Governors and Convents of the aforesaid late Religious houses into the hands of the aforesaid Lord King, to his own use and to that of his heirs and successors for ever, as in separate acts of such surrender or resignation under the Conventual seal of the aforesaid late monasteries and Religious houses thereby returned by the Commissioners of the Lord King for that purpose appointed, and by the same is certified in the Chancery of the same King, and therein remaining under the same seals, may more fully stand and appear, namely from the feast of St. Michael the Archangel in the twenty second year of the Reign of the said Lord King that now is, Henry the VIII.th to the same feast of Saint Michael the Archangel then next ensuing in the twenty third year of the same Lord King, to wit for one whole year.

as below.

* * * *

Minister's Accounts, 151, 30—32 Hen. VIII. (Great Malvern).

Scit' nuper Mon maioris Malu'nie cum terr dnic, etc
Firm scit' man'ii dict' nup monastii cum terr dnic etc, cum ptinen
Rectoria de Malu'ne
Firm' cuiusd'm prati voc' Trowbridg medowe in Radnall pcell terr duic' tempe x me. et citra x ma. dimiss p Indent'
Firm' cuiusd'm pastur de terr dhic' voc ffurners more in Baldnall dimiss p xndent' citra x ma.
Firm' man'ii voc Motte Courte pcell terr dnic tempe me. x dimiss p Indent citra x ma.
Firm' man'ii ne Garleford existen infra dum de Maluerne
Firm' Grange de Newlond
Firm' manerii de Powyke in com. Wigorn.
Firm' molend de Powyke
Firm cuiusd'm lesu'r voc Swynelesue in Powyke p'dict'
Diu's firm' infra dum de pyxham dius pson' dimiss p Indentur citra supius x me.
Firm, man'ii de Wodesfeld in Com. Wigorn
Firm' Rect' de Powyke in Com. Wigorn
Do. Do. Upton Snodysbury in Com. Wigorn
Man'ium de Newlond in Com. Wigorn
Civitas Wigorn
Dum de Dowles et Meaton infra dum de Dowles in Com. Salopp
Dum de Wodesfeld in Com. Wigorn
Rectoria de Wodfilde
Dum de Falford in Com. Staff.
Dum de Longney in Com. Glouc.
Firm manii de Longney
Firm Rect de Longney
Man'ium de Lollesey cum homscastell in Com. Wigorn
Firm ecclie sive capelle sci miclas voc HolmeChapell in Com. Wigorn
Sutton ? parua Sen'nestoke Estnore longdon Chadley Mowrton Suckeley Mathon Brad et de Duham
Firm' x ne. in Matho et styngton cum at
Battial ffon in Com Heref. Salopp Wigorn et Wilxt (sic)
Firm' Rtorie de Knyghton & Stowe
Estleche Merton al Brondruppe Cote londe Bromesbarowe ffertyngton al ffordhamton Stamforde et penc[iones] in Lantony
Hillamton et Mereden in Com Heref.

The site of the late Monastery of Great Malvern with the demesne lands, etc.
The farm of the site of the said manor of the said monastery with the demesne lands etc., with the appurtenances
The Rectory of Malverne
The farm of a certain meadow called Trowbridge-mead in Radnall parcel of the demesne land, in time of the tithe and over the tithe, leased by indenture.
The farm of a certain pasture of demesne land called ffurners more in Baldnall leased by indenture over the tithe
The farm of the manor called Motte Court parcel of the demesne land, etc.
The farm of the Manor of Garleford being within the demesne of Malverne
The farm of the Grange of Newlond.
The farm of the manor of Powyke in Co. Worcester
The farm of Powyke Mill.
The farm of a certain field called Swynelesue in Powyke aforesaid
Divers farms within the demesne of Pyxham leased to certain persons by indenture, over the above title.
The farm of Wodesfeld manor in Worcestershire.
The farm of the Rectory of Powyke in Worcestershire.
The farm of the Rectory of Upton in Snodysbury in Worcestershire
The Manor of Newlond in Worcestershire
The City of Worcester.
The Demesne of Dowles and Meaton within the demesne of Dowles in Co. Salop
The Demesne of Wodesfeld in Worcestershire.
The Rectory of Wodfilde.
The Demesne of Falford in Co. Staff.
The Demesne of Longney in Co. Glouc.
The farm of Longney Manor.
The farm of Longney Rectory
The Manor of Lollesley with Homscastle in Worcestershire.
The farm of the Church or Chapel of St. Michael called Holme Chapel in Worcestershire.
Sutton parva, Severnstoke, Eastnor, Longdon, Chadley, Morton, Suckley, Mathon, Brady, and Durham.
The farm of the tithe in Matho (?) and Estington, etc.
The "Bailliwick foreign" in Co. Hereford, Salop, Worcestershire, and Wiltshire.
The farm of the Rectory of Knyghton and Stowe.
Est Leach, Merton, *alias* Brondruppe, Cotes land, Bromesbarrow, Fertyngton *al* Fordhampton, Stamforde, and pensions in Lantony.
Hilhampton and Mereden in Herefordshire.

Following these are accounts of possessions of Priory of Abecote in Co. War., cell of Great Malvern.

The following copied from Dugdale's *Monasticon*, shows us that before the end of Mary's reign the number of annuitants on the funds of the dissolved monastery had considerably decreased.

Return on Sharp's Roll of 2nd and 3rd Phil. and Mary, *Malvern Major.*

				Per An.
Fees	Thomas Botteseye Auditor	xls.		Per An.
	John Russell	lvis.		" "
Annuities	Roger Ligon.	xxs.		" "
"	Edward Porter	ivs. ivd.		" "
"	William Cokesey	ivs. ivd.		" "
"	Robert Burghill	xxvis. viiid.		" "
"	Richard Lechmore	xxs.	"	" "
"	Richard Ligon	xl.	"	" "
"	Richard Alen ..	xxs.	"	" "
"	Thomas Sherle	xls.	"	" "
"	Anthony Kingston Knight	lxxxs.	"	" "

CHAPTER XX.

SALE OF THE CHURCH.

"Mute is the matin bell, whose early call
Warn'd the grey fathers from their humble beds;
No midnight taper gleams along the wall,
Or round the sculptur'd saints its radiance sheds."

THE Priory domain, farm, cloisters, domestic buildings, and church, were alienated to William Pinnock, who very speedily sold the same to Mr. John Knotsforde, servant to King Henry VIII. He in turn soon began to make what he could out of his purchase. The cloisters, dormitories, chapter-house, and other of the domestic offices were taken down, and the materials disposed of. The Lady Chapel was razed to the ground, and so much of it sold as was marketable. The south transept was also demolished; the lead off the church was taken away, and other demolitions made.

The church itself was spared by the parishioners offering to buy it. The parishioners were poor at the time, the great part of Malvern's wealth being held by Mr. Knottsforde; but somehow funds were forthcoming, and, as the little church of St. Thomas was in decay, they bought the Priory Church for the parish services for £200, a sum equal to £2,000 or more of present money. An act more to a people's credit, or one evincing more of clear foresight, or of public spirit, has seldom been recorded.

To the parishioners of that day Malvern owes the rich inheritance of their noble church, with all its treasures of ancient stained glass, old tiles, and historical associations.

Mr. Knottsforde took up his residence at the Prior's house, which was remodelled and added to as suited his taste. He had five daughters, all of whom married, viz.: Mary, to Thomas Price, Esq., of Manaty; Eleanor, to John Champion, Esq.; Elizabeth, to Wm. Ridgeley, Esq.; and Frances to Thomas Kirle, of Marcle. The eldest daughter, Anne, lived to raise a beautiful alabaster monument to her parents' memory. She married William Savage, Esq., of Cheshire, and continued to inherit the Priory estate. Three of these weddings took place at Malvern, as the parish registers show; it would be interesting to know with what attendant pomp and circumstance.

Mr. John Knottsforde lived—the great man of the parish—through the remainder of the reign of Henry VIII., through the reign of Edward VI., that of Mary, and thirty-three years of the reign of Elizabeth, a witness of all the vicissitudes and changes of thought, religion, and policy that characterised those remarkable reigns. In Mrs. Lawson's book, "The Nation in the Parish," mention is made of a servant who died in Mr. Knottsforde's house, named Edward Hall, who gave to the parish of Upton-on-Severn "fifteen messuages and lands," but who afterwards died in poverty,—a fact suggestive of the inference that others beside Mr. Knottsforde obtained riches out of the dissolved Monastery of Great Malvern.

The old Parish Church of St. Thomas the Apostle stood, as already mentioned, at the north-west corner of the churchyard, a spot on which has recently been built a music saloon. For two hundred and fifty years or more it was the parish church. It had fallen into decay, and before the date of the convent's dissolution efforts had been made to repair "ye byldyng." In Mr. Noake's "Life of Prior Moore," amongst other payments is mentioned an entry about the year 1521, "to ye sexten of Moche Malv'ne to ye byldyng of ye Parish Church there 5/s"; and at the same time, "to p'r Lyttul Malv'ne towards ye losse of his chaleses being stolen 11s. 3d."

When the Priory Church of Malvern became that of the Parish, the church of St. Thomas was taken down, its valuables were removed, and its font taken to St. Leonard's, Newland. On removing soil when making foundations for the music saloon, a "piscina," of early date, and portions of a floriated cross were dug up. It is sad to have to record that at a time so recent the site of this church should have been used for such a purpose, and that a building for purely secular use, in no recognizable style of architecture,—ugly as most people think,—should have been built there, obstructing as it does one of the best views of the venerable Priory Church.

A memorable day it must have been for Malvern, when its scattered inhabitants were called together for worship in its newly acquired Priory Church, to hear the Scriptures read aloud in the "*vulgar tongue*," and to have their services said or sung in ***English*** for the first time

The following earnest missive came to Malvern, amongst other places, in the year 1537, from the devout Bishop Latimer. It was entitled:—

Injunctions gyven by the Byshop of *Worcester* in his Visitacion to all Persones, Vicars, and other Curatties of his Diocesse, the yere of oure Lord God MDXXXVII. *Anno Regis* HENRICI *Octavi* XXIX.

HUGH, by the goodness of God, Byshop of *Worcester*, wysheth to all his Bretherne Curates, grace, mercy, peace, and true knowlege of Gods Worde, from God oure Father, and oure Lord *Jesu Criste*.

For as moche as in this my Visitation, I evidently perceyve the ignorance and negligence of diverse Curates in this Deanery to be intollerable, and not to be suffered, for that thereby doth reigne Idolatry and many kindes of Supersticians, and other enormities. And consideryng witnall, that our Sovereigne Lord the Kyng for some parte of remedy of the same, hath granted by his most gracyous Licence that the Scripture of God may be redde in *English* of all his obedient Subjects. I therefore wyllyng youre reformation, in most favorable maner, to your least displesure, do hertely require you all and every on of you, and also in Goddes behalfe, commaunde the same accordyng as youre dutie is, to obey me as Goddes Minister, and the Kinges, in all my lawfull and honeste Commaundementes, that you observe and kepe inviolably all these Injunctions, following, under payne of the Lawe.

First, Forasmoche as I perceyve that ye nether have observed the Kinges Injunctions, nor yet have them with you, as willyng toe observe them. Therefore ye shall from henceforthe bothe have and observe diligently and faythfully, as well speciall commaundementes of Prechynges, as other Injunctions geven in his Graces Visitacion.

Item, That ye and every on of you provyde to have of youre owne a hole Byble, yf *ye can convenyently or at the leaste a* New Testament, bothe in *Latin* and *Englishe*, before the Feste of thee Nativite of oure Lord nexte ensuyng.

Item, That ye and every on of you do rede over and studye every day one Chapiter at the least, conferrying the *Laten* and the *Englishe* together, procedying from the Chapiter from the begynning of the Boke, to the ende, havyng no necessarie let to the contrarye.

Item, That you, and every on of you provyde to have of youre one a Boke, called *The Institution of a Christene Man*, lately set out of the Kyngs Graces Prelates, by his Graces Commaundement.

Item, That ye, and every on of you from hensforth bydde Beades no otherwise, than accordyng to thee Kinges Graces Ordinance, lest long Bedde tellyng lett frutefull preeching of Goddes Worde.

Item, That ye, and every one of you, as often as ther is any Maryage within your Paryshe, exhort and charge youre Parishyoners openly, in the Pulpytt, amongst other thynges in your Sermonds, that they nether make, nor suffer to be made any privy Contracte of Matrimonye, as they woll avoyde the extreme payne of the Lawe certeynly to be executed upon them.

Item, That ye, and every on of you, that be *Chauntre Prestes*, doe instructe and teache the Children of youre Paryshe, suche as will come to you, at the least, to rede *Englishe*, so that thereby they may the better lerne how to beleve, howe to praye, and howe to lyve to Goddes Plesure.

Item, That no Parson, Vicar, Curate, nor Chauntre Prest from hensforthe doe discourage any Lay Persone from the reding any good Bokes, eyther in *Latin* or *Englishe*, but rather animate and encourage them unto suche thynges.

Item, That ye, and every on of you, not only in Prechyng, and open communicacion, but also in secret Confession, and makyng of Testamentes, excite and sterre youre Paryshoners from wyll Workes, to the necessary Works of God, Works of Mercy and Charite.

Item, That ye, and every on of you, do at all tymes the best that you can, to occasion your Paryshoners to Peace, Love, and Charite, soe that none of ye suffur the Sonne to set upon thyer Wrathe.

Item, That ye, and every on of you, provyde to have a Copye of these myn Injunctions within xiii days at the uttermoste.

Item, That you, and every on of you, shall from hensforth suffre no Religiouse Persons, Fryar, or other, to have any Service in your Churches, eyther Trentall, Quarter Servyce, or other.

Item, That Prechyng be not set asyde for any manner of Observaunce in the Churche, as Procession, and other Ceremonyes.

Item, That ye, and every on of you, doe not admytt any yong Man or Woman to receyve the Sacrament of the *Aultar*, untyll that he or shee openly in the Churche after Masse, or Evensong, upon the Holyday, doe recite in *Englishe* the *Pater Noster*, the *Crede*, and the *Ten Commaundements*.

Item, That in prase time no . . . . body be browgth into the Church, but he browgth into the Churchyard, that the peryl of ynfeccion therby may the better be avoyded.

Item, That no Curate commaund the Evyn to be fasted of any Abrogat Holydaye.

The "Kinges Injunctions" referred to by Latimer, which had not been observed, were, amongst other things, as follows:—"ministers and incumbents" were "to procure one bible and set it up publicly in the church, and encourage all persons to read it, as being the Word of God, which every man ought to believe and follow."

CHAPTER XXI.

THE REFORMATION COMMUNION TABLE.

"O hallow'd memories of the past,
Ye legends old and fair,
Still be your light upon us cast,
Your music on the air."

IN the year 1596 there died at Newland, "Penelope, wife of Robert Walweyn, Gentleman." She was daughter of "Richard Ligon, of Maddresfield," and direct descendant of the great Beauchamp family, who were Earls of Warwick. This lady was buried in Malvern church, and a very beautiful tomb was erected to her beloved memory, *on the site of the former high altar* of Malvern. There for many years it stood, in the exact place where eyes for centuries had been wont to gaze upon the consecrated host! The lady's high lineage was shown on three sides of the tomb by no less than thirty-five coats, or quarterings, of arms, and at her feet were the following lines (the side next the wall was plain) :—

"Hic pia Penelope Walwine conditur uxor,
Iamdudum morbis languida, docta mori;
Docta mori, vitæ que breves transcendere metas;
Nunc anima cœlum possidet, ante fide."

For forty years, certainly, and probably for a longer period, the tomb remained where it had been placed. In Abingdon's day (1630), thoughts of its removal were entertained. He writes, "The first monument which presenteth itself in the choir of

Malvern is that which cannot continue there, because it standeth where the altar sometimes was, and the communion table is now designed to be." When the removal took place is uncertain. In 1825 Mr. Southwell* speaks as if it had occurred within the memory of those living. The slab of the tomb was then on the "north side of the communion table," and the "handsome pew of Sir Anthony Lechmere," says the record, "partly rests upon it." It is likely this tomb was not taken down till the reign of Queen Anne. The communion rails removed at the late restoration were of painted deal, of pattern and general character that would indicate an approximation to the influences of that period, as would also an altar piece, to be shortly referred to. Whilst the tomb occupied its *high-altar* position, the question naturally presents itself—where was the communion table? It certainly did not stand on or near the the site it now occupies, as witness Abingdon's testimony. Then where was it? The communion table of Malvern, of the Reformation period, still exists, minus its board, and its mute testimony will help somewhat to answer the enquiry. It has little likeness to an altar, but is a real, honest English table, of substantial build; such as might have been owned by any well-to-do citizen of that time. The legs are massive, turned and carved; the four sides of its upper frame-work are carved also. It has the appearance of being intended to stand, not against a wall, but in an open space, where all its surroundings could be seen. The board originally belonging to it is gone, and it has now a poor wooden top of later and much more degenerate workmanship. We may easily conceive this fine Elizabethan "*board*," with its richly carved edges, standing in the church, altogether independent of its *high-altar* position. And we may also imagine how, in exact accord with the rubric's directions at "communion time," with its "*fair linen cloth*" thereon, it stood in the "*body of the church*, or in the chancel," length-ways, from east to west, "the Priest standing on the north side" to consecrate the elements, "before" and in sight of the people kneeling or sitting

* Southwell's Guide.

round him. One thing is indisputable, that for many years no table or altar in Malvern did stand in the place to which it is supposed to be entitled. A picture belonging to Upton-on-Severn, spoken of in Mrs. Lawson's charming book, contains an illustration of the communion office as it existed about 1676. There "the celebrant in some sort of dark robe" stands at the "*north side*" of the table, "the ends of which stand east and west." And as indicative of the prevalence of such custom, we are told in the same book of the unsuccessful attempt, made in 1640, to establish by canon that the table should be called "an altar," that it should be placed at the east end, and not in "the centre of the chancel, and that it should be fenced." At the venerable Saxon church of Deerhurst, below Tewkesbury, the communion table still occupies the middle of the chancel, carved oaken seats and kneelings for communicants being fixed against the north, east, and south walls. The date on the carved seats is 1605.

In 1746, the Walwyn tomb had been removed and the communion table had taken its place. The antiquarian, Cole, who visited Malvern in that year, says, "a *new* and elegant altar-piece, erected on ye old one, which is standing," "extremely high from top to bottom." This altar-piece had been painted, says Chambers, by a gentleman of the name of Ponty, and he describes it as not so "despicable as a work of art, and as composed of the Virgin Mary, Moses, and angels descending and singing Hallelujahs." The height was afterwards considered such an eye-sore, hiding as it did much of the east window, that the practical parishioners of 1812 or 1814 thought it right to cut it in two; but so regardless were they of this "work of art" that the "heads of Moses and the Virgin were so cut across the throat as to present a risible appearance."* The portion cut off went to ornament the top of the present organ-loft, where it remained till lately. The other part continued to do duty over "The Lord's Prayer," "Belief," and "Commandments," which were shown in gold letters "between and under columns and entableture of the Ionic order."

* Chambers' Malvern.

CHAPTER XXII.

AFTER THE DISSOLUTION (EDWARD VI.).

"Times doe shift, each thing his turn doth holde;
New things succeed, as former ones grow old."

HERRICK.

THE late king's treasury had been filled by funds accruing from ruinated monasteries, but something more had to be done. The convents were gone, but there remained, attached to parish churches, a rather numerous class of small foundations, known as chauntries, etc., devoted to what had come to be regarded as *superstitious* uses :—viz., for the support of priests to say masses for the dead , or "obits." For the suppression of these an act was passed in the reign of Henry VIII., but was not put into execution. A more ample and complete act came into force in the sixth year of the reign of Edward VI., under which order was given "to bring, or send, such books, registers, inventories, as hath heretofore come into their hands touching the sums, number, and value of any goods, plate, jewels, vestments, and bells, or ornaments, of any churches, chapels, and such like," and "proceed to the due search and inquisition of the wants, or defaults, of any of the said goods." They were also to enquire by what default great quantity of the plate, etc., had been embezzled by private men. Mackenzie E. Walcot, Esq., F.S.A., has taken the trouble to prepare, and the

Worcester Architectural Society to publish copies of these inventories, as drawn up for the king's commissioners for Worcestershire, and, by aid of this pamphlet, I am able to give reports from the churches of Great Malvern, Little Malvern, Newland, Madresfield, and other churches immediately surrounding Malvern.

The purpose, without doubt, of these visitations, was to find out what value there was, that without too great an appearance of indecency could be plundered. The wealth of the convents had already been appropriated, as the king's treasury showed; it was now to be seen what the parish churches would yield.

The inventory for Great Malvern runs as follows:—

MOCHE MALVERNE, Aug. 8.—a lytle pyxe of sylver, a chalyce of sylver, a coope of redd velvett, a coope of redd sylke, a coope of redd wolsted, a cheasable of blewe sylke with the albe, a cheasable of grene sylke with the albe, a peyre of candylstykkes of brasse, a crosse of coper, iiij bellss in the steple, a saunce bell, a lytle sacrynge bell, a lyche bell,* a peyre of orgaynes, a sensar of coper. A chalice of sylver was solde in the iij yere of K. Edwarde the Syxte before the makynge of the iventorye to paye the church debtes & to repare the churche. RIC. GYLHAM, Vicar.

It thus appears that the parish had been in debt, and that the church was needing repair.

LITTLE MALVERN—j chalys of sylver by estymacon ix unces, iij olde copes of course here not being sylk, ij vestments, j albe of hockarte, j crosse of copper, ij small bells whereof on is not our own.
Ser THOMAS BELL, Curate.

NEWLAND CHAPPELL, Aug. 7.—j chalys of sylwerr, j lytel pyxe of sylwer, j cope of blew saten with branches, j cope of grene crewle, j westment of red saten with branches, j westment of grene crewle, j westment of yowlow crewle with albs, stolys & fannels, iij aulter clothes, ij surplesys, in the stepull too bells, j lych bell, j sacryng bell, ij crewetts of pewter, j lyttle botell† of pewter, ij corperasses with casys of sylk, j crosse of bras, ij candelstylks of bras, j tynacull of bras, j senseur of bras with the schyppe, j chrysmatory of leed. WILL. ROBYNS, Curett.

MATHAN, Aug. 9.—j chalys of sylver & gylte weying xx unces, a pyx of sylver weying iij unces, ij copes of redd velvett, a chesable of blew velvett with albes thereunto, a crosse of coppre, a censer of copper, a lampe of latten, ij candelsticks of latten, a tennacle of brasse, iiij bells in the steeple, a saunce bell, a lyche bell, a sacryng bell. Item; they say they have j other chalyce weying vii unces, & remaneth in the hands of Ric Cave in gage‡ for xxs of hym borowed & bestowed upon barnes. WILL PACKER, Vicar.

Newland Chapel belonged to Malvern, and its inhabitants, till recent times, sought Great Malvern church, or churchyard, to bury their dead; as did also the rich people of Madresfield.

MADRESFELDE, Aug. 8.—a chalys, a paten of sylver parcell gylt, an old vestement with a surples, ij litle bells in the steple, with a crosse of tynne, a litle lyche bell, with a redde vestement of sylke. JO. YAUNES, person.

* Rung before the corpse on the way to burial.
† For the wine ‡ Pledge

CLYVELOD, Aug. 8.—j chalice of sylver & gilte, i lytle bell, j vestment of yeolow sylke. Jo. GRENEWAY rector.

LYGH.—j crosse of sylver parcell gylte with ij ymages SS. Marie & John, ij chales of sylke parcel gylt, j cope of blew velvet, j vestment of chrymsen velvet with his albe, j vestment of taunye velvett with his albe, v grete bells in the styple with a sanctus bell, ij serplyssis. * H. P. 340.

CASTLE MORTON, Aug. 9.—ij chalyces of sylver parcell gylte weyenge by estamacon xiiij unces, ij copes j of crymson velvet, and the other of olde damaske, iiij peyre of vestments of velvett, ij of them redd & thother crymson, j peire of vestments of white damaske, ij or iij peces of olde torne vestments, j crosse clothe of blewe sarsenett, and iij olde banner clothes, ij crosses of copper or brasse, a senser, ij peire of candelstyks of brasse, a canapy of brasse wherein the pyx hangeth, ij aulter clothes, and ij olde towells, iiij bells in the steple, a saunce bell, a lyche bell, iij sacring belles.

Sir Wm. Houghton, Knt., gave for his obit "j kow preased at xiis." so Richard Yate for lamps at Hanbury gave "ij kine preased at xiis. the kow" and at South Lyttleton "iiij kyne were preased at xiis. the kow to maintain 24 lamps and certen tapers." At Bredon there was an endowment of "fyve kyne," and at Stockton of "ij kyne at xs. the kow." At Tenbury the lampe field was similarly appropriated to provide iijs. iijd.

BRAUNCEFORD, Aug. 8.—a chalis, a paten of sylver parcell gylte which lyeth in cage (gage) with John Broke for xxxiijs. iijd. plegged to hym, viij yeres passed for the great sute betweene the said parishe & the parishe of Lygh, thys chalyse ys used dayly in the churche, iij vestements, j of red sylke, & ij of grene worstyd, ij albes, j other vestement of crymsyn velvet lying to gage for xxxs. with william lynton & Rychard Halle viiij yeres passed in the same sute, a coope of grene sylke, a aulter cloth, asurples, a pyxt, a crosse of copras, ij litte bells in the steple, a senser of brasse, ij cruetts of pewther.

As at Mathon, so here, the valuables of the parish were in "gage" *(pledge)*, the "chalyse" though in pledge being used "dayly in the churche."

CHACELEY.—They reported :

Mem (we had a brasse crosse with a staff brass brased & j olde holly water pote of bras, which crosse according as we were comanded, did deface, and brake the same, & so lefte there in the churche. which watter pote & broken peces of the crosse hath ben embezzled forthe of the churche.)

HOLTE :

They say that there was sold about vii yeres past, by the concente of all the paryshoners, j chalys weying xii unces, lacking a quarter a once, for iii li lacking xxd. which was bestowed as ffolloweth, that is to say ffor a byble xxiijs. for a paraphrases xiis. for omyles viiid. and xvs. for the reparacon of the churche.

These reports show the state of the national church in Worcestershire at the time, and, what concerns us most reveals somewhat about Malvern and its dependent chapels. It will be seen that, whether for use or not, almost everywhere the richly embroidered vestments and other grand things belonging to former observances in religion had been kept, and that separation therefrom was not so distinct and decided as we have been led to believe. Only here and there did the now time-honoured *surplice* appear.

* Houseling People, or communicants.

There is record that a bible had been bought, and homilies and paraphrase, at Holte. In some few parishes "carpet for the table" takes the place of "altar cloth," and "table or boards" occurs instead of "altar," and "communion cup" instead of "chalice;" but for the most part the old nomenclature was in force.

Nothing occurs in these inventories about "relics," but a few years earlier Bishop Latimer preaching before his clergy is reported to have said:—"I think ye have heard of St. Blesis's heart which is at Malvern and of St. Algar's bones, how long thay deluded the people; I am afraid to the loss of many souls. Whereby men may conjecture that all about in this realm, there is plenty of such juggling deceits, and yet hitherto ye have sought no remedy. But even still the miserable people are suffered to take the false miracles for the true, and to lie still asleep in all kind of superstition. God have mercy on us!"

CHAPTER XXIII.

THE PARVICE.

"The good old rule
Sufficeth them,—the simple plan
That they shall take who have the power
And they shall keep who can."

WORDSWORTH.

IT is an interesting subject of enquiry for what use and purpose the room over the north entrance to the Priory church was anciently intended. Was it merely an ornamented covering to the porch, or what was it? It was built during the re-construction of the church in the reign of Henry VII., and is entered by a stair from the inside of the church. Till recently the entrance was from the outside* from the old Abbey House, and without doubt it was in former times connected with a passage or apartment existing outside the large west window, from which, by small apertures or squints, still existing, a view was had of the whole body of the church, as well as of the high altar. A fire-place exists in this room which does not appear to be modern, but there is no trace of an altar. It has windows looking north, and giving full view of the entrance to the churchyard and the way to the church. There is also in the north east corner a window looking east. Many such rooms as this exist in different parts of England, and they are generally

* Accounts have been given the writer of over 30 Parvices belonging to churches, but only a very small number have communication with the church from the *inside*.

PORCH AND PARVISE, MALVERN PRIORY.

distinguished by the name of "Parvice," a name anciently given also to law offices. The English poet Chaucer speaks of

"A Sargeant of law, ware, and wise,
That often had been at the *Parvise*,"

meaning without doubt a court of law. In the 16th century, says a writer on Parvices, "Certan antiquarians adopted the word Paradise, or rather its contracted form *Parvie*, to signify not the porch but the room over the porch, which we find in many churches to exist."

The use to which such rooms were put was various. At Westbury-on-Trym, a chauntry priest had residence in an apartment of this kind "so formed as to enable him to descend into the mortary chapel there to watch by bodies of the dead, or to perform the offices which devolved upon him." In other places they were the habitations of priests who attended to lights burning before a shrine. Hawkhurst church in Kent had a room in the porch which was "commonly called the treasury," and there are often instances in which chests are to be found in such rooms, where valuable books, records, or documents, were stored. The places near Malvern having a "parvice" are Worcester Cathedral, St. Mary's, Shrewsbury, Chipping Campden, Dursley, St. Lawrence, Ludlow, and Chipping Norton. In an account of Sherborne Abbey we read, "above the groining of the porch is a *parvice*, having two Norman window openings. In former days this chamber was constantly inhabited by one of the sextons, who acted as watchman." To which of these various uses, or to what use, the Parvice of Malvern was devoted, cannot be known. That it was used as a watch tower is not improbable.

In later times this Parvice has had less dignified experiences. Whatever were its ancient uses it was always in some manner associated with religion. After the Reformation it no longer remained so devoted. For years the old Abbey house possessed it, and under its custody it was made a servants' hall; and there are persons living who have drunk and feasted in it, and have there danced Sir Roger de Coverley, and other merry jigs, to badly played violins and tambourines. Till 1849 it remained in private hands. There was *inside the church*, also belonging to the Abbey House, a "*littel room*" entered by a private doorway, where as was reported *someone slept*. In 1849 this scandal came to an end. After debate and bargainings both places were got into possession of the parish. The records in the parish books, under date 18th Feb., 1849, run thus:—"Mr. Archer attended and stated that he would *give to the parish* the room over the south side, and agreed to accept £100 for the room over the entrance porch. George M'Cann voluntarily collected the sum required for the purpose. Thanks of the meeting were given to Mr. Archer for his great liberality in giving the room over the south entrance to the parish." 15th March, 1849, "Mr. Archer declined to sell the room for other purposes than as a vestry room." The ancient Parvice of Malvern became a vestry room for parish meetings from that time henceforward, and so still remains.

CHAPTER XXIV.

THE BELLS.

"How many a tale their music tells
Of youth, and home, and that sweet time
When first we heard their soothing chime."

"Prayers ascend
To heaven in troops at a good man's passing bell."

"To call the folks to church in time,
We *chime*.
When mirth and joy are on the wing,
We *ring*.
When we lament departing soul,
We *toll*.

COLE tells us, in 1746, that he was informed that three bells had been sold out of the Malvern steeple fifty or sixty years before his visit, and that then only six remained. The three were sold to "St. Mary Overy's church in Southwark." Cole probably did not take notice of the little "*sanctus bell*" which still remains in addition to the six large bells mentioned. This little bell is without rope and does not appear to have been used for many years.

One bell of unusual interest is in the tower, viz., the tenor bell. Dr. Card thus describes it, "It is the most musical and the most ancient of them all, bearing the following inscription, in what appears to be Lombardic character,"

Virginis egregiæ vocor campana Mariæ (I am called the Virgin Mary's bell).

"The antiquity of this bell may be startling to some of our readers who are not aware that bells were used in the times of the Anglo Saxons." This bell was the famous "vesper bell" of the convent for calling people to evening prayers. It belongs to the twelfth century.

Sir T. Browne, in the *Religio Medici*, says, that at the hearing of such bell everyone, in whatsoever house or street, betook himself to prayer to the Virgin Mary; and he then makes this simple comment:—"I never could hear the Ave Mary bell without an elevation, nor think it a sufficient warrant, because they erred in one circumstance, for me to err in all, that is, in silence and dumb contempt. Whilst, therefore, they direct their devotions to her, I offer mine to God, and rectify the errors of their prayers by rightly ordering my own."

Of the use to which these two bells, the "*sanctus bell*" and the "tenor bell," were put, in the many years of their Malvern history, it is hopeless to conjecture. In the dark days of the church such bells were often used for superstitious purposes, and their power over the imagination of the ignorant was often very great. "The bell," says an ancient writer "is hallowed and rung that by its sound the faithful might be stirred up, and the bodies and minds kept sound, enemies drawn away, and all stratagems defeated. The violence of hail, tempest, storm, and thunder allayed, lightening and winds restrained, and all evil spirits and powers of air vanquished." For ringing at "great thunderings" charges are often made in parish books as late as the last century.

At sound of the sanctus bell of Malvern many a ploughman, within its hearing, has stayed his team and prostrated himself on the ground,and devotees to her worship have often raised prayers to the Virgin Mary at the booming sound of the Priory's ancient tenor bell.

"If that the thunder chaunce to rore, and stormie tempest shake,
A wonder is it for to see the wretches how they quake.
Howe that no fayth at all they have, nor trust in any thing.
The clarke doth all the belles forthwith at once in steeple ring:
With wond'rous sound and deeper farre than he was wont before,
Till in the loftie heavens darke the thunder bray no more.
For in these christned belles they think, doth lie much power and might;
As able is the tempest great and storme to vanquish quight.
'By name I Mary called am, with sound I put to flight
The thunder crackes and hurtfull stormes, and every wicked spright.'"

Paulinus, Bishop of Nola, A.D. 400, and Pope Sabianus, A.D. 604, have the invention of *church* bells generally assigned to them.

The "passing bell," rung in the Christian's mortal agony, was formerly regarded as able to scare away evil spirits, who might otherwise worry the departing soul.

CHAPTER XXV.

THE PARISH REGISTERS.

"The abstracts and brief chronicles of the time."
SHAKESPEARE.

BY the kindness of Rev. I. Gregory Smith, Vicar of Malvern, I have been permitted to get a look at the old registers of the parish. They begin with the year 1556, and are most interesting documents. The first three books, or rolls, are of parchment,—very long strips. From the year 1556 to that of 1597 they are in the writing of a single hand, and have been copied from an earlier document in accordance with an "injunction" given by authority in the latter year,* the purport of which was that parchment should be used for all parish registers, instead of paper; and that all former paper registrations should be copied into the new parchment books. The scribe who copied the Malvern registers did his work

* Lord Cromwell, Henry VIII.'s Vicar General, soon after the dissolution of the monasteries, *i.e.*, in 1538, enjoined that "Every parson, vicar, or curate for every church keep one book or register, wherein he shall write the day and year of every wedding, christening, or burial, made within his parish." "And for the safe keeping of the same book, the parish shall be bound to provide of their common charges, one sure coffer, with two locks and keys, whereof the one to remain with him, and the other with the wardens of every parish wherein the said book shall be laid up, which book (he was) every Sunday to take forth, and in the presence of the said wardens, or one of them, write and record in the same, all the weddings, christenings, and burials made the whole week afore."

The act of 1597 differed from those that went before chiefly in this respect, that it ordered that the register book should be of parchment. The LXX Canon, published in 1604, was, in the main, only a reinforcement of the existing laws relating to parish registers. Like the act of 1597, it enjoined that "the day and year of every christening, marriage and burial which have been in the parish, shall be entered (in the parchment book) since the time that the law was first made in that behalf, so far as the ancient books thereof can be procured, but *especially since the beginning of the reign* of Elizabeth. This will account for so many register books commencing with the year 1588.

The Malvern registers, it will be seen, begin in Mary's reign, 1556.

with the greatest neatness and care, the only apparent alterations being in the spelling, which has evidence of having been altered to the style then prevailing, and we miss the quaintness of the early orthography. The title page contains the following descriptive memorandum, written partly in *old text :*

> The Register book of Great Malvern, began the 1st day June Anno Dom, 1556. Now newlie written in parchment according to the constitution set forth Anno Dom. 1597.

The inner, or second page, which had originally been left blank, contains memoranda of various dates of "ministers and preachers of the word," who had at different times preached at Malvern, as note the following :—

> Anthony Donney, Master of Arts, and a preacher of the word ; preached at Malvern the 7th day of April in the year of our Lord God 1629 being licensed by the Lord Bishop.

For what purpose these entries were made, or by what necessity, does not appear. Were the men mentioned of note as preachers, or was it that the advent of strange preachers was so uncommon that the event was deemed worthy of such record ?

The beginning of each year of the registers is marked in the margin by the date, and by a carefully written old text, for the first word.

To have made anything like an exhaustive search of registers beginning with the year mentioned (1556), and continued till 1885, would have taken many days of careful toil, especially as every succeeding vicar's hand writing and style has to be carefully studied before his entries can be made out. The most I have been able to do has been to notify the valuable mine of information contained in these interesting records. For the most part the entries are made with care and clearness.

The first object I had in consulting these venerable documents was to see what light they would throw on Malvern's inhabitants and history, after the dissolution of the monastery. Did those persons to whom the place fell as an inheritance care for the same, and did they, or any of the monks, continue to live thereat ? These things are amply answered by the registers.

The second entry under the heading of "Weddings" has

reference to the Knottsforde family who bought the rich Priory domain and church.

John Campion and Elnor. Knotsfford were marryed on xvii day September 1556.

In the same year "Maculine Coleman," a former monk of Malvern, is mentioned thus :—

Maculine Coleman and Elizabeth Neade were marryed on vi day February 1556.

The name of Neade, or Need, occurs several times in the early registers. The death of this *Elizabeth* in the following year is thus registered :—

Elizabeth Colman wiffe of Maculine Colman was buried the 5th day August 1557.

Robert Ffarr and Johan Skelton were marryed the vi day June 1557.

A "Walter Ffarr" was amongst the late monks; Robert was perhaps a relative. Johan Skelton was probably a daughter of Richard Skelton, who was an officer of the late monastery, and who is mentioned in the accounts as receiving "Ffees." This same Robert Ffarr, or one of like name, was "marryed" in the year following to Elizabeth Strange, and a family afterwards, of the name, appears in the registers.

William Ridgeley Gent, and Elizabeth Knotsfford, daughter of John Knd. Esqr. were marryed the fifth day of April 1562.

In the same year a "pensioned" monk by name "Poole" is registered amongst the wedded ones.

Richard Poole, and Blanch Gylham were marryed vi of April 1562.

A "Ric Gylham" was Vicar of Malvern at the time, and "Blanch" was most likely his daughter. The Pooles appear to have had a numerous family, and, for many years in the registers of "Weddings, Christenings, and Burials," the name occurs.

Richard Wheelar and Anne Pinnock were marryed xxxiv day Sep 1564.

William Pinnock was the first possessor of the Priory domain after the Dissolution, he selling the same to John Knotsford. This entry looks as if the family continued to reside at the place.

Mention is made above of a Richard Skelton; the following entry records, most probably, his second marriage.

Richard Skelton and Sibbell Goodyear, were marryed xxii day of October 1564.

A "Goodyear" was an annuitant of the dissolved monastery.

Thomas Kirle and Frances ....fford, Wid, were marryed xxiv day Sep 1550.

Thomas Kirle was a gentleman of Much Marcle, one of the "Man of Ross" family. We know from another source that he married "Frances, daughter of John Knotsfford, Gent.," but why the above entry should conceal part of her name, and why it should be succeeded with the word "Wid," is far from clear.

John Russell Gent, and Jane Markys were marryed xii day of August 1570.

A "Sir John Russell Knight" was "high stuart" of the monastery, and is several times mentioned in the "Scudamore Papers" as receiving "Ffees."

Amongst the registers of "Christening" are the following :—

Stephen Gwylham was baptized the 18 June 1588.
Jane Ffar daughter of Robert Ffar was baptised 7 day June 1559.
Francis Campion Son of John Campion was baptized 24 day Ffeb 1559.
Richard Poole was baptized the 2 day June 1566.
William Campion Son of John Campion was baptized 30 day of April 1576.

There were twenty-six baptisms in 1581. In the seven years from the commencement of the register no less than forty-seven marriages occur, in 1559 ten took place, and in the year 1561 eleven.

This shows us that Malvern, after the dissolution of the monastery, was not so denuded of inhabitants as it is sometimes thought to have been; and that, so long ago as then, it had amongst its parishioners and near neighbours persons of substance and position.

As the registers proceed through the 16th to 17th and 18th centuries many suggestive entries occur. I quote a few :—

A woman child was brought to Thomas Bennet of Balhon the xxii day Jany. and was baptized at Malvern the xxiii of the same January 1591.

Matthew the son of a wandering woman was born and baptized the xxiii day of October 1603.

Richard the son of Margaret Lewis, being baseborn, was baptized the 31st day April A.D. 1616.

William Bennett, sometime a monk, incumbent of Cleveload, was buried the 23 day April 1562.

A certain groom called Jono which died at Maddresfield was buried the 3 June 1576.

A certain stranger was found in a ditch at Newland and was buried the last day of June 1576.

Thos. Ligon the son of Richard Ligon of Maddresfield Esquire, buried 25 Dec. 1579.

A certain widdow called Margery, was delivered in a chamber of John Knotsfords Gent, without a midwife, and was buried 1 February 1581.

"The son of a wandering woman," the "sometime monk," the poor "groom called *Jono*," the "stranger *found in a ditch*," the great "Esquire of Maddresfield," and poor "widdow Margery" all on a level! occupying as much space the one as the other in both grave and register.

> "Weighed in the balance, hero dust
> Is *vile* as vulgar clay;
> Thy scales, Mortality, are just
> To all that pass away."
>
> BYRON.

> Francis the son of William Savage was buried the 23rd day April 1581.

"William Savage," was son-in-law to the Mr. John Knotsford, and afterwards possessor of the Priory estate. The previous year a grand-daughter of the same John Knotsford was buried, by name "Jane Campion."

In the margin of the Register for 1569, a note is fastened with a pin, of children baptised by *midwives* in 1565, 1566, 1567, 1568, and 1569. The numbers in each year, except that of 1568, are torn off, but there are often entries like the following:—

> A little girl born in Baldenhall, named Joan, was baptized of the midwife the 6 day April 1581.
>
> Francis Ffield the son of William Ffield was baptized of the midwife at home, the 1 day of March, and buried the same day 1561.

The deaths of John Knotsford and his wife, Jane, are mentioned in the registers as follows:—

> Jane Knotsford the wife of John Knotsfford was buried the 26 of October 1582.
>
> John Knotsfford Esquire dyed the 24 day November, and was buried the 28 day of November 1589.
>
> Elizabeth the wife of Thomas Abingdon of Malvern, was buried the 27 day Sep 1589.

"Thomas Abingdon," the "*learned antiquarian*," who lived at Hindlip, and who was implicated in the Gunpowder Plot conspiracy. This entry looks as if he lived at Malvern before he took up his residence at "*Hindlip House*."

It will be noted that wherever a person of rank is registered some fulness of description is given, greater than that to people of less importance.

Under date *1651* we read as follows:—

> Jarmin, son of John Need, and Francis his mother was baptized, the 21 day of ye month, as is supposed by Mr. Tayler, and forgotten to be registered, by reason of the *troublesome times*.

John filius, John et Margery Lawrence, baptized by Mr. East, in Mr. Pantings time, and absence, 1657, 29 day of ye month.

Widow Cook (midwife) buried from Newland Sep. the 22 1665.

Memorabile.—Ann the wife of Francis Tyler was the first child she brought into the world, and the last woman that she layd.

Strangers were sometimes buried at Malvern, as "John Walwyn from Powick," and amongst others:—

Frances Nott widow of Shellesley was buried here Sep 5 1666.

Anonyma filia Joannis Tippin et Elizabeth, uxoris ejus (circiter mensem nata) et negligentiâ, aut pertinaciâ, non baptista tamen sepulta 10/15.

In English

The nameless daughter of John Tipping and Elizabeth his wife, about a month old, and by the negligence, or obstinacy, of her parents not baptized, yet nevertheless buried (*i.e.* in consecrated ground).

A noticeable feature of Malvern parish registers is the records of burials in "*wool*," which by statute (30 Charles II., cap. 3) was made imperative. Persons dying were to be buried in woollen* on pain of forfeiting £5, and an affidavit had to be made of each burying before a justice of the peace, under like penalty. Entries of this period, in addition to the ordinary record, have these words added, "Affidavit was brought within eight days." Three of such records I quote in full:—

Thomas Moore was buried the 30 day of August.
These are to certify that Thomas Moore of Great Malvern was buried in wool, according to the present act of Parliament, now in force, on friday 30 day August Anno Dom. 1678. Oath was made before me.

Row: Bordley.

Jane Moore }
John Moore }

Richard Nicholas was buryed Septr. 27. Affidavit was brought within eight days.

Penelope Nicholas of the parish of Great Malvern in the County of Worcester widow maketh oath, that her late husband Richd. Nicholas of the parish of Gt. Malvern in the County of Worcester aforesaid, lately deceased, was not put in, wrapped, or wound up, or buryed in any shirt, shift, sheet, or shroud made or mingled with flax, hemp, silk, hair, gold or silver or other than what is made with sheeps wool only, nor in any coffin lined or faced with any cloth stuff, or any other thing whatsoever made or mingled, with flax, hemp, silk, hair, gold, or silver, or any other material but sheeps wool only.
Dated this 2nd day of Oct. in the 30th year of the reign of our sovereign Lord Charles II. King of England, Scotland, France and Ireland A.D. 1678. Scribed & subscribed by us, who were present as witnesses to the swearing of the aforesaid affidavit.

Robt. Tranter
Fr. Childe

* This act came into force in 1678. Its intention was stated to be for "lessening the importation of linnen" and "the encouragement of the woollen and paper manufactures of the kingdom." The act was not repealed till 54 George III.

John Godwin was buried January 26th. Affidavit was brought within eight days after.

These are to certify that John Godwin of Gt. Malvern was buryed in wool according to the present Act of Parliament now in force, on Sunday the 26 day of Jany Anno Dom 1678/9.

Oaths whereof were made before me Thos Savage.*

James Badger
Thos. Sanders

George son of William Lygon of Madresfield was buryed April 3rd 1680. Affidavit was brought April 9th.

Sybil Silman of ye parish of Madresfield in ye County of Worcester maketh oath, that Mr. George Lygon of ye parishe of Maddresfield in ye County of Worcester, lately deceased, was not put in, wrapped, or wound up, in any shirt, shift, sheet, or shroud, made or imaged with flax, hemp, hair, gold or silver, cloth or other than what is made of sheep's wool only; nor in any coffin lined or faced with any cloth stuff or any other thing which was made or mingled with hemp, flax, silk, hair, gold or any other material but sheep's wool only. Dated this seventh day of April in the 32nd year of the reign of our sovereign Lord Charles II. King of England, Scotland, France, Ireland Anno Dom. 1680. Sealed and subscribed by us who were present as witnesses to the swearing of the above affidavit. Elizabeth Montuor

Fr. Childe

A poor anonymous man, said he was of Wiltshire was buryed March 22/1713.

All the early registers are signed at the bottom of the page by the Vicar and two persons who are called "guardians."

The *copied* registers from the year 1556 (the commencement) to 1597, bear the signatures of

William Jermyne, Vic
John Knight }
Ric Batger } *guardians.*

* Married John Knotsford's eldest daughter and lived on the Priory farm.

CHAPTER XXVI.

DISAFFORESTATION OF THE CHASE.

"Those days are gone; but still a share
Of glory shall remain."

AN event involving the weal or woe of many of the near inhabitants of Malvern in the 17th century, was the disafforestation of the "Malvern Chase." From the times of Malvern's existence as a habitable region, its huge forest oaks, its beech trees, its elms, and black fir trees, together with its tangled bramble thickets, had covered over thousands of acres of the valley beneath it. For miles toward the north it was forest. Down to the Severn's bank was forest; away into Gloucestershire, and still it was forest. Mighty men had been its lords. The great D'Abitot had claimed it as his property. The mighty De Clares had made it their hunting ground; and many lords besides them wielded over it almost absolute sway. The great Earl of Warwick, "the king maker," was at one time its ruler, and from the grey gothic tower of his castle of Hanley had sent forth the life and death warrants of his authority. Ladies of royal lineage and kings themselves had enjoyed sport therein. It was now to be disafforested. King Charles I. had a proprietary interest in the forest, and a kingly spirit of spoliation, if not of robbery, was again in the ascendant.

This time, however, the king had not to deal with simple monks, tired of their vows and longing to be set free, as

Henry VIII. had, but with haughty "lords of manors," "*mean* lords," and a multitude of "commoners." These, to the number, as was reported, of "800 to 900," claimed "common of herbage and panage," besides "estovers" in the "twoo wooddes" called the "Bishopps woode" and the "Erles woode." It was also said that "10 thousande poore people were concerned," and that "nott haveinge and enjoyeinge thereoff maye turne to their utter overthrow, and undoeinge." In the act of 1600 it was acknowledged that every holder of "messuage and tennaunt" in 13 parishes had right to "Hous-boote, Hay-boot, Cart-boot, Plough-boot, and Fire-boot." But whatever became of others, the king determined that his interest should be made into money, and this could be done by nothing less than disafforestation. Accordingly an act was passed by which the Chase was declared disafforested "froom the game of Deere and jurisdiction of fforest lawes." One third of the waste land was allotted to the king, and the rest of the said forest or chace was to remain "for ever in common." Claims came to be made by others as "Sir Thomas Russell, and John Hornihold" and some "meane lords of manors," and a decree was made that composition should be given them, "and bee performed out of the third part allotted or to be allotted to his magesty and his assynes." "Sir Cornelius Vermuden, and his heires," in 1632, became possessors of the king's part.

The manor of Malvern, which had been acquired by the crown on the dissolution of the Priory in the sixth year of Edward VI., was demised to Thomas Fysher, gentleman, for twenty years at the rent of £56 17 4½, by the following description: "all the lordship and manor of Greater Malvern, in the County of Worcester, lately belonging to the Priory of Malverne, and all lands, commons, wastes, furzes, heaths, marshes, rents, reversions, services, court-leet, &c., in the Greater Malverne and Baldnall."

In the reign of Queen Mary, 1553, the advowson of the church of Malvern fell to John Lumley, Lord Lumley, to hold in tail male of the crown.

With the disafforestation disappeared the king's deer, and very soon the noble ***antler bearers***, which for so many generations of men had hid, and been hunted in the forest thickets, were no more to be seen. Great dissatisfaction arose, and riots took place, where the king's thirds became enclosed. At gatherings of the people everywhere violation of common rights became the topic of conversation and grievous complaints were made. Plots resulting in open disturbances, as well as secret assassination, characterised in many places the forest inhabitants. Eventually, time the soother of griefs, if not repairer of wrongs, brought forgetfulness. The great men who had enclosed lands were permitted to hold them, and the Chace itself became peaceably submissive to the jurisdiction of its "Court-leets" and "Court barons."

At the coronation of Charles I. many Worcestershire men were summoned by the court to have the honour of knighthood conferred upon them, an act without doubt intended to bring fees into the king's treasury, and we learn from the "booke of the Composition of Knighthood" of 1630, that amongst those who refused to attend in Worcestershire, and were fined accordingly, were :—

John Hornihold, Hanley	amount	27	10	0
John Russell, Gent., Great Malvern	,,	12	0	0
Francis Rosse, Great Malvern	,,	12	0	0

The difference in the value of money made these sums far from being as insignificant as they now appear. Some of the Worcestershire men paid fines as high as £1000.

CHAPTER XXVII.

MALVERN IN THE SEVENTEENTH AND EIGHTEENTH CENTURIES.

"Pause we awhile, and from Oblivion's gloom
Snatch old tradition in his infant bloom."

IN the year 1612 the Rev. Edmund Rea became Vicar of Great Malvern. The living had been conferred upon him by the king, who then held the advowson. He held his post for twenty-eight years. At his death a tomb inside the church was erected to his memory.

There is little doubt this gentleman was the author of the old song inserted below, with which Malvern has become familiar. Mr. Barratt, who wrote a notice of Malvern late in the last century, affirms that the lines were composed by "the Parish Clerk," that they remained in M.S. till 1778, and then were first published by Nash, in his *Worcestershire*. Dr. Card, in a note at page 43 of his work on the Priory Church, says: "We have seen an old commonplace book of the Rev. John Webb, in which it is said that Edmund Rea, who was Vicar of Great Malvern in 1612, was the author of the song, though we desire not to be understood as contending for the positive certainty of this assertion." Webb was Vicar in 1708, and from what we know of him, would not have been likely to fix the authorship of the song without good grounds for what he wrote. The song bears evidence of the date of its composition. It was clearly written before the disafforestation of the chase, and at a time when the healing power of Malvern's waters for various diseases had attracted notice.

OLD SONG.

"As I didde walke alone,
  Late in the evenynge,
I heard the voice of one
  Most sweetlie syngyne;
Which didde delighte me much,
Because the songe was such,
As endedde with a touch,
    O Prayse the Lord.

The God of sea and lande
  That rules above us—
Staies his avengyne hand,
  Cause he doth love us,
And doth his blessyngs sende,
Altho' we doe offend,
Then let us alle amende,
    And Prayse the Lord.

Grete Malverne on a rocke
  Thou standyst surelie;
Doe not thyself forgette,
  Lyvynge securelie.
Thou haste of blessynges store,
No countrie towne hathe more,
Doe not forgette therefore
    To Prayse the Lord.

Thou haste a famous church,
  And rarelie buildedd:
No countrie towne hath such,
  Most man have yieldedd,
For pillars stoute and stronge,
And wyndowes large and longe,
Remember in thy songe
    To Prayse the Lord.

There is Godd's service rede
  With reverence dulie;
There is his word preachedd
  Learnedd and trulie;
And everie sabbath-daie
Syngyne of psalms they saie
Is sure the onlie waie
    To Prayse the Lord.

The sun in glorie grete,
  When first it riseth,
Doth blesse the happie sete,
  And thee advyseth
That then its time to praie,
That God may blesse thy waie,
And keep thee all the daie,
    To Prayse the Lord.

That thy prospect is goode
  None can denie thee;
Thou haste grete store of woode
  Growynge harde by thee;
Which is a blessynge grete,
To roaste and boil thy mete,
And thee in colde to hete,
    O Prayse the Lord.

Preserve it I advyse,
  Whylst now thou haste it ;
Spare not in any-wyse,
  But doe not waste it ;
Leste thou repent too late,
Remember Hanlie's fate,
In time shut up thy gate,
    And Prayse the Lord.

A chase for royal deere
  Rounde doth besette thee,
Too many I do fere,
  For aught they gette thee ;
Yette tho' they eat awaie
Thy corn, thy grasse, and haie,
Do not forgette I saie
    To Prayse the Lord.

That noble chase doth give
  Thy bestes their feedynge,
Where theye in summer live
  With littel heedynge,
Thy sheepe and swine there go,
  So doth thy horse also,
Till winter brings in snow,
    Then Prayse the Lord.

Turn upp thyne eyes on high,
  There farelie standynge ;
See Malverne's highest hille,
  All hills commandynge.
They all confesse at wille,
Their soveraigne Malverne hille ;
Lette it be mightye stille,
    And Prayse the Lord.

When westerne wyndes do rocke
  Both towne and countrie,
Thy hille doth breke the shocke,
  They cannot hurte thee ;
When waters grete aboundc,
And many a countrie's drown'd,
Thou standyest safe and sounde,
    O Prayse the Lord.

Out of thy famous hille
  There dailie springeth,
A water passynge stille,
  That always bringyeth
Grete comfort to alle them
That are diseased men,
And makes them welle again
    To Prayse the Lord.

Haste thou a wound to heale,
  The whyche doth greve thee ;
Come thenn unto this welle,
  It wille releive thee,
"*Noli me tangeries*,"
And other maladies,
Have theyre theyr remedies,
    Prays'd be the Lord.

To drinke thy waters store,
  Lye in thy bushes
Mayne with ulcers sore,
  Mayne with bruises,
Who sucor finde from ille,
By monie gyven stille,
Thanks to the Christian wille,
    O Prayse the Lord.

A thousande bottles there
Were filled weeklie;
And manye costryls rare
For stomachs sicklie;
Some of theme into Kente,
Some were to London sente,
Others to Berwicke wente,
O Prayse the Lord.

If the Rev. Edmund Rea was the author of this "old song," as appears probable, we may see how proud he was of his church, what delight he had in the Malvern Hills, and what a soul of praise there was in him, because of the glad surroundings of his earthly dwelling place. It is altogether unlikely that a "Parish Clerk," as we now understand that term, should have been the author.

To the same writer may be given the honour of the following:

"Hark! speaking to themselves,
Are Malvern's sweet nine bells:
How they troll, troll, troll."

Of this Rev. E. Rea's interest in all that belongs to Malvern evidence is seen in the fact, that out of the small emoluments of his cure he gave £100 "in order to get the queen's bounty towards the augmentation of the vicarage." He was buried, as has been said, inside the church, and "all round the edge of his grave" was the following inscription in tiles:—

"Here lyeth the body of Edmund Rea, late Vicar of Much Malverne, deceased the 23 Dec., anno. do. 1640."

To the Rev. John Webb we owe the publication of the following document. It shows that a state of things surrounded Malvern in those days with which we are now, happily, altogether unfamiliar. We can hardly bring ourselves to understand how the gathering of tythes in kind, as there set forth, could have been practicable.

CUSTOMS OF OLDEN TIMES.

Reprint of the Ancient Terrier, containing a true and perfect Account of the Tythes and Oblations belonging to the Parish Church of Great Malvern, in the County and Diocese of Worcester, as they have been Acknowledged, Paid, and Received, and are now reputed, taken, and agreed to by JOHN WEBB, *the present Vicar, the Church Wardens, and the Chief Inhabitants of the aforesaid Parish, this 20th day of June, in the 13th Year of the Reign of our most gracious Sovereign Lady* ANNE, *by the Grace of God, of Great Britain, France, and Ireland, Queen, Defender of the Faith, and in the Year of our Lord,* 1714, *as followeth:—*

IMPRIMIS,

There are antiently belonging to the Vicar of the said Parish Church for the time being, one House and Garden, and Church-Yard adjoining.

OFFERINGS.—At *Easter*, Offerings are due and payable from all Persons whatever that are Sixteen Years of age and upwards, in these proportions following: viz., for a Man and his Wife, Four-pence; for Widowers and Widows, not in Service, Two-pence a-piece; for Children and Apprentices, Two-pence a-piece; for all Men Servants and Journeymen of Trades, Six-pence a-piece; and for Women Servants and Workers of Trades, Four-pence a-piece,

These Rates or Sums have customarily been paid, Time out of Mind by all abiding in our said Parish at Easter.

SMOKE AND GARDEN.—All House-Dwellers are accustomed to Pay One Penny for Smoke, in lieu of Tythe-Wood, and One Penny for Garden, if they have any, at *Easter*.

COCKS AND HENS.—Likewise there is a custom to pay Three Eggs, or Three Farthings for every Cock: or an Half-penny, or Two Eggs for every Hen: But here is no Modus for Ducks, Pigeons, or Turkies.

KINE.—The Milk or White of Kine is only One Penny for each Cow, and payable at *Easter*.

CALVES.—For Calves, when reared, only Three Half-pence for each; when Killed by the Owner, the Left Shoulder; when sold to the Butcher, the Tenth Penny; and when sold with the Cow, according to Law.

COLTS.—Fourpence only is due when each colt is foaled.

PIGS.—Here is nothing due for Pigs when but Six, or under; but when Seven or upwards, the Third best; and when Seventeen, or upwards, the Third and the Thirteenth-best are due when they are three weeks old, * e without the Dam.

LAMBS.—Tythe Lambs are due the Third Day of *May*, and if the Number be under Seven, only one Half-penny is due for each Lamb; but when Seven, the Third-best; when Seventeen, the Third and Thirteenth-best; when Twenty-seven, the Third and Thirteenth, and the Twenty-third best are due, paying back Three Half-pence for the Three they lack of Ten, Twenty, or Thirty; and so proportionably for any greater number whatever. When the number of Lambs is Eight, One is due, paying back One Penny; when Nineteen, Two are due, paying back one Half-penny; and when Thirty, Three are due, without paying back anything; likewise One Half-penny is due for each above Ten, Twenty or Thirty, and yet under Seventeen, Twenty-seven, or Thirty-seven, &c.

SHEEP.—All Wool shorn here is tytheable at Shear-Day, and has been valued at Three Half-pence per Fleece; but the Vicar may have the Third-best, when they are seven; the Third and Thirteenth-best, when they are Seventeen; and the Third, the Thirteenth, and Twenty-third best when they are Twenty-seven, paying back three times Three Half-pence, or Four-pence Half-penny, for the Three Fleeces they lack of Ten, Twenty, or Thirty, and so proportionably for any greater or less number, as before in the Lambs.

PASTURE.—But if any Person, to evade the Parson of Tythe-Wool, doth shear his Sheep on Tythe-free Land, or use any other Way or Means to defraud the Vicar or Incumbent of his Dues in this Matter, then, and in such case, such Person or Persons ought to pay Two-pence per Month for every Ten Sheep he or they do or shall keep, or depasture on any Tytheable land whatsoever, and so proportionably for any greater or less Quantity.

EXCEPTION.—Except all the Tythes of Wool and Lambs, and of One Hundred and Fifty Sheep only, to be kept on the Lands belonging to the Capital Messuage of *Thomas Savage*, Esq., which shall at any Time of the Year be depastured on the Commons or Commonable Places belonging to the said Parish of *Great Malvern*.

GEESE.—Geese are Tytheable at *Midsummer*, and payable as follows: viz., when under seven nothing is due; but when seven, or any other number under Seventeen, only the Third-best is due; and when Seventeen and yet under Twenty-seven, the Third and the Thirteenth-best are due; and so proportionably for any greater or less number whatever.

CHERRIES.—The Tenth of Cherries and all other Marketable Fruit, whether Apples, Pears, or Plumbs, is due at the Tree when gathered.

DRINK.—Two-pence per Hogshead only is due for all Drink made with Unmarketable Fruit.

* Document torn.

HEMP AND FLAX.—Hemp and Flax are payable in Kind, as in other Places.

HOPS.—Hops are paid in Kind here, as in other Places.

BEES.—The Tenth of Honey and Wax is due for Bees, when they are taken by the Owners; and the Tenth Penny when they are sold.

TURNIPS.—When Turnips are eaten with unprofitable Cattle, Herbage is due for the Ground; and when the Roots are gathered, the Tenth Bushel is due.

HERBAGE.—Herbage is due for all Pasture Ground grazed with unprofitable Cattle.

GREAT TYTHES PAID TO MADRESFIELD, SMALL TYTHES HERE.—All Lands in this Parish that pay the GREAT TYTHES to the Rector of *Maddresfield*, have always been accustomed to pay the SMALL TYTHES to the Person or Persons that the said SMALL TYTHES of the said Parish of *Great Malvern* were paid to, and are now payable to the said Vicar.

MORTUARIES.—Mortuaries are accustomed to be paid here according to Law.

MILLS.—There being two Water Corn-Mills in this Parish, for the uppermost of them *John Bellers* (in whose Possession it now is) doth pay One Shilling and Four-pence, as a Modus; and for the lower Mill *John Powell* (in whose occupation it now is) pays One Shilling as a Modus.

CHANCEL BURIALS.—Here hath been a custom to pay Six Shilling and Eight-pence to the Vicar, for every Burial whatever in the Chancel.

The above-mentioned, with all and every other Offering and Offerings, Tythes, Oblations, Obventions, Fruits, and Profits whatsoever, which have been, now are, or may hereafter be esteemed, reputed, taken, or known to be Small, Privy, or Minute Tythes, whether Predial, Mixed, or Personal, are due and payable to the Vicar or Incumbent of the aforesaid Parish Church of *Great Malvern* for the Time being for ever. IN WITNESS WHEREOF WE, the said Vicar, Church-Wardens, and other of the Inhabitants of the said Parish, have hereunto set our Hands the Day and Year first above-written.

JOHN WEBB, Vicar, Ib.

EDWARD WILLSON, RICHARD BULLOCK } Churchwardens.

MAR. WEBB.
JON. WARNER.

CHAPTER XXVIII.

SUCCESSIVE RESTORATIONS.

"Thou too, fair pile, in beautiful old age
Smil'st at the spoiler and his baffled rage."

"Running adown
The long time avenues."

THE end of the 18th century beheld the church of Malvern in a desperate condition. The ample funds the monastery formerly possessed had not been available for its reparation. Its friend the Rev. Edmund Rea was no more; Webb had gone to his rest. A period of neglect had set in. Nothing about the church was cared for; coldness, indifference, and neglect, reigned supreme. The destroying tooth of time had been left to do its work, and in 1788 ruin beyond recall began to appear. Rain came into the church in many places. Its many-times whitewashed walls were green in some places, and black in others with damp. The place had a vault-like smell. The few people who attended its once-a-week services had to wrap themselves up and take other precautions against catching their deaths. A death-like chill exuded from its old stone walls. In the year mentioned the church became in "too ruinous a state to be used with safety." A beholder of that day thus described the place in the *Gentleman's Magazine*:

I made a survey of this edifice, where I am free to declare, I was shocked to the utmost sense in beholding so sumptuous a pile, another Westminster Abbey church, though of smaller dimensions, doomed to the worst of defilement and neglect. On the north side of the church was a play ground for unrestrained youth, whose recreations consisted in throwing stones at the numerous windows, all full of the finest stained glass; and adjoining this play ground was a kennel of hounds, whose hideous yells filled up at intervals (service time or otherwise) the cry of the headstrong juvenile assailants. In the interior of the church on the north side, is a chapel dedicated to our Lord, and called Jesus chapel. Here I saw actually stuck up on its eastern wall a large pigeon-house, belonging, as my conductor informed me, but to which I could not give any credit, to the person presiding over the sacred place wherein I then stood, he being equally happy to see the flights of such innocents through the aisles and vaults, as to hear the harmonious sounds of the surrounding canine rangers of the sportive fields.

Not till fourteen years afterwards was much, if anything, done. Then a Mr. Tatham was employed, and he reported, "that he was of opinion that the church was capable of such repair as might render it fit for divine service, and preserve the building for many years;" and, as a further inducement to the undertaking, he added, "that its antiquity, magnificence, and beauty, combined to render it worthy of being preserved as a specimen of Gothic architecture, in which respect it is little inferior to any in the kingdom." Soon after £976 3 0 was raised by voluntary contributions, and £25 17 0 was made up by a parish rate. From a subsequent report it appears that that sum and £1000 more was expended "in repairing & in restoring the ceiling, and in contributing" some more whitewash to its walls; this was done before the year 1812. Chambers reports that in that year "Although neatness, or at least cleanliness, reigned above, ruin and desolation bore sovereign sway below." The eminent architect Mr. Smirke was then employed. He did little, and was soon dismissed. The reason for his dismissal was probably the failure of hopes that had been raised of funds coming in, as the result of a document, which, as it is connected with the history of the church, I shall take the trouble to transcribe. It is the "great Malvern church brief" which was issued in the king's name (49th George III.) to "all and singular Archbishops, Bishops, Archdeacons, Deans," and to "preachers" of every kind including the "*Quakers*,"—calling upon them, in all England, and to the farthest extent of Wales and "Berwick upon Tweed," to ask and receive "christian and charitable contributions;" and the Quakers, by "persuasive motives and arguments," were earnestly to "exhort" their congregations to "liberal contributions." The trustees appointed included one bishop, one earl, two esquires, and ten private gentlemen. Some extracts from this brief I give as follows:

GREAT MALVERN CHURCH BRIEF.

George the third by the grace of God of the United Kingdom of Great Britain and Ireland King Defender of the Faith TO all and singular Archbishops Bishops Archdeacons Deans and their Officials Parsons Vicars Curates and all other spiritual persons And to all Teachers and Preachers of every separate Congregation And also to all Justices of the Peace Mayors Sheriffs Bailiffs Constables Churchwardens Chapelwardens Headboroughs Collectors for the Poor and their Overseers And also to all Officers of Cities Boroughs and Towns Corporate and to all other our Officers Ministers and Subjects whomsoever they be as well within Liberties as without to whom these Presents shall come Greeting Whereas it hath been represented unto us as well upon the humble Petition of the Minister Churchwardens and Principal Inhabitants of the Parish of Great Malvern in our County of Worcester as by Certificate under the hands of our trusty and well beloved Justices of the Peace for our said County of Worcester assembled at their General Quarter Sessions of the Peace held at Worcester in and for our said County on the eleventh day of July in the Forty-ninth year of our Reign That the Parish Church of Great Malvern aforesaid is a very ancient structure and now become very much decayed and that it is necessary that a large sum of money should be laid out in repairing the same although the said Parishioners have from time to time laid out large sums in the repair thereof That the truth of the Premises hath been made appear to our Justices assembled at their General Quarter Sessions of the Peace aforesaid not only by the said Inhabitants but on the Oath of John Stephens an able and experienced Architect who hath carefully viewed the said Church and the repairs necessary to be done thereto which on a moderate computation will amount to upwards of One thousand four hundred and forty-seven pounds which sum the said Inhabitants are not able to raise among themselves They have therefore humbly besought us to grant unto them our most gracious Letters Patent Licence and protection under our Great Seal of Great Britain to empower them to ask collect and receive the alms benevolence and Charitable Contributions of all our loving Subjects throughout England our Town of Berwick upon Tweed and our Counties of Flint Denbigh and Radnor in Wales to enable them to repair their said Church unto which their humble request we have graciously condescended not doubting but that when these Presents shall be known by our loving Subjects they will readily and cheerfully contribute their endeavours for accomplishing the same Know ye therefore that....in pursuance of the tenor of an Act of Parliament made in the fourth year of the reign of the late Queen Ann entitled "An Act for the better collecting Charity money on Briefs by Letters Patent and preventing abuses in relation to such Charities" Our will and pleasure is and we do hereby for the better advancement of these our pious intentions require and command all ministers Teachers and Preachers Churchwardens and Chapelwardens and the Collectors of this Brief and all others concerned that they and every one of them observe the directions in the said Act contained and do in all things conform themselves thereunto and that when the Printed Copy of these Presents shall be tendered unto you the respective Ministers and Curates Churchwardens and Chapelwardens and to the respective Teachers and Preachers of every separate Congregation and to any person who teaches or preaches in any Meeting of the People called Quakers that you and every one of you under the Penalties to be inflicted by the said Act do receive the same And you the respective Ministers and Curates Teachers and Preachers and Persons called Quakers are by all persuasive motives and arguments earnestly to exhort your respective Congregations and Assemblies to a liberal Contribution of their Charity for the good intent and purpose aforesaid...... And We do by these Presents nominate constitute and appoint The Right Reverend the Lord Bishop of Worcester The Right Honorable Lord Beauchamp Anthony Lechmere Benjamin Johnson Esquires John Wilson Richard Benbow John Bellers John Bullock William Bullock John Amphlett Robert Richards John Beard John Stevenson Salt Gentlemen and the Minister and Churchwardens of the said Parish for the time being Trustees and Receivers of the Charity to be collected by virtue of these Presents......... In Witness whereof we have caused these our Letters to be made Patent and to continue in force for One whole year from Lady day next and no longer Witness ourself at Westminster the ninth day of December in the fiftieth year of our Reign.

Humphrys.

British Museum, Ch. Br., B. L. 4.

We do not know what use was made of this ponderous document only a portion of which has been quoted. We have no information as to its reception in the "Friends' Meeting Houses," at Berwick-upon-Tweed, or the County of Denbye; nor do we know how many penalties were made due, by non-observance of its kingly demands; all we do know is that that no mention is made in statement of accounts for 1809 to 1814 of any money being contributed under it, but in the subscription list for years 1814 to 1818 there does appear an item running thus:

Brief, and interest 9 19 0

and this would seem to be all that resulted from this pompous proceeding. The fable of a mountain in labour to produce a mouse is not altogether inappropriate. This Parliamentary method of collecting money was, in fact, an abortion. As some compensation to this disappointment, a grant was made by the Government of £1000, and further restorations were proceeded with. From February, 1816, to June of the same year, the church was closed for repairs. Much was done in the meantime, so that it was deemed sufficiently "repaired." When opened again for worship, the "crumbling roof," we are told, "no longer dropped on the uplifted eye of devotion;" and pews, lined with "crimson cloth," and other "costly mode of fitting up," made an imposing appearance. One of the Worcester papers spoke of the restoration of that day as "an instance of rare and successful exertion, that reflected the highest credit on the Vicar, the Rev. Dr. Card."

Mr. A. Welby Pugin visited Malvern in 1833. He wrote:

> I next shaped my course to Malvern to see the Abbey there, and the celebrated Hills. Here is a church in which the stained glass has not fallen a victim to Protestant zeal. It is truly magnificent, and the drawing of the figures is correct and beautiful, the colouring rich and varied. These windows may be rated among the finest specimens of English glass of the fifteenth century. The paving-tiles are likewise decidedly the finest in the kingdom; such a variety of patterns, and such a quantity of tiles I never saw anywhere. A few years ago a meeting of the fashionables of Malvern was called to subscribe towards the repairs of the dilapidated building, and by the help of raffles, &c., a few pounds were collected. Two hodfuls of mortar were got to repair the church, and the remainder of the money expended in putting in a window of the aisle, and the arms of the subscribers in stained class, with their names in full, a monument of their folly and arrogance. The very mullions in which the glass is placed, are rotten and falling. The church itself is in dreadful repair; fall it must, and all that is to be hoped is, that in its fall it may annihilate those whose duty it was to have restored it; but of this we may be sure, that if it falls while there is a congregation within its walls, it will clear some away that ought to be got rid of, for such a set of lounging idlers as the fashionables of Malvern are only to be matched at Brighton or Cheltenham.

Pugin's ill-natured remarks have been multiplied by others, till it has become a fashion to abuse Dr. Card, and the restorations with which he had to do. The truth is, the taste for restoration of churches was not then so advanced as now, and he did *what he could.* He had to please those associated with him, or nothing in the way of money had come in. To say the least, he *saved the noble church from falling down*, and becoming a ruin; and those who have complained and derided him by name, as they have frequently done, should have remembered that, but for Dr. Card's exertions, no church would have remained in Malvern till our time, for a more correct taste to restore.

In 1834, Dr. Card was again engaged in the church's restoration. Considerable repairs of a substantial nature were then done to the exterior of the church, and the battlements, and pinnacles of the nave and porch were restored, and at the same time soil to the depth of two to three feet was removed from the foundations on the north side, which side of the church was thoroughly renovated. In 1841, the remainder of the exterior of the church,—the tower excepted,—was restored. The Rev. Dr. Card died June 26, 1844, and the *Gentleman's Magazine*, in a brief memoir, deplored his loss, and said: "Looking at all that Dr. Card has done for Malvern Church, we may safely affirm that his name will be handed down to posterity, as one of its greatest benefactors; and by his deeds, as there shown in such bold characters, he has raised a monument to his memory, which will endure until the edifice itself shall cease to be."

But of all the restorations on record, none were so complete and satisfactory as that begun in 1852, by the Rev. John Rashdall, M.A., Vicar, and followed up with such energy by his distinguished successor, the Rev. George Fisk, L.L.B. Under the auspices of the first, the tower of the church was overhauled, and made secure, its battlements repaired, and other work done. Under the latter's leadership, a work was accomplished, so great, that it deserved to be remembered. No record can reveal its full extent. New roofs were made for every part of the building, beautiful ceilings, from ancient patterns, were formed, and, from roof to basement, the walls and pillars were divested of their long accumulated coats of white wash. All were cleansed and repaired, so that its ancient masonry was again laid bare. Rubbish of all kinds was swept away, and there was much of it. The famous "*crimson lined pews*," as well as some ugly obstructions beneath the tower were removed. Floors were renewed, windows made secure, and much besides done, till Malvern Church, so long neglected, and sometimes much desecrated, was again made beautiful. Something of its ancient glory was made to reappear, and enough was done in the way of restoration to afford a well-grounded hope that the inhabitants of Malvern for many generations to come would possess a church suited to their needs and justly claiming the admiration of the beholder.

CHAPTER XXIX.

ANCIENT CARVINGS ON THE MONKS' STALLS.

"Malvern, may'st thou remain serene, secure;
O'er thy sweet scenes may no rude tempest blow;—
Long as revolving time may'st thou endure,
And streams meandering through thy valleys flow."
ELIZABETH SMITH, 1829.

ONE feature, and that not the least amongst Malvern's beautiful antiquities, is the stalls of the monks, under the seats of which are carvings of no ordinary character. To these I now direct attention. The seats of these stalls are moveable, that is to say, they hang on hinges, and can be turned up, or let down as may be desired. When turned up they exhibit the carvings, which I propose to describe; they also form a kind of ledge or little seat on which persons without absolutely sitting can rest themselves. The general conclusion is, that these turned-up seats were a permitted indulgence to the monks during their long and constantly recurring services. They were not permitted to sit but could lean back on this ledge, and rest themselves in a certain degree, and it is intimated that, when these "misereres" act properly, should the worshipper be so negligent as to fall into a slumber, a thing not always to be guarded against, even amongst monks, the seat would throw him forward, slam down, and so expose his indolence. Similar stalls exist in the ancient Cathedrals of Worcester,

Gloucester, and Hereford, in Stratford-on-Avon Church, the Abbey Churches of Pershore, Tewkesbury, and Ludlow, and in many other conventual and Collegiate Churches. So great a similarity exists in the manner, style, and subject of their sculpture, as to suggest the idea that both in England, and on the continent, those who produced them worked under like inspiration, if not from common models. It would appear as if anciently such curiously carved stalls were considered a necessary appointment in the arrangement of the choir of Churches.

The number of old stalls in Malvern Church is twenty-four, but there is evidence that additional ones formerly existed, their probable number being thirty. The seats are in good preservation, the carvings of two seats only are missing, and, though some are mutilated, yet, considering the times and dangers through which they must have passed, it is a matter of congratulation so much has been preserved to us.

Conjecture has often wearied itself as to the meaning and significance of these carvings, and it would be unfair to attempt to explain or interpret them, except by reference to their general character.

Often exceedingly grotesque and full of humour, they sometimes are keenly satirical, at others homely or commonplace. Now they represent, very seriously and sagely, events of Holy Scripture, and anon we find them depicting acts and deeds that appear to us very materialistic, if not obscene.

Persons of some intellectual acuteness have been wont to regard them, even in their apparent grossness and frivolity, as symbolising the deepest and most vital mysteries of the Christian faith, and the fact of important events of biblical history being included in such carvings, as is the case at Worcester and other places, would give some force to this view. Seeing too, that these ancient works of art occupy parts of churches usually regarded with peculiar reverence, it would be agreeable if we could give to them so serious an interpretation ; but, unfortunately, there is too much of a secular character about some of them to admit of this, and those who are most desirous to take the serious view are driven to seek for a further explanation. All through the middle ages there existed considerable rivalry and jealousy between the various classes of society, and notably between the religious orders, and the several grades of each ; and through the literary works of that period a good deal of invective is found to exist, and these grotesque carvings may in the first place be interpreted in the light of satires upon one or other of these classes. A fox in a monk's hood—as at Malvern—suggests the cunning craftiness of the monk, as do foxes preaching to geese before devouring them, and, as at Worcester, a fox in garb of a monk offering up mass.

Great oppression was exercised upon the masses of the people in the middle ages, by the monastic orders, as by others in high place, and these satires may be interpreted as indicating the rising conviction that oppression's days were numbered.

In the fourteenth and fifteenth centuries such sentiments had become popular, and a hare represented as riding upon a dog, as at Worcester; and three rats hanging a cat, as in carvings at Malvern (see engraving), may be regarded as representing the prevalent belief, that the oppressed would ere long rise up, and overthrow their oppressors, and there is little doubt such representations were, in their day, well understood, and keenly felt.

After all is said, that can be, of the scope and intention of these works of ancient art, there still remains much that needs explanation, and there are some of them, for instance, those at Worcester, which we can hardly look at without being led to the belief that there was sometimes an intention to illustrate events of Holy Scripture. Such subjects as the "JUDGMENT OF SOLOMON," the "IDOLATRY OF THE ISRAELITES," the "CIRCUMCISION OF CHRIST," and the "PRESENTATION IN THE TEMPLE," there portrayed, must have been depicted with a *serious* intention of illustrating those subjects.

These carvings exhibit the notions of Natural History then prevalent, as they also illustrate the popular literature of the age. The cockatrice, syren, or mermaid and dragon, are all found at Malvern, as are also some of the fabulous monsters of Eastern legends.

The popular amusements of the period, such as ball playing, morrice-dancing, and its field sports, the various seasons of the year, and the domestic arrangements and occupations of our forefathers are all included in the range of subjects represented.

In fact, so far from these ancient works of art being executed with any *one* object, the more they are thought about, and enquired into, the more will they be seen to have a *breadth* of purpose, and a pictorial significance that at first sight does not appear to belong to them, as they in a remarkable degree illustrate the habits, thoughts, and belief of our forefathers.

Having spoken of their probable scope and intention, I proceed to describe in detail some of these carvings. They exist, as has been said, underneath the seats of four rows of stalls in the choir of the Church, there being six ancient stalls in each row, and others of modern workmanship, and for the sake of simplicity I will divide them into, first, those upon the north side, twelve in number, and secondly, those on the south side, also numbering twelve.

Taking the front row on the north side I begin with the stall next to the tower. This contains a somewhat remarkable carving, that of a Benedictine monk elevating in each hand a very large chalice, the chalice being in size out of all proportion to the monk, and nearly as large as his head. A table on tressels is before him, and on the table, which seems to form an extemporised altar, is a knife and a loaf of bread; and between the two a pile of Eucharistic wafers. The head-dress of the figure is not of an ecclesiastical pattern, and, unlike monks generally, he has long curls of hair hanging on each side his face. The carving evidently represents the consecration of the sacramental elements. The fragile tresseled table, which is covered with a cloth and other details, would seem to indicate that the carving records some event, the history of which has been lost, but which was known to the monks, and was thought worthy of being commemorated in the way we see it.

The eminent archæological writer, Charles Boutell, Esq., speaking of this figure says, "his habit resembles that of Prior Nelond, in his noble brass at Cowfold, in Sussex." In this carving there evidently was a serious purpose to represent sacred subjects. On each side are two large heraldic roses. These side carvings, in most other cases, have a like significance to the central subject to that which supporters have to a shield of arms in an heraldic achievement.

The elbow or arm of this stall has a figurehead carved upon it, much resembling that of a fox, the head being enveloped in a *monk's hood.*

On the next stall eastward is seen what appears to be an agricultural labourer of the period. He wears a plain frock without buttons or ornamentation of any kind; his shoes have pointed toes, his legs are covered with hose, and his forehead is furrowed with deep wrinkles, as if by care. His occupation is that of weeding, and the carving may for that reason be intended to exemplify the month of July. The implements, which he is using, are, first the "wedehoke," a long staff, at the end of which is fixed a short sickle-shaped instrument, held in the left hand; secondly, in his other hand the "crotch," a double-pronged staff, with which large weeds were held down, to be cut with the "wedehoke." A weed of somewhat large dimensions is being wrought upon, and an equally large one is near at hand. In our days of advanced agriculture such huge weeds do not exist, and consequently the "crotch and wedehoke" of the pattern here set forth have ceased to exist. This figure carving of an agricultural labourer is akin to, and happily determines the character of figures existing in a "miserere" at Worcester Cathedral, the implements in the hands of which figures are for the most part broken away, whereas in the Malvern carving both the figure and implement are unbroken and distinct. The side carvings are two birds with long claws, probably intended for wood pigeons or ring doves. On the elbow a most singular compound monster is carved.

The next carving, the most noticeable of the whole series, is one, about the meaning of which conjecture has often been busy. It consists of three mirthful rats in the act of hanging a cat, and the subject is designed and executed with great humour and skill (see illustration). Mr. Thomas Wright, F.S.A., says, "Next

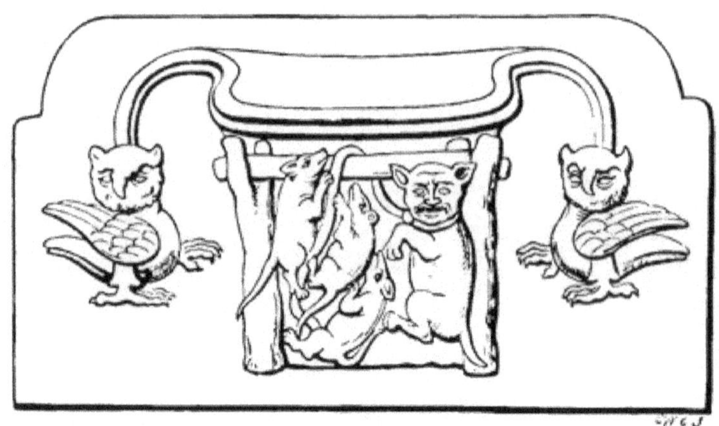

RATS HANGING CAT. *Malvern.*

PRIORY CHURCH, MALVERN.

to the Beastiaries, the most popular books of the middle ages were the collection of fables known under the titles of "Ysopets and Avnets." With these was intimately connected the large romantic, or rather satiric, cycle of the history of "Reynard the Fox," which enjoyed an extraordinary degree of popularity. The fables and romance of Reynard are frequently represented over the stalls. The fable of the rats hanging the cat is represented very grotesquely on the stalls of Great Malvern." Mr. Charles Boutell describes it thus: "Cat hanged on rude kind of gallows, the executioners being rats, or probably mice, three in number, and represented of a comparatively large size *in order to give prominence to the idea.*"

The gallows is a very rude one, being formed of two upright forked trees, with beam fixed cross-ways thereon, of equally rude material. The rope, in running noose, is round the cat's neck, and the cat's protruding eyes, and open mouth, indicate that the end is near. The three rats are enjoying the operation greatly, and are actively employed in tightening the rope. Executed with great skill, it possesses considerable satirical importance. The side ornaments are two owls, believed to be emblematical of wisdom.

The moral of the carving is not far to seek. It is expressive of the sentiment then fast becoming popular, that the oppressed, who were the many and least influential, would rise, ere long, and overcome their oppressors.

Against whom this satire was directed is not so plain. It might have been against the great barons of the period who held their fellow-men in the thraldom of serfdom, and were very insolent in their demeanour. Or this carving may have been directed against ecclesiastical magnates, who then, with something of monarchical despotism, were lording it over God's heritage.

The monk of Malvern, at a period before the existence of the carving says:—

"Now is religion a rydere,
A romere about,
A leader of love-days (or merry meetings),
And a land-buyer,
A prickere on a palfry,
Fro manor to manor,
And heep of hounds at his ears,
As he a Lord were."

And the oppression of the great barons is often spoken of in his pages.

The same monk tells us, by way of pointing a satire against this latter class, the fable of "the rats belling the cat," intimating therein that it is no use belling the cat (who represents the king), if the kittens, who are more numerous, and are pictures of the barons, are not also kept in order.

The carvings of the next stall represent a man holding a scythe, dressed in a short frock or tunic, with plain hip-belt. He has very long curls on each side his face, but no beard. His legs are covered with tight-fitting hose, and his shoes have pointed toes. The implement he is using is a scythe, in form resembling those in use at the present day, with the exception that the upper handle is below the shaft instead of above as is usually the case. In Somersetshire, this kind of handle is still in fashion, showing that the art and device of five centuries of time have done but little to alter the form of this useful implement. This carving represents the month of July, when hay for winter's provision had to be cut down and gathered in.

This figure has recently most incorrectly been said to represent "Old Time," with his scythe, as if it were possible in those "*ages of faith*," for a pagan device to occupy such a position in the Church of Great Malvern.

The next, or fifth stall, like the one last described, represents a workman of the period, in this case a gardener. His dress is similar, but without hip-belt, and with the addition of eight large buttons down the front of his frock or tunic. He has a basket on his right arm filled with rounded fruit, probably apples, or pears; and is holding uplifted in his left hand what appears to be a large pine-apple, without its crest.

The side subjects consist of two large well-carved conventional leaves. The elbow of the one stall has a curious figure thereon partly resembling a boar, and partly like a lion. The other elbow contains a grotesque hooded head of a monk, with protruding lips, receding brow, and face strongly indicative of humor.

The sixth stall has a representation of the ancient notion of a cockatrice, composed of a cock's head and breast, with two legs of a quadruped, and a long tail in serpentine form of the dragon type.

In all artistic works of the middle ages, great partiality was shown for compound monsters, a partiality inherited, as is believed, from our Teutonic forefathers, by whom in a single figure parts of beasts, birds, and reptile forms, are added to the human figure. They were believed to represent spiritual monsters that were then supposed to be inhabiting this lower world. No spirit essence was too ethereal to be incapable of receiving *material* embodiment. Such combinations were the outcome of the exuberant fancies of the artists of those days.

A general belief then prevailed in the actual existence of the most grotesque monsters. The "BEASTERIES," or books of Natural History of the middle ages, are full of such monstrosities. And this belief was without doubt greatly fostered by the magnified and extraordinary accounts given by travellers of the wonderful things they had seen or heard in various parts of the world.

Knowledge was then in the dim dawn, or grey morning of its existence; few things were perfectly understood, and the little known only gave mysterious importance to the great world of truth that lay in darkness beyond.

Others of these carvings do not call for particular notice or description, but the whole of them are worth the most careful attention.

One carving, probably representing the month of May, shows a man holding in each hand branches of roses in full bloom. There is a similar subject portrayed in manner almost identical at Worcester. Compound monsters of the dragon type appear on other stalls, and underneath one seat will be found, as side subjects, very nicely executed, monks' heads in cowls. A winged human figure, of anything but etherial proportions or appearance, on another stall (south side, front row), represents an angel sitting upon a bench and playing a cithern.

On the stalls on the south side (front row), are represented:

1st, a bearded face, with its supporters two beardless faces with long curls; and 2ndly, on a seat adjoining, there appears the half figure of a civilian, without beard, also with curls. These faces are all executed with great skill and spirit. On one of the stall elbows, also, there appears a very well-carved intellectually-shaped head, with a bearded face. These carvings may be taken to represent different orders of men moving before the monks in the fourteenth century.

The carving on one of the back stalls on the south side, showing a man in bed covered with drapery up to his waist, and supported by kneeling attendant, has been referred to in an early chapter of this book, as probably representing the merchant Swelf, and it will repay careful examination (see illustration). The attendant at his head appears to be a woman, the figure at the feet may either be taken to represent a priest with a cup, or, as already suggested, receiving a bag full of money hitherto hid away in concealment. A similar vessel or bag is on the right of the attendant, which the person in bed may either be supposed to be giving up, or about to receive, according as the whole subject may be interpreted. This carving is full of spirit, and, were it divested of the accumulated paint with which it has been for some time covered, it would bear additional evidence of the considerable skill manifest in its execution.

One other subject portrayed on these stalls must have careful attention. It is the figures of the mermaid,* or syren, and the merman, which will be found on one of the second stalls in the back row, on the north side of the chancel. No existences were more firmly believed in, in the middle ages, than the mermaid, and

* "Apollodorus has preserved a fragment of Berosus, which furnishes an early notice of a merman. We gather from his statement that there appeared in the Erythrean, or Persian Gulf, a creature called Oanes, which resembled a fish, but under the fish's head was that of a man, and to it's tail were conjoined women's feet; and further, that it spoke a language which the Chaldeans understood. Oanes taught them many useful arts during the day, and when night came on he plunged into the sea."

"Gervaise of Tilbury (13th century), asserts that mermen and mermaids live in the British ocean; and there is no lack of indications that our ancestors were well acquainted with the form of such creatures."

"Some of the classic poets describe the Sirens with wings."

"Pliny and other writers relate that Tritons and Nereids, or in other words merman and mermaid, have been seen both alive and dead."

"MERMAIDS," *Archæological Journal*, March, 1882

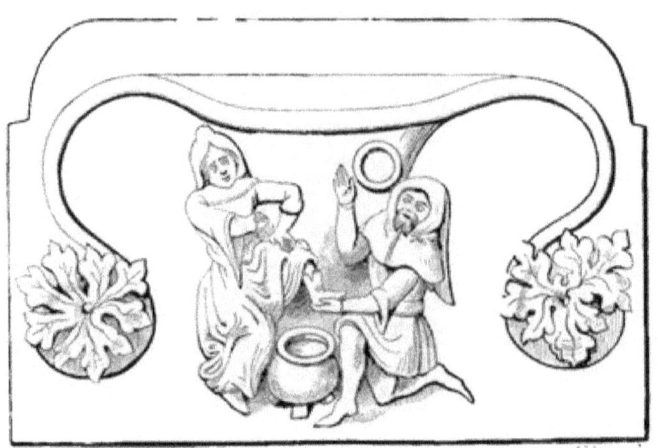

FROM HEREFORD.

CARVER'S MARK FROM LUDLOW.

MERMAID, WITH MIRROR AND COMB.

St. Lawrence, Ludlow.

to none was more attention given in early works of art. "It was one of the most usual of designs on 'Misereres.'"* In Winchester Cathedral, a merman and mermaid are side subjects on a stall. The mermaid with a comb performing her toilet, her long hair covering great part of her body; the merman holding a fish; a frightful sea monster forming the central subject. On stalls at Boston, Lincolnshire, two men, apparently sailors, are in a boat, in attitudes of astonishment at the "sea-maids' music." The head of one is bent down to the water, as if listening intently to the melody of a horn, played by the mermaid. At Bristol Cathedral, the merman is alone with a mirror and large comb. One of the most complete carvings of this kind is found at Lyons Cathedral, in which appears a little family group of these strange creatures. A mermaid is there seen nursing her young in a very affectionate and natural manner, the merman meanwhile playing a fiddle for their mutual edification. Shakespear gives utterance to the belief in mermaids. In "Midsummer Night's Dream" we read:

> "I sat upon a promontory
> And heard a mermaid, on a dolphin's back,
> Uttering such dulcet, and harmonious breath,
> That the rude sea grew civil at her song;
> And certain stars shot madly from their spheres,
> To hear the sea-maid's music."

The merman at Malvern is represented with a beard, and holding a circular mirror in his left hand; the mermaid in her right hand holds a large comb. The side subjects to the stall are two birds' necks and heads.

The illustration of a stall carving at Ludlow (see engraving) showing a mermaid engaged at her toilet is from an accurate drawing, made and obligingly placed at my disposal, as an illustration of the general subject, by W. G. Smith, Esq., of Dunstable, draughtsman and engraver on wood to the "*British Archæological Association.*" To Mr. Smith's skill as an artist I owe the great beauty of most of the illustrations in the present work.

Mr. Smith remarks:—"The misereres in the Church of St.

* Professor Lewellyn Jewett.

Lawrence, Ludlow, are *remarkably fine examples,* and eight of the *best specimens,*—decidedly the best,—are marked with the peculiar mark. It is probable that this mark would be found elsewhere if sought for. It would however require looking for, as, owing to the grain of the wood and the dark colour, the marks (altho' large) are very unobtrusive, and may be easily overlooked." The mark in question accompanies the engraving from Ludlow.

On one of the back stalls, on the south side of the choir, is carved a monk with a pair of bellows, and demon. This remarkable and somewhat indelicate looking carving is engraved in *Carter's Ancient Painting and Sculpture.* There have been many far-fetched and extravagant fancies and conjectures about it, and some have thought there is deep religious significance in it. The *monk* figure there portrayed has been thought to mean the arch enemy of man in religious disguise. The *demon* has been supposed to represent a human being, whose head and long ass's ears shadow forth his stupidity and *vanity*, the use made of the bellows indicating somewhat grossly and profanely the inflation with pride and vanity to which some persons are so willing to submit.

I do not think that anything indelicate was intended by the ancient carvers, and to the men of that day I doubt not the carving had a meaning and significance of which we must content ourselves perhaps to remain in ignorance.

The sower is shown on a stall at Malvern (north side), and a like subject appears in Worcester Cathedral. At Malvern a man in tunic or frock, but without belt, has a box or "hopper" strapped across his person over the left shoulder. Near him is a sack of seed corn, partly emptied. This subject is emblematical of one of the seasons of the year when sowing is performed, that is to say, either spring or autumn. Two birds on the wing form the side subjects, ready perhaps to devour any seed not completely covered.

On one of the back stalls, on the north side, another subject presents itself, a similar one to which is found at Hereford (see illustration). It is thus described by Mr. Boutell:—" Man kneeling on right knee, who is taking off boot from right foot of woman seated opposite to him; woman's uplifted arms are broken off, she has lappet sleeves, and a kerchief hangs down from her hair; behind her is a large jug. Man has his cloak folded up, and tucked into his belt behind him; over his head are ends of some broken object that evidently was held by the woman."

It is remarkable and especially characteristic of these "miserere" carvings everywhere, that scriptural or religious subjects are very rare.

One other carving, underneath the monks' stalls of Malvern, remains to be described. It is that of a man beating down acorns for his swine to eat (north side, second row). Two pigs, of large dimensions, form the side subjects of this piece of work. The man wears a belt. There are similar subjects on stalls at Worcester and other places. It may be that this carving exemplifies the months of October or November.

Mr. Noake, to whose books I have frequently had to refer, says, speaking of a similar carving at Worcester: "It cannot escape notice how frequently the porcine race is introduced into these carvings, together with acorns, oak foliage, &c., of course in illustration of the times when the country was mainly covered with extensive forests, in which millions of these animals found pannage at certain seasons, and in their turn yielded their flesh as substance to their owners. The consumption of so much salted meat throughout the winter, when neither the turnip cultivation nor adequate provision of hay for the cattle in the winter had led to the supply of fresh meat in that season, occasioned the frequency of scurvy and other diseases, to us at the present day comparatively unknown."

The same writer expresses his opinion in another of his works, that, "In general, these monstrous carvings are intended to be typical of evil thoughts and bad passions which are engendered by a life of ease."

CHAPTER XXX.

RECORDS AND REMAINS

"Gather the rosebuds while ye maye,
Olde tyme is stil a-flying,
And the same flower that smiles to-day
Tomorrow will be a-dying."

HERRICK.

"What is a life?—the flourishing array,
Of a proud summer meadow, which today
Wears the green plush, and is tomorrow hay."

QUARLES.

HILLHAMPTON, in the northern portion of the parish of Ocle, Pytchward, county Hereford, anciently belonged to the *Monastery of Malvern Magna* Since the general dissolution of religious houses by Henry VIII. it has been repeatedly sold, and affords no materials worthy of particular note. In the reign of Elizabeth, it was held under the crown by military service, and was considered as possessing *manorial* rights."—*Duncomb's Herefordshire.*

"Manorium de Hill Hampton, nuper monasterio Magnae Malvern nudum spectans, tenetur de dominâ Reginâ *in capite per servitium militare.*"—*Harl. Bibl.* 762.

COLE'S ACCOUNT OF THE CHURCH.

GREAT MALVERN CHURCH IN WORCESTERSHIRE.

June 21, 1746. This Priory Church stands on ye Worcestershire Side under ye Brow of ye vast Ridge of Mountains which are called Malvern Hills. The Priory Church is compleat and a noble Structure it is; a Print of which together with an Ichnography of it may be seen in Dr. Thomas's *Antiquitates Prioratus majoris Malvernie*. When I was here I took an exact account of all ye arms in each of ye Windows, together with all ye Epitaphs which I conceived might be added since ye Publication of Dr. Thomas's Book. But when I came home, finding all ye said Arms in ye Windows not only exactly described by the said Dr. Thomas in his History of this Place, but also by Mr. Abington in his *Account of Great Malvern* Priory added to his History of Worcester Cathedral, p. 204, I shall only mention two or 3 particulars omitted or since put into ye said Church. For an Account of it see also Bp. Tanner's Monastica, p. 625.

The Tower is very beautifull and stands in ye middle of ye Church between ye Nave and Choir and has six Bells remaining in it: 3 others, as I was informed by ye clerk, were sold some 50 or 60 years ago to St. Mary Overy's Church in London. The Pillars which separate ye Nave from ye Side Isles are as heavy and clumsy as ever I saw. There is a new and elegant Altar Peice erected on ye old one which is standing and a very fine and curious peice of work, which is semi-circular and covered both before and behind extreamly high from top to bottom by yellow Tiles with ye arms of several of ye Nobility which shall be mentioned afterwards. The Altar is upon an eminence of a great many steps. The stalls which formerly surrounded ye Choir are all now removed into ye North Isle. Within ye Rails and just before ye Altar on a black marble Slab are these arms, viz: Quarterly, 1 and 4, 2 lions passant for Lygon, 2 and 3, on a chief three crows for Corbyn .. impaling a Chevron inter 3 attires of a stag fixed to the Scalp for Cocks. Under them is this Inscription:—

William Lygon Junr. of Madresfeild.
Esqr. obiit 4 September 1716
Ætatis 26.

This Gentleman was first Husband to ye present Right Honourable the Lady Hardwick of Wimple in Cambridgeshire, and wife to ye Right Hon: ye Lord Chancellor of Great Britain and at this time of writing July 29, Lord High Steward of England. Close to this on ye N. on another these arms at top viz. Lygon.

* * * * *

John Webb. A.M.] He gave 100 pds. in order to get the Queen's Bounty towards the Augmentation of ye Vicarage, which is about 55 pds. per an. His wife was sister to Dr. Baron of Baliol College in Oxford, as ye clerk informed me.

* * * * *

John Wodehouse.] Mr. Blomefeild, p. 769, vol. 1 of his Antiq. of Norfolk says that he lies buried at Watton; but I suppose that must be a mistake and he himself in another part of his Book p. 587 refers to Dr. Thomas's History of this Church. His lady was Daughter to Sr. Denner Strutt of Little Warley in Essex, Bart. His sister Margaret Wodehouse married Thos. Savage of Elmley Castle, Esqr. which was ye Reason of his Interment here where he lived with his said sister who lies buried close to him as ye clerk informed me.

* * * * *

John Whittingham.] Dr. Thomas, p. 36, speaks of him in his History of this Church, as an ingenious Man and a good Herald in these words: Qui fuit vir ingeniosus et in Re Heraldica optime visus.

* * * * *

The South Transept Isle is demolished. There is a handsome Gate of ye Priory standing at ye W. End of ye Church: near which there is a tradition that King Henry ye 7th lived sometimes. The Rev: Mr. Smith is ye present Vicar.

* * * * *

Length of Great Malvern Church from East to West, exclusive of the Lady Chapel, about 180 foot. The Lady Chapel at East end, which is pulled down is 50 foot. Bredth of the Body and Side Isles is 63 Foot: Height of the Tower to the Top of the Pinnacles is 150 Foot. *MS. Note of Mr. Browne Willis.*

British Museum, Add. 5811, f. 119, &c.

The omitted parts are notices of monuments, heralds, and designs on tiles.

LELAND'S ITINERARY. HEARNE. SECOND EDITION. OXFORD, 1744.

Malverne Hilles vol. 4, pt. 2d. 184 b. I marked at *Worcester*, that the high Crestes of Malverne Hilles be to the sight neare to Worcester; but it is 6 Miles to Great Malverne Priory which standeth at the Roote of those Hilles.

Malverne Hilles lye a greate waye in length from South to North. The North-East be the highest. One Gilbert de Clare E. of Gloucester, and* Johanna de Aires. Da. to K.E.I. his wife caused a Fosse to be made in the Crestes of Malverne Hilles in the 3 Prejudice of the Limits and Liberties of the B. of Hereford and Worcester.

Malvern v. 7. pt. 1st 25. The Chase of Malver*n* is bigger than either Wire or Fekenham, and occupiethe a greate parte of Malver*ne* Hills. Great Malver*ne* and Little also is set in the Chase of Malvern. Malverne Chase (as I here say) is in lengthe in some places a XX miles, but Malverne Chase dothe not occupi all Malverne Hills.

LELAND COLLECTANEA DE REBUS BRITANNICIS. HERNE. EDITIO ALTERA. LONDINI, 1770.

Malvern. I. 419. Anno D. 1140. Aldewinus fundator monasterii de Malvern obiit.

Malverne Major. I. 65. Prioratus or. S. Benedicti de Malverne Major. Cella est. Westmonaster. (Wigorn).

Capella S. Joannis Bapt. vicina Prioratui, ubi S. Werstanus martyrium pertulit.

Quidam Aldwine hermita cum suis fratribus incepit ædificare domum de Malverne xviij. anno Gul Conquestor. Gul Conquestor & Henricus ejus filius adjecerunt possessiones.

Henricus deClare comes de Glocestria. Osbernus Pontinm and Richardus Pontium benefactores hujus domus. Avicot in comit. Warwic. cella, ubi sunt 4. monachi.

DEERHURSTE IN GLOUCESTERSHIRE.

Deirhurste v. 6. 78. 79. It standeth as Severne ryver commith doune in læva ripa a mile benethe Theokesbyri.

The site of the Towne, as it is now, is in a manner of a medow, so that when Severne much risith the water commith almoste about the Towne.

It is to be supposed that it was of old tyme lesse subject to waters, and that the Botom of the Severne then deper withoute Chokinge of Sandes dyd at Flouddes less hurte.

It is now but a poore village, and the Lordship longgid of late partely to the Abbate of Theokesbyri. Such parte as Westminstre had was longing to Persore Abbay tyl William Conqueror gave it away. *Derehurst* Abbay had the Residew afore that the House of Derehurste was alienated from the Monasterie of S. Dionise by Varise, to the which it was a Celle, and one Hugo Magason a Monke of S. Dionise was the laste Prior aliene there yn King Edwarde the 4 Dayes, and about that tyme it was dissolvid, and moste of the Landes of it given to Foderingey, and Eton College, as it is said, had sum title. After Sute betwixte the Colleges and the Abbay of Theokesbyri Debatinges was, and after long tracte a final Ende made in Henry the 7 days that the Priory of Goldecliffe, longging then newly to Teokesbyri, should go with the landes to Foderingey College, and *Dehor*hurste onto Theokesbyri.

Bede maketh mention that yn his tyme there was a notable Abbay at *Dere*hurste. It was destroyed by the Danes. Werstanus fledde thens, as it is sayde to Malverne.

---

* Joanne of Acres St.

SITE OF ST. WERSTAN'S ORATORY.

That there was a chapel dedicated to St. Michael, with a residence for seculars, where Banister's cottage* now stands, appears evident, as the cottage is erected on part of the walls. In many places in this cottage are the same kind of curiously inscribed tiles as those which formed part of the pavement of the ancient church. Very many of like tiles have been frequently dug up out of that part converted into a garden. The chimney-piece in the house is formed out of a fine stone, with mouldings, and has the appearance of having been some part of the chapel. It is equally evident that the orchard belonging to the same cottage was a burial-place, from the coffin furniture and bones which are constantly found. As a further proof that it was a cell or hermitage for anchorites, the ancient writings of the house refer to it as "the Hermitage." The proprietor, in removing the earth behind the cottage, found some earthenware pipes constructed so as to slide one into another, evidently for the purpose of conveying the water from St. Ann's well.

SOUTHWELL'S *Guide*, *1825*.

CHARTER FROM THE LAMBETH PALACE LIBRARY.

The following charter or "letter," concerning a visitation to the Malvern Priory of the Archbishop of Canterbury in the 13th century, has been obtained from the Lambeth Palace library, but too late to appear in its proper place. I here insert it because of its intrinsic value, and because of the light it throws upon the condition of the monks in that remote time.

It refers to the reign of the notoriously wicked Prior of Malvern, Wm. de Ledburg, or Ledbury. In the controversy which preceded this Prior's induction into office, the Archbishop is not mentioned as taking any part, and, for the first time, he here claimed right of visitation. He did so as "Primate of all England" and by "Metropolitan right," and in person "directed his steps to the said monastery." He appeared, without doubt, with large retinue, and with considerable pomp, and so presented himself at the Priory gate. When he arrived the Prior was absent, by "reason of certain and lawful reasons," and the Sub-Prior locked and barred the gate against him, and resolutely and persistently refused him admission; and the Archbishop had to turn away, slowly descend the slope of Malvern hill, and return to Canterbury. The Pope of Rome thereupon promulgated "sentence of greater excommunication" against all the official brethren of Malvern. With "an obdurate mind," and "enticed by wicked advice," the monks maintained their refusal for "long space." Eventually, sounder

* The site of "Banister's cottage" is now occupied by a dwelling house, "Bello Sguardo."

counsel prevailed, humbly and devoutly "pardon of the same father" was sought, and after his "corrections" had been submitted to, the brethren of Malvern "reverently accepted the Archbishop's visitation." The "corrections," amongst other things, consisted of a demand for large sums of money, to repay the expenses of the first visit, and it was no doubt a costly affair to the monks.

The following charter completes this page of monkish history.

Littera super visitacione facta in Prioratu Majoris Malvernie in Diocesi Wigorniensi.

Vniversis presentes litteras inspecturis ffrater Willelmus de Alencestre Supprior monasterii majoris Malvernie et ejusdem loci Conventus salutem in domino sempiternam. Ad universitatis vestre noticiam volumus pervenire quod cum reverendus in Christo pater dominus Johannes dei gratia Cantuariensis Archiepiscopus tocius Anglie primas olim Wigorniensem diocesim metropolitano jure visitaret, ac ad dictum monasterium nostrum personaliter declinasset causa sue visitacionis inibi exercende, nos ipsum ad visitacionem hujusmodi admittere recusavimus minus juste. Et quia ipsius visitacionem suscipere noluimus ea vice competenter moniti et inducti ipse papa hoc in fratrem Willelmum de Ledebyre Priorem me Suppriorem .. Precentorem .. Sacristam et Celerarium dicti monasterii nostri majoris excommunicationis sentenciam promulgavit quia pravo seducti consilio per longa tempora sustinuimus animo indurato. Nunc autem saniori usi consilio super hiis ab eodem patre veniam petivimus, et eum personaliter ad visitacionem hujusmodi venientem die Jovis quinto die Mensis Julii instantis, Anno domini Mo. cco. LXXXo. quinto admisimus et ipsius visitacionem suscepimus reverenter, atque correcciones quas fecit ibidem subivimus humiliter et devote, presente et consenciente dicti .. Prioris nostri certis et legitimis ex causis tunc absentis procuratore ad visitacionem dicti patris suo nomine suscipiendam specialiter constituto . In quorum omnium testimonio presentes litteras fieri fecimus sigillo communi Capituli nostri munimine roboratas . Actum et datum publice in Capitulo nostro . Anno Mense et die superius annotatis.

Letter concerning a visitation made in the Priory of Great Malvern in the Diocese of Worcester.

To all those about to inspect the present letters, Brother William de Alencester (or William of Alcester), Subprior of the Monastery of Great Malvern, and the Convent of the same place, greeting in the Lord everlasting. We will that it come to the notice of all of you that when the reverend father in Christ the lord John by God's grace Archbishop of Canterbury, Primate of all England, before this time visited the Diocese of Worcester by metropolitan right, and personally directed his steps to the said our monastery with the intent of exercising his visitation therein, we refused to admit him to such visitation unjustly; And because we were unwilling to receive his visitation, although on that behalf well advised and warned, the Pope himself thereupon promulgated a sentence of greater excommunication against Brother William de Ledbury the Prior, me the Subprior,—the Precentor, and—Sacristan and Cellarer of the said our Monastery, because enticed by wicked advice we for a long space of time maintained our refusal with an obdurate mind; But now using more sound counsel upon these matters, we have sought pardon of the same father, and have admitted him coming personally to such visitation on Thursday the fifth day of this present month of July in the year of our Lord one thousand two hundred and eighty five, and have reverently accepted his visitation, and undergone humbly and devoutly the corrections which he made therein, in the presence and with the assent of the proctor of the said Our Prior, then absent by reason of certain and lawful reasons, specially appointed to receive the visitation of the said father in his name. In witness of all which things we have caused the present letters to be made, corroborated by the impression of the Common Seal of our Chapter. Done and given publicly in our Chapter, in the year month and day above mentioned.

Malvern, and the Church of St. Andrew, Pershore.

Resignacio Prioris et Conventus Malvernie super Ecclesia Sancti Andree de Perssora.

Vniversis Christi fidelibus presens Scriptum inspecturis Thomas de Wychio Prior Majoris Malvernie et ejusdem loci Conventus salutem in domino. Vestra noverit universitas quod spontanea voluntate unanimiter et imperpetuum concedimus et dimittimus venerabili patri Willelmo Dei gratia Abbati nostro Westmonasteriensi et fratribus nostris ejusdem loci totum jus quod habuimus in advocacionem ecclesie sancti Andree de Perssora et in ipsa ecclesia et in omnibus Capellis et rebus aliis ad eam pertinentibus necnon et in dominicis decimis ejusdem Abbatis nostri et in omnibus aliis decimiis tam majoribus quam minutis tam in manerio de Perssora quam in adjacentibus villis. Item volumus quod idem Abbas noster et fratres nostri Westmonasterienses habeant similiter grangiam nostram et viam ad eam cum toto redditu quem in eadem villa de Perssora tempore istius concessionis habuimus Et ne liceat nobis inposterum aliquo ingenio vel arte quicquam juris in predictis ecclesia vel aliis rebus vendicare ! omnibus instrumentis que de omnibus supramemoratis habuimus vel habemus imperpetuum renunciamus. Vt igitur hec nostra concessio irrefragabiliter perpetua firmitate nitatur presentis scripti testimonio et sigilli capituli nostri munimine eam duximus roborandum. Hiis testibus Domino S. Episcopo Wygorniensi et cetera.

Resignation of the Prior and Convent of Malvern concerning the Church of St. Andrew, Pershore (1217)

To all the faithful of Christ about to inspect the present writing Thomas de Wyche, Prior of Great Malvern, and the Convent of the same place, greeting in the Lord. Know all of you that of our own free will unanimously and for ever we grant and demise to the Venerable father William by the grace of God our abbot of Westminster and to our brethren of the same place all the right which we had in the advowson of the Church of St. Andrew, Pershore, and in the same church and all in the Chapels and other things appertaining thereunto, moreover also in the demesne tithes of the same our Abbot and in all other tithes both great and small as well in the manor of Pershore as in the adjacent vills. Also we will that the same our Abbot and our brethren of Westminster have likewise our grange and the road thereto with the whole rent which we had in the same town of Pershore at the time of that grant. And, that it be not lawful for us henceforward by any device or artifice to claim aught of right in the church or other things aforesaid, we for ever renounce all the instruments which we have had or have concerning all the things above mentioned. In order, therefore, that this our grant inviolably may possess perpetual validity, we have thought right that it should be corroborated by the testimony of the present writing and by the protection of the seal of our chapter.

These being the witnesses, the Lord Silvester, Bishop of Worcester, etc.

ADDITIONAL MSS., IN BRITISH MUSEUM, RELATING TO MALVERN.

CARTÆ ANTIQUÆ. H 29.

Henry I. to Malvern Priory, "Quietanciam de assartis in foresta de Malvern 1128."

An account of Malvern Church by Vertue. Chiefly inscriptions, 1737-1747

Land held by Malvern Priory in Kidderminster 1267-1274.

Decree relating to disafforestation of Malvern Chace 1632-1664.

Grant of Land in Longdon.

Exchange of land in Morton 13th century.

Church notes and drawings (about 1748).

Grant of land in Malvern (temp Henry 3).

Grant by John Prior of Grange at Eston A.D. 1275.

Many documents relating to the Priory of Little Malvern.

AGARD'S "INDEX," Vol. 41, XCIV. p. 322.

SALOP.—TWO WARRANTS, ROLL 23.—20 EDW. I.

Prior of Great Malvern claims to hold pleas of the Crown and to have the goods of the condemned and fugitives in Doules.

Prior holds 2 Courts in the Manor of Doules.

GLOUCESTER.—TWO WARRANTS, ROLL 23.—15 EDW. I.

Prior of Great Malvern claims to have view of Frank pledge, etc., in Langeney Manor, co. Glouc.

Prior says his Priory is a cell of Westminster, and that he is perpetual Prior, and on his privileges generally.

REV. R. W. EYTON'S NOTES ON ROYAL CHARTERS OF HENRY I. (Brit. Mus. 31943 f. 76)

NOTE ON HENRY I.'s CHARTER TO MALVERN MAGNA, PRINTED IN DUGDALE'S *MONASTICON*, Vol. iii., p. 447.

About Sept. 1126.

Simon, Bishop of Worcester, was elected May 8, 1125.

Richard, Bishop of Hereford, died Aug. 15, 1127.

The king after May 8, 1125, was next in England, Sept. 11, 1126. The deed therefore passed between Sept. 11, 1126, and Aug. 15, 1127. We have no historical notice of Henry I. being at Hereford in that interval. This deed proves the fact.

Milo de Glocester attests, but there is reason to believe that his father is alive, and attests even later, *i.e.*, Aug., 1127. Milo's eldest son, Roger, was married and knighted in or before 1141. One plea of Walter de Gloec is recorded in the Pipe Roll of 1130. (Rot. p. 107.)—But it is certain that then he was dead, for Milo is in perdonis de daneg'. . . . Milo had therefore then inherited from Walter, ergo Walter was dead. The king probably visited Hereford in Sept., 1126, while conveying his prisoner, Walleran, to Bridgnorth.

MALVERN VICARS.

"So life, a world of shadows, passes on!
And after some few joys and many cares
Our journeys end: our weary heads repose
In their last resting place."

MALVERN MAGNA.

PATRONS.	INCUMBENTS.	REGISTERS.
Prior et Conventus Majoris Malverne.	Randulphus de Pidele, id. Dec. 1269 ..	Giff. f. 29. a.
	Gareland de Ledebury, pbr. 1287	ib. f. 289. a.
	Robertus de Bruera, cap Jun. 1313.. ..	Reg. sede. vac. f. 816
	Thomas de Blourton, 4 Kal. Apr. 1338 ..	Hem. f. 15. b.
	Thomas Alyn, pbr. 20 Kal. Feb. 1338 ..	R. sed. vac. f. 148. b. 149
	Nicholaus le Smythes de Poywyke, pbr. 10 Julii. 1349	Wolst. v. 2. f. 17, a.
	Thomas le Clerk de Hereford, pbr. 21 Aug. 1349	Reg. sed. vac. f. 128. a.
	Will'us Martyn, pbr. 9 Nov. 1354	Brian. f. 11. b.
	Joh. Smythes, 6 Julii, 1362..	Barnet f. 2.
	Nicholaus Bacon, 6 non Julii, 1367.. ..	Wittlesey, f. 15. a.
	Henricus Cantelopp, pbr. 7 Apr. 1385 ..	wak. f. 41. a.
	Jeronymus Orchard, Cap. 1 Maii, 1424 ..	Morg. f. 26. b.
	Ric ap Gryffyth, cap. 17 Jan. 1471	Carp. v. 2. f. 23. b.
	Johannes Stevyn, cap. 20 Maii, 1475 .	ib. f. 70. b.
	Ricardus Robyns, alias Glover, cap. 21 Aug. 1490	S. Gygl. f. 3. b.
	Will. Jermyne, 1556	
Johannes Lumley mil d'us Lumley.	Will'us Jermayne, cl. 18 Maii, 1575.. ..	R. 32. Bul. f. 11. a.
Jacobus Rex.	Edmundus Rea, cl. A. B. 10 Sept. 1612 ..	ib. Parry. f. 99. a.
Carolus Rex.	Nicholaus Garret, cl. 26 Febr. 1640 ..	R. 33. f. 22. a.
Henricus Bromley de Holt, arm.	Johannes Ballard, cl. A. B. 12 Mart. 1643 ..	ib. f. 30. a.
	Ricardus Smith, cler. 1656..	Reg. Parochial.
	Jacobus Badger, 1669	Reg. Parochial.
Gul. Bromley de civ. Wigorn. Arm.	Thomas Hassel, cl. 15 Apr. 1692	R. 34. f. 55. a.
Gul. Bromley de Holt	Thomas Beardmore, cl. A. B. 5 Oct. 1698 ..	ib. f. 66. a.
Gul. Bromley de Holt	Harricus Hill, cl. 17 Feb. 1701	ib. f. 80. a.
Johnnes Bromley de Holt, arm. et de Horseheath.	Johannes Webb, cl. A. A. 24 Jan. 1708 ..	ib. f. 94. a.
Johnnes Bromley de Holt, arm. et de Horseheath.	Johannes Smith, cl. A. B. 12 June, 1730 ..	R. 35. f. 15. b
Thomas lord Foley.	Thomas Phillips, B. A. 8. Jan. 1758 ..	
Hon. Edward Foley.	Richard Graves, D. D. 19 Sept. 1801 ..	
dw. Thos. Foley, Esq.	Henry Card, M. A. 30 June, 1815	
Lady E. Foley.	T. Wright, M. A. 1844	
" "	John Rashdall, M. A. 1850	
" "	George Fisk, L. L. B. 1856	
" "	I. Gregory Smith, M. A. 1872	

CHAPTER XXXI.

CONCLUSION.

WITH the "Records and Remains" of the last chapter, and the brief account of the Incumbents of Great Malvern, my book comes to an end.

Concerning its antiquities much more might have been written, and many additions could have been made to the history of the church and monastery. I have described, to the best of my power, the commencement of the Priory, and have taken much pains to be as full and accurate as possible. I have opened up to the reader some chapters of monkish history, have told the inner life, labours, trials, difficulties, and worldly vicissitudes of the monks. Matters hitherto involved in obscurity I have laboured to make plain. Through many an old book have I waded, seeking for information. Documentary evidence of considerable magnitude has been sought for and found, as mentioned in the preface; and in connection with the dissolution especially, but with other points as well, I have given very much of hitherto unpublished information. Of the church's history subsequent to the Reformation, in the reign of Edward VI., and other successive reigns, I have been able to say something. Last of all, of the various restorations of the church, beginning in the middle of the last century, and reaching down to the present time; of all these I have been able to add considerable items of reliable notices. Much that could have been done has not been done. I have taken no notice of the Priory's unrivalled collections of old tiles, or tesselated pavement, and no adequate description has been given of its rich store of ancient glass paintings. These together are of sufficient interest to form subject matter for a second volume.

To produce a work such as this, or to see such work undertaken by another, has been the dream and desire of a portion of my life-time. As already stated, often have I urged upon gentlemen, in every way competent, the execution of such pleasant duty: and to several I have offered the use of materials in my possession. I did so in vain, and at length have found the realisation of my desire forced upon myself. I am conscious of many shortcomings, and of much inability, but the work, such as it is, I now give to the public. Its success, or non-success, I commit to the arbitration of time. My work has ended,—my last page has been reached.

"What is writ, is writ;
Would it were worthier."

Since thine unbroken early day,
How many a race has passed away,
In charnel vault to moulder;
Yet nature round thee breathes an air,
Serenely bright, and softly fair,
To charm the awed beholder.

Thy past is but a gorgeous dream,
And time glides by us like a stream,
While musing on thy story;
And sorrow prompts a deep alas!
That like a pageant thus should pass
To wreck such human glory.

APPENDIX.

I.

The Priory of Great Malvern is only once mentioned in the following grant, but is so in a remarkable connection. It appears that a Lord John de Rivers, of Burgate, had certain possessions in the manor of Kidderminster, and property in and over certain "men" within that manor, "as well free as villein." These *men*, with the " lands tenements and all other appurtenances," he grants and gives, in "free pure and perpetual alms," to "Brother John Prior of Mayden Bradley" (county Wilts), "and the leper sisters of the same place, and the brethren serving God"; and amongst a great number of others so disposed of and dealt with, the "Prior of Malvern" is mentioned.

Malvern Priory owned land in Kidderminster, as well as the adjoining manor of Dowles and Mitton, and had secured to it, by the charter Henry I., the "Land of Northwood between Hawebrooke and Lyndringesich, from Henedwye in the Severn"; and more than one Malvern Prior was involved in suits at law and had to pay annual fees for the right of holding courts, or "pleas of the Crown," in the manor. It may be that Lord de Rivers in some of these suits had obtained property in the adjoining possessions belonging to Malvern, and that it was this he had devised to the "leper sisters of Mayden Bradley."

Dowles and Northwood remained the property of Malvern Priory till the Dissolution in the sixteenth century. Whatever it was Lord de Rivers had to demise pertaining to the Prior of Malvern, this charter shows us that at that time property was claimed in "men," as being "bound in all service," as well as "in rent."

It is also clear the said deed claims right of transfer of "all fealties and services," "with all things which by any means can arise to the aforesaid *land* or *men*." The said Lord de Rivers in so granting and disposing absolves himself "absolutely from all manner of suits or earthly demands," either in the tenements or the "men."

British Museum, Harley Charter, 55 D. 25.

Grant by John de Rivers, Lord of Burgate, co. Dors.' (?) to John, Prior of Mayden-Bradley, co. Wilts., and the lepers there, of certain "men" within the Manor of Kidderminster, co. Worc., in exchange for other "men" and their lands within the Manor of Burgate, which the said Prior held by gift of the ancestors of the said John.

Obs.—In the following Latin documents the punctuation of the MSS. is in the main preserved.

Omnibus Christi fidelibus presens scriptum visuris vel audituris Johannes de Ripariis dominus de Burgate eternam in domino salutem.

Noverit universitas vestra me concessisse et in escambium atque in liberam, puram, et perpetuam elemosinam dedisse et hoc presenti scripto confirmasse fratri Johanni Priori de Maydenebradeleg'e et sororibus leprosis ejusdem loci et fratribus ibidem Deo servientibus et eorum successoribus omnes homines subscriptos tam liberos quam villanos in Manerio de Kyddeministro cum eorum terris, tenementis, et cum omnibus pertinentiis suis, videlicet Ricardum de Petra, Ricardum de la Lake, Robertum de la Holeweye, Henricum de Frenis, et totum servicium et redditum predictorum Prioris et conventus de Maydenbradeleg'e in quibus nobis pro tenementis suis seu aliis rebus infra manerium de Kydeministro tenebantur, Magistrum Hugonem de Cancia, Willelmum de Wythinton', Ricardum Franceys, Willelmum Fuzel, Letitiam de Trimpeleg'e, Nicholaum Aufre, Johannem Le Bule, Robertum le Turnur, Ricardum Ravenig', Priorem Malvernie, Hugonem de Bosco, Henricum de Caldewelle, Robertum de Bruneshope, et terram que vocatur Fazenacre, Henricum de

Hodenhale, Adam de Assevenne, Matillidem Cuppild, Symonem Champeneys, Cristinam Becke, Willelmum de Chiltenham, Walterum Gest, Robertum Parvum de Northewode cum eorum terris et tenementis, homagiis, fidelitatibus, serviciis, et liberis consuetudinibus, redditibus, releviis, eschaetis, sectis, placitis, Herizetis, et perquisitis, et cum omnibus pertinentiis suis, et rebus omnibus que de predicta terra et hominibus cum pertinentiis quocunque modo accidere possint. Dedi etiam eisdem et concessi omnes villanos subscriptos in predicto manerio habitantes, videlicet, Nicholaum Pukel, Henricum Le Parde, Willelmum Pukel, Hugonem de La Hulle, Adam filium Petronille, Margeriam viduam, Henricum filium Ade, Walterum filium Tecle, Johannem de la More, Willelmum Coleman, Robertum Bercarium, Henricum Driu, Walterum Red, Editham de Haberlega, Osbertum de Haberlega. cum eorum terris et tenementis. et sequelis eorum et cum omnibus catallis suis mobilibus et immobilibus. serviciis. Redditibus. auxiliis. tallagiis. consuetudinibus. Bosci liberationibus operacionibus. et Bensipes. attachiamentis. placitis. querelis. amerciamentis sectis. et cum omnibus aliis pertinentiis suis et rebus quocunque modo nominentur que de predictis hominibus tam liberis quam villanis quocunque modo vel aliquo jure accidere possint.

Habendum et tenendum de me et heredibus meis predictis Priori de Maydenebradeleg'e, et sororibus leprosis ejusdem loci. et fratribus ibidem Deo servientibus et eorum successoribus omnes homines predictos tam liberos quam villanos cum eorum serviciis et cum omnibus aliis pertinentiis et rebus pretactis predictos homines et terras tangentibus quocunque nomine nominentur in omnibus libertatibus et liberis consuetudinibus ad predictos homines et terras spectantibus in liberam puram et perpetuam elemosinam absque ullo retenemento mihi et heredibus meis, Libere Integre et pacifice. solute. et quiete. ab omnimodis sectis. querelis. et exactionibus mundanis inperpetuum. videlicet ita solute quod omnes homines predictorum Prioris et Conventus infra manerium de Kydemnster' habetantes nec eorum tenementa in nulla re nobis et heredibus nostris pertinente nec alicui sint intendentes vel respondentes nisi tantummodo predictis Priori et conventui et eorum successoribus et Curie sue inperpetuum. Et Ego Johannes de Riperiis et heredes vel assignati mei omnes predictos homines tam liberos quam villanos cum eorum terris. serviciis. redditibus. sectis. sequelis. catallis. consuetudinibus. et cum omnimodis aliis pertinentiis et rebus omnibus quocunque nomine nominentur predictos homines et terras tangentibus predictis Priori et sororibus leprosis de Maydenebradeleg'e et fratribus ibidem Deo servientibus sicuti liberam puram et perpetuam elemosinam contra omnes homines et feminas mortales tenemur inperpetuum warantizare. acquietare. et defendere.

Pro hac autem donacione. concessione et carte mee confirmacione predicti Prior et sorores leprosæ de Maydenebradelege et ejusdem loci fratres dederunt concesserunt et quieteclamaverunt pro se et successoribus suis michi Johanni de Ripariis et heredibus meis omnes homines subscriptos cum eorum terris et tenementis. serviciis. et cum omnibus pertinentiis suis. quos scilicet predicti Prior et conventus de dono antecessorum meorum quondam habuerunt infra manerium de Burgate. videlicet. Johannem de Brumhore. qui tenet tria tenementa cum pertinentiis suis. Johannem Trapel. et Agnetem relictam Roberti Trapel. et Aliciam Dorkes. et Johannem clericum de Forde qui etiam tenet tria tenementa cum pertinentiis suis. et Thomam Papam. Godefridum le Turner. et Magistrum Hospitalis de fforde. Agnetem Bordel. Johannem Bordel. Radulphum Grucy cum eorum terris homagiis fidelitatibus. Wardis. maritagiis. releviis. Redditibus serviciis. Hereztis. escachetis. et cum omnibus aliis pertinentiis suis et rebus omnibus que de predictis terra et hominibus quocunquemodo accidere possint.

Dederunt etiam et concesserunt predicti. Prior de Maydenebradelege et ejusdem loci conventus et quieteclamaverunt pro se et successoribus suis predicto Domino Johanni de Ripariis omnes villanos subscriptos infra predictum manerium de Burgate. videlicet. Robertum Opin. Ricardum Le Nywe. Godefridum Mercatorem. Reginaldum Wranne. Reginaldum Le Nyweman. Ricardum Ailmer.

Cristinam viduam. Johannem Wranne. Ricardum de ffrogeham. Robertum de ffrogeham. Rogerum Cole de ffrogeham. Robertum de La Hulle. Constanciam relictam Johannis Coci. Radulfum Dun. Philippum Joldewyne. Walterum de Hazlewelle. Ricardum Cridiho. Willelmum Sumer. Walterum Brunig. Ricardum de Marisco. Walterum Wendekake. Johannem Le Chnizt. Robertum Le Pur. Ysabellam relictam Kywel. cum eorum terris et tenementis et sequelis eorum et cum omnibus catallis suis mobilibus et immobilibus, serviciis, Redditibus. auxiliis. tallagiis. consuetudinibus attachiamentis placitis querelis. amerciamentis. Sectis. et cum omnibus aliis pertinentiis suis et rebus quocunque modo nominentur que de predictis hominibus tam liberis quam villanis quocunque modo vel aliquo jure accidere possint.

In cujus rei testimonium ego predictus Johannes de Ripariis parti illius scripti que penes predictos religiosos remanet pro me et heredibus vel assignatis meis sigillum meum in robur perpetue firmitatis apposui. Et predicti Prior et conventus illi parti que penes me et heredes meos residet commune sigillum suum una cum sigillo Prioris pro se et successoribus suis apposuerunt.

Hiis testibus. Dominis. Nicholao de Menles. Johanne de Kernet. Rogero de Mewe..., Elya de ffaleyse. militibus. Johanne de Wutton. Roberto Ernys. Henrico de Hacche. Randulfo de Mere. Henrico de Padenore, Magistro Hugone de Cantia. Ricardo de Muleford. Hugone de Bosco. Willelmo de Heymore Henrico de Caldewelle. Thoma de Stone. Et multis aliis.

The words "Carta Cyrographata" cut through at the top by an indented line.

Seal of arms of John de Riveres.
(in fine preservation.)

TRANSLATION.

. To all the faithful of Christ about to See or hear the present writing John de Rivers, Lord of Burgate, everlasting greeting in the Lord.

Let the whole body of you know that I have granted and given in free, pure, and perpetual alms, and confirmed by this present writing to Brother John, Prior of Mayden-Bradley, and the leper sisters of the same place and the brethren therein serving God, and their successors, all the "men" hereafter written as well free as villein, in the Manor of Kidderminster with their lands, tenements, and with all their appurtenances, namely Richard de Petra, Richard de La Lake, Robert de La Holeweye, Henry de Frenis, and all the service and rent of the aforesaid Prior and Convent of Mayden-Bradley, whereby they are bound to us for their tenements or other things within the Manor of Kidderminster, Master Hugh de Kent, William de Wythinton, Richard Franceys, William Fuzel, Lettice de Trimpelege, Nicholas Aufre, John Le Bule, Robert Le Turner, Richard Ravenig', the Prior of Malvern, Hugh de Bosco, Henry de Caldewelle, Robert de Bruneshope, and the land which is called Fazenacre, Henry de Hodenhale, Adam de Assevenne, Matildis Cuppild, Symon Champeneys, Christina Becke, William de Chiltenham, Walter Gest, Robert Parvus (Little ?) of Northwood, with their lands and tenements, homages, fealties, services and free customs, rents, reliefs, escheats, suits, pleas, heriots and perquisites, and with all their appurtenances, and with all things which by any means can arise from the aforesaid land and men; I have given also to the same, and granted, all the villeins undermentioned inhabiting in the aforesaid manor, namely, Nicholas Pukel, Henry Le Parde, William Pukel, Hugh de La Hulle. Adam son of Petronilla, Margery Widow, Henry son of Adam, Walter son of Tecla, John de La More, William Coleman, Robert Bercarius (Shepherd ?), Henry Driu, Walter Red, Edith de Haberley, Robert de Haberley, with their lands and tenements and their suits (*i.e.* families), and with all their chattels, moveable and immoveable, services, rents, aids, tallages, customs, wood-deliveries, operations, and reaping-services (or Bedripes), attachments, pleas, complaints, amerciaments, suits (*i.e.* court service), and with all other their appurtenances, and things by whatever manner they are called, which may arise by any means and in any right from the aforesaid men as well free as villeins.

To have and to hold of me and my heirs, to the aforesaid Prior of Mayden-Bradley and the leper sisters of the same place, and the brethren therein serving God and their successors, all the men aforesaid as well free as villein, with their services and with all other appurtenances and things beforementioned touching the men and lands aforesaid by whatever name they are called in all the liberties and free customs belonging to the men and lands aforesaid, in free, pure, and perpetual alms, without any reservation to me and my heirs, freely, wholly, and peacefully, absolutely and quietly, from all manner of suits, complaints, and earthly demands, namely so absolutely that all the men of the aforesaid Prior and Convent within the Manor of Kidderminster dwelling, and their tenements be answerable or responsible in nothing appertaining to us and our heirs or to any one else, except only to the aforesaid Prior and convent and their successors and their court for ever. And I John de Rivers and my heirs or assigns am and are bound for ever to warrant acquit and defend all the aforesaid men, as well free as villein, with their lands, services, rents, suits, followings, chattels, customs, and with all manner of other appurtenances, and all things by whatsoever name they are called concerning the aforesaid men and lands, to the aforesaid Prior and leprous sisters of Mayden-Bradley and the Brethren therein serving God, as free, pure, and perpetual alms against all mortal men and women.

But for this gift, grant, and confirmation of my charter the aforesaid Prior and leprous sisters of Mayden-Bradley and the Brethren of the same place have given, granted, and quit-claimed for themselves and their successors to me John de Rivers and my heirs all the men undermentioned with their lands and tenements, services and with all their appurtenances, those namely which the aforesaid Prior and convent formerly held by gift of my ancestors within the Manor of Burgate, namely, John de Brumhore, who holds three tenements, with their appurtenances, John Trapel, and Agnes relict of Robert Trapel, and Alice Dorkes, and John clerk of Forde who also holds three tenements with their appurtenances, and Thomas Pope, Godfrey Le Turner, and the Master of the

Hospital of Forde, Agnes Bordel, John Bordel, Ralph Grucy with their lands, homages, fealties, wards, marriages, reliefs, rents, services, heriots, escheats, and with all other their appurtenances and all things which may arise in any way whatever concerning the aforesaid land and men.

Also the aforesaid Prior of Mayden Bradley and the convent of the same place have given and granted and quit-claimed for themselves their successors to the aforesaid Lord John de Rivers all the villeins undermentioned within the aforesaid manor of Burgate, namely, Robert Othin, Richard Le Nywe, Godfrey Mercer, Reginald Wranne, Reginald Le Nyweman, Richard Ailmer, Christina widow, John Wranne, Richard de Frogeham, Robert de Frogeham, Roger Cole of Frogeham, Robert de La Hulle, Constance relict of John Cook, Ralph Dun, Philip Joldewyne, Walter de Hazelwelle, Richard Cridiho, William Sumer, Walter Brunig, Richard de Marisco, Walter Wendekake, John Le Chnizt, Robert Le Pur, Isabella relict of Kywel, with their lands and tenements and their suits and with all their chattels moveable and immoveable, services, rents, aids, tallages, customs, attachments, pleas, complaints, amercements, suits, and with all other their appurtenances and things by whatever manner they are called, which can in any manner whatever or by any right arise concerning the aforesaid men, as well free as villein.

In witness whereof I the aforesaid John de Rivers have appended to the part of that writing which remains in possession of the aforesaid religious persons for myself and my heirs, my seal as a corroboration of the perpetual stability thereof. And the aforesaid Prior and convent have appended to that part which rests in possession of me and my heirs, their common seal together with the seal of the Prior, for themselves and their successors.

These being the witnesses: Sirs Nicholas de Menles, John de Kevnet, Roger de Mene..., Elyas de Falaise, Knights; John de Wutton, Robert Ernys, Henry de Hacche, Randulf de Mere, Henry de Padenore, Master Hugh de Kent, Richard de Muleford, Hugh de Bosco, William de Heymore, Henry de Caldewelle Thomas de Stone, and many others.

II.

Translations of the following documents, from Cotton MSS. in British Museum (Faustina A. III), have been given on pages 45 to 48 of this work.

Privilegium Adriani Pape quarti de cella Sancte Marie Malvernie.

Adrianus Episcopus servus servorum Dei dilectis filiis Gervasio abbati ecclesie sancti Petri Westmonasteriensis ejusque fratribus salutem et apostolicam benedictionem. Quociens a viris ecclesiasticis talia postulantur que et equitati conveniant. et a racionis tramite non recedant animo nos decet animo libenti concedere et petencium vota effectu debemus prosequenti complere. Eapropter, dilecti in domino filii, vestris justis postulacionibus gratum impertuum assensum. et ecclesie beati Petri Westmonasteriensis in qua divino mancipati estis obsequio jura et omnia bona sua integra volentes et illibata servare cellam sancte Marie de Malverna quam monasterio vestro pleno jure constat esse subjectam cum omnibus pertinentiis suis vobis et per vos ecclesie vestre auctoritate apostolica confirmamus. et presentis scripti patrocinio communimus. Statuentes ut nulli omnino hominum liceat futuris temporibus hanc paginam nostre confirmacionis infringere vel ei aliquatenus contraire. Si quis autem hoc attemptare presumpserit indignationem omnipotentis Dei et beatorum Petri et Pauli apostolorum ejus se noverit incursurum. Datum Laterani. viij Kl'. Jun'.

Carta Godefridi Wygorniensis Episcopi quod in Cella Majoris Malvernie nullam habeat jurisdictionem.

Universis Christi fidelibus ad quos littere presentes pervenerint, Godefridus permissione divina Minister ecclesie Wygorniensis salutem in domino.

Litteras apostolicas non cancellatas non abolitas nec in aliqua sui parte viciatas inspeximus continentes quod Abbas et Conventus Westmonasteriensis Londoniensis Dioceseos cum omnibus cellis suis et Prioratibus et precipue cum Prioratu Majoris Malvernie. et Monachis earundem cellarum et Prioratuum ad Romanam ecclesiam nullo pertinent mediante et ab omni lege Dioceseos ac jurisdiccione ordinaria sint exempti. Nos itaque pro nobis et successoribus nostris predictam exempcionem in ipso Prioratu majoris Malvernie nostre Dioceseos veraciter agnoscentes, predictum Prioratum et Monachos loci ejusdem ab omni jurisdictione Episcopali ac ordinaria exemptos et liberos profitemur. necnon. solis Abbati et Conventui Westmonasterii subesse debere. secundum quod in Privilegiis diversorum retro Romanorum Pontificum concessis eisdem plenius continetur. Ad hec cum inter predictos... Abbatem et Conventum Westmonasteriensem, ac Priorem et Monachos Majoris Malvernie supradicte ex parte una et nos ex altera super jure patronatus dicti Prioratus necnon super possessione vel quasi jure visitandi dictum Prioratum et Monachos ejusdem ac corrigendi corrigenda removendique removendos ac procuraciones racione visitacionis ab eisdem petendi exigendi et recipiendi exorta esset materia questionis, nos pro nobis et successoribus nostris jus patronatus sive advocationem in ipso Prioratu et eciam omnimodam jurisdictionem legitimam Dioceseos et ordinariam in predictis Prioratu ac monachis ejusdem ad eosdem Abbatem et Conventum Westmonasteriensem pleno jure recognoscimus pertinere, et omne jus et clamium que habemus vel habere poterimus in futurum seu possessionem vel quasi legitime Dioceseos seu ordinarie jurisdictionis nobis seu predecessoribus nostris quandocunque et qualitercunque acquisitam sponte pure et absolute remittimus et eisdem Abbati et Conventui Westmonasteriensi pro nobis et successoribus nostris concedimus per presentes. Nec Priores Prioratus ejusdem qui pro tempore fuerint aut Monachi ad obedienciam prestandam nobis vel successoribus nostris pro Prioratu ipso aut pertinentibus ad eundem aliquatenus teneantur exceptis dumtaxat ecclesiis parochialibus porcionibus et pensionibus ecclesiasticis ad dictum

Prioratum pertinentibus quas in proprios usus optinent in quibus quidem ecclesiis porcionibus et pensionibus ecclesiasticis canonicam jurisdictionem nobis et successoribus nostris reservamus. Ita tamen quod procuraciones aliquas ab eisdem ecclesiis porcionibus et pensionibus seu personis racione eorundem exigere non possimus. In cujus rei testimonium sigillum nostrum presentibus est appensum. Datum apud Westmonasterium die Veneris in vigilia sancti Leonardi Abbatis. Anno gratie Mo. CCo. octagesimo iijo.

Compositio inter Westmonasterium et Malverniam.

Vniversis Christi fidelibus presens scriptum inspecturis Thomas de Wychio Prior Majoris Malvernie et ejusdem loci Conventus salutem in domino. Vestra noverit universitas quod cum ex concessione venerabilis patris nostri Willelmi Dei gratia Abbatis et fratrum nostrorum Westmonasteriensium liceat nobis de nostra vel eorum congregacione vacante Prioratu nostro nobis Priorem eligere ne liberalitas sua eis sit capciosa, concedimus et profitemur nos eis esse subjectos in hunc modum videlicet quod electum nostrum Abbati nostro et fratribus nostris presentabimus apud Westmonasterium eorum assensum requirentes et eleccione ejus dum tamen ydoneus fuerit ab eis approbata idem electus noster faciet ibidem abbati nostro obedientiam de parendo ei secundum Regulam beati Benedicti hoc salvo quod per Abbatem Maliciose non amovebitur. Abbas autem noster Westmonasteriensis visitabit imperpetuum domum nostram singulis annis semel tantum cum xx. equis de suis et eum honorifice admittemus ut decet et moram ibidem faciet per duos dies et duas noctes sumptibus nostris et ingredietur Capitulum nostrum ut Abbas et libere corriget corrigenda tam in persona Prioris nostri quam Monachorum secundum Regulam Sancti Benedicti dummodo malitiose sine ratione nichil attemptet. Ita eciam quod non licebit ei monachum ammovere de Malvernia vel alium de Westmonasterio illuc mittere sine assensu nostro. Volumus eciam ut monachi domus nostre apud Westmonasterium secundum consuetudinem antiquam faciant professionem suam abbati et facta professione sua libere Malverniam revertentur. Preterea idem Abbas noster recipiet Hospicium suum in Manerio de Poywike secundum consuetudinem antiquam singulis annis semel cum hoc tamen moderamine quod in equitaturis numerum viginti equorum de suis non excedet nec malitiose in gravamen domus nostre extraneos secum adducet. Sequelam etiam hundredi et visum liberorum plegiorum et omnes alias consuetudines quas hactenas Abbas et Monachi Westmonasterienses de Manerio de Poywike habere consueverunt, ita decetero habeant non obstante carta alicujus Abbatis Westmonasteriensis super sequela ejusdem hundredi optenta. dummodo super aliis articulis in eadem carta contentis nullum nobis prejudicium generetur. Vt autem hec omnia perpetue stabilitatis effectum optineant presenti scripto ea confirmamus et sigillorum nostrorum munimine roboramus. Hiis testibus etc.

Rex Edwardus confirmat formam pacis factam inter Dominum G. Wygornensem episcopum et Westmonasterium super Cella Malvernie.

Edwardus Dei gratia Rex Anglie Dominus Hibernie et Dux Aquitanie omnibus ad quos presentes littere pervenerint salutem.

Inspeximus litteras patentes quas venerabilis pater Godefridus Wygorniensis episcopus fecit Dilectis nobis in Christo Abbati et conventui ecclesie Sancti Petri Westmonasterii et Priori et Conventui Celle Majoris Malvernie de forma pacis super quibusdam contencionibus et discordiis inter eos habitis per amicabilem composicionem inite et firmate in hec verba:—

Vniversis Christi fidelibus, et cetera. Sicut patet in secundo folio precedenti.* Et quia forma pacis predicte coram nobis et consilio nostro nobis mediantibus de assensu et voluntate parcium predictarum ordinata fuit inita et firmata, ut perpetua rei geste

* See pages 186—9.

memoria plenius et cercius habeatur formam et composicionem predictam sic initam et firmatam tenore presencium testificamus et eciam pro nobis et heredibus nostris quantum in nobis est concedimus et confirmamus sicut littere patentes predicte racionabiliter testantur. In cujus rei testimonium has litteras nostras fieri fecimus patentes.

Teste me ipso apud Herefordiam. xv. die Novembris Anno Regni nostri. xj.

Item Ratificacio ejusdem de pace facta inter Abbatem et Conventum Westmonasterium et Priorem et Conventum Malvernie.

Edwardus Dei gratia Rex Anglie, et cetera.

Omnibus ad quos presentes littere pervenerint salutem.

Inspeximus litteras patentes quas Dilecti nobis in Christo frater Willelmus de Ledebury Prior Majoris Malvernie et ejusdem loci Conventus fecerint dilectis nobis in Christo fratri Ricardo Abbati Westmonasteriensi et ejusdem loci Conventui de ratificacione pacis inter ipsos Abbatem et Priorem et Conventus predictos ex una parte et venerabilem patrem Godefridum Episcopum Wygorniensem et Capitulum suum de quibusdam contencionibus et discordiis inter ipsos motis coram nobis et consilio nostro inite et firmate nobis mediantibus in hec verba :—

Per presentes pateat universis quod nos frater Willelmus de Ledebyrie Prior Majoris Malvernie et ejusdem loci Conventus ratificamus et ratam habemus pacem factam per dominum Edwardum Dei Gratia Regem Anglie et suum consilium inter venerabilem patrem Dominum G. eadem gratia Episcopum Wygorniensem et suum capitulum ex parte una atque R. ejusdem permissione Abbatem Westmonasteriensem et Conventum et nos ex altera, eam complere et confirmare volentes atque futuris temporibus firmiter observare, Volumus eciam quod si contravenerimus quod absit quod Dominus Rex et sui heredes nos ad ipsius observacionem per quoslibet suos ministros compellat et compellant sub pena quarumlibet rerum nostrarum amittendarum seu distrahendarum mobilium et immobilium et quibuscunque eis placuerit assignandarum quam sibi nobis placuerit infligendam. In cujus rei testimonium presentibus litteris et Capituli nostri fecimus apponi sigillum. Datum apud Malverniam vij idus Octobr'. Anno regni regis ejusdem xjo. finiente.

Nos autem ratificacionem predictam in predicta forma factam ratam habentes et gratam eam pro nobis et heredibus nostris quantum in nobis est concedimus et confirmamus. prout littere patentes predicte racionabiliter testantur. In cujus rei testimonium has litteras nostras fieri fecimus patentes. Teste meipso apud Herefordiam Quinto decimo die Novembris anno Regni nostri Vndecimo.

Assensus Prioris et Conventus Malvernie super ordinacione Domini Edwardi Regis.

Ista littera continetur de verbo ad verbum in pagina precedenti.

INDEX.

A.

B.

C.

D.

E.

F.

G.

H.

I and J.

K.

L.

M.

N.

O.

P.

Q.

R.

S.

T.

V.

W.

SUBSCRIBERS.

The Right Honourable The Earl Beauchamp, Madresfield Court (three copies)

Lord Alwyne Compton, Dean of Worcester

Rev. I. Gregory Smith, M.A., Vicar of Malvern, Prebendary of Hereford

Thomas Rowley Hill, Esq., M.P.

Alderman Noake, Worcester

Councillor W. B. Williamson, Esq., Worcester

,, George B. Williamson, Esq., Worcester

William Charles Lucy, Esq., F.S.S., Gloucester

Rev. Wm. Thorn, Worcester (two copies)

,, S. I. Pettigrew, Puddlestone Rectory, Leominster

,, J. B. Wilson, Knightwick Rectory

,, George Sandford, Sherborne, Malvern Wells

,, J. B. Wathen, Guarlford Rectory, Malvern

,, R. C. Cordiner, Yarnton Lodge, Malvern

,, W. W. Gedge, Malvern Wells

,, F. W. Davenport, Christ Church, Malvern

,, C. L. Banister, Wyche, Malvern

Thomas H. Abbott, Esq., Nailsworth, Gloucestershire

T. L. Smith, Esq., Worcester

Thomas C. B. Griffiths, Esq., Bromyard (two copies)

Stephen Ballard, Esq., Colwall, Malvern

W. F. Fox, Esq., Malvern Link

—. Cadbury, Esq., Birmingham

—. Cadbury, Esq., Birmingham

J. H. Raper, Esq., Kensington, London

James Wilkie, Esq., Bristol

E. W. Elmslie, Esq., Malvern

J. W. Kearns, Esq., Malvern

Samuel Iles, Esq., Bristol

Richard Jones, Esq., Leighhurst, Malvern

Samuel Clarke, Esq., Small Heath, Birmingham

D. Kendall, Esq., Broome Lodge, Malvern Link (two copies)

Charles Williams, Esq., Richmond, Surrey

G. W. Shepherd. Esq., Birmingham

Thomas Cox, Esq., Glanelly, Malvern

Wm. Franklin, Esq., Southville, Bristol

John S. Burrow, Esq., St. James's House, Malvern

George Morriss, Esq., Worcester

R. V. Vassar Smith, Esq., Charlton Park, Cheltenham

Walter B. Burrow, Esq., Eaton Lodge, Malvern (two copies)

Edward Edwards, Esq., Fenchurch Street, London (two copies)

Alfred Robinson, Esq., Fishponds, Bristol (two copies)

Dr. Tyrrell, Claremont House, Malvern

Mrs. Henry Burrow, Hurst Lea, Malvern

Rev. C. Y. Potts, Ledbury

Edward Nevison, Esq., Malvern (two copies)

T. King, Esq., Soho Square, London.

Mrs. James Leigh, Malvern Wells

R. T. Mence, Esq., Malvern

Rev. C. Bathurst, Oriel House, Malvern

Rev. C. E. Rankin, St. Ronan's, Malvern

Mr. Alfred Sparkes, Malvern

„ Samuel Price, Leigh, Malvern

„ Thomas R. Franklin, Hughenden, Malvern

Miss Haddock, Hughenden, Malvern

Mr. Norman May, Malvern

„ W. Elzie, Malvern

„ J. Ransome Corder, Malvern

„ William Davis, Malvern

„ William Elliott, Malvern

Mr. J. H. Jones, Malvern
,, William Haynes, Malvern
,, T. Sanderson, Malvern
,, Thomas Fox, Malvern
,, E. Gwynn, Malvern
,, C. H. Chapel, Malvern (two copies)
,, Ben Jones, Malvern
,, Edward Ward, Birmingham
,, Henry Jones, Malvern Link
Miss Rayson, Fort Royal Hill, Worcester (four copies)
Mr. H. Cox, Dymock, Ledbury
Messrs. Eaton & Son, Worcester (two copies)
Mr. Thomas Nott, Brockmanton Court, Leominster
Miss Fletcher, Cambridge House, Malvern Wells
Miss E. E. Lambert, Summerside, Malvern
Mr. James Coombs, Worcester (four copies)
,, William Nott, Martin's Castle, Bromyard
,, Joseph Jones, Malvern
,, H. R. Stanhope Clarke, Malvern
,, A. Stallard, Church Street, Malvern

www.ingramcontent.com/pod-product-compliance
Lightning Source LLC
Chambersburg PA
CBHW030323270326
41926CB00010B/1486

* 9 7 8 3 3 3 7 2 4 9 8 6 1 *